I STOOD ALONE

Christopher Price

Copyright © 2010 Christopher Price

All rights reserved. No part of this book may be reproduced or transmitted in any form or by any means, electronically or mechanically, including photocopying recording or by any information storage or retrieval system, without permission in writing from the author.

International Standard Book Number: 978-0-9829776-0-6

Acknowledgements

First, I would like to thank Tarik Daniels for his confidence, expertise, and unwavering support—you are invaluable!

Thanks to Lincoln Jude for the beautiful cover design; it is more than I could have ever conceptualized! I am indebted to you!

Thank you to my family. The love and care you all bestowed upon me as a child helped to sustain me through my troublesome years.

Lastly, thanks to my daddy and my step-mother for providing me with food and shelter during the tedious process of completing this true labor of love…Mere words cannot adequately express my sincere gratitude to you both!

Dedications

To the Creator for giving me the vision and the tenacity to write this book, and to my parents who the Creator saw fit that my gifts and talents should flow…

I Stood Alone

Alone I Stood in the Eye of the Storm:
Blistering Winds Ripped Across My Face,
Turbulent Waters Rose Beneath My Feet,
The Spirit of God Propelled Me at My Back.

I Stood Alone in a Den of Ravaging Lions and Bloodthirsty Vultures.

I Reached for Them.
I Called upon Them.
I Prayed to Them.
They had Abandoned Me-
My Friends
My Loved Ones.

I Stood Alone.

Lonely, Fatherlessly, Motherlessly, Lovelessly, Alone.
I Stood.

I Stood Alone

Begging for Comfort
Leaning on My Virtues
Gaining Sustenance from His Love.

I Stood—He and I.

Table of Contents

Chapter One 7

Chapter Two 19

Chapter Three 37

Chapter Four 49

Chapter Five 71

Chapter Six 89

Chapter Seven 103

Chapter Eight 123

Chapter Nine 145

Chapter Ten 161

Chapter Eleven 185

Chapter Twelve 201

Chapter Thirteen 223

Chapter Fourteen 237

Chapter Fifteen 267

Chapter Sixteen 289

Chapter Seventeen 313

Chapter Eighteen 325

Chapter Nineteen 353

Chapter One

"Come on, Ms. Leslie! Girl, you always the last to get dressed," Erin chided. "Chile, by the time you get all dolled up, the carnival will be over, and we woulda missed all the boys, honey!" Erin continued, disapprovingly.

"Chile, I'm going as fast as I can! Shit, it take time to get beat!" Leslie shouted.

Bleeeep! Bleeeep! The whine of a car horn could be heard clearly throughout Leslie's rather large home. The sound was quick, yet elongated, suggesting urgency.

"Chile, these people always sittin' on they damn horn for one reason or another around here! I guess that shit just come along with livin' in the damn hood," Leslie exclaimed.

Bleep! Bleep! Bleep! The driver continued to pound.

"Chris," a high-pitched female voice screamed!

I quickly turned toward the sound of my name being called.

"That's Tookie!" I shouted to my best friends, Leslie and Erin, as I hurried down the stairs.

The three of us rushed to the front door. As I swung open the door, I saw Raylene, or Tookie as our family affectionately calls her, running up the porch stairs, "Come on, Chris!" She urged. "This White boy pushed me and called me a Black bitch!"

Leslie, half-dressed, ran upstairs to put on her clothes. Erin, close on her heels, ran to retrieve his shoes.

I walk-ran to Tookie's small black car, "Come on, Chris!

Get in!"

As I opened the passenger door to her car, I heard a barely audible Voice whisper, "Don't go."

I disregarded the Voice, thinking it was my apprehension about going with Tookie to mediate an argument between her and a White boy. I would have much rather had gone to the carnival with my friends, yet I got in the car.

My mind was racing, "pushed...Black bitch," Tookie's voice echoed in my mind. I was livid, to express the least, but I was not at all surprised. We were, after all, in Toledo, Ohio, said to be one of the most racist cities in America. I was born and reared there. The practice of racism was the status quo, and I was all too familiar with its ugly tentacles.

With our car doors closed firmly, Tookie pushed down on the accelerator of the car. As we sped off, I asked her, "So tell me again what happened, and start from the beginning."

Tookie, in her usual fast speech, told me what occurred: apparently Tookie, along with her eighteen-month-old daughter, was driving on Maumee Street where she narrowly avoided hitting a young couple walking across the street. The guy, irate from nearly being hit, swore at Tookie, "Stupid bitch, you need to slow down!" Tookie heard the guy.

She haphazardly parked her car, running toward the guy, she screamed, "What did you say, mutha fucka?" With her breast nearly resting on the guy's chest and her index finger pointing directly in his face, she repeated herself, "I said, what did you say?"

The guy stepped back, yet pushing Tookie as he did. As she stumbled backwards, he roared, "You heard me! And, stay out of my face, Black bitch!"

Tookie jumped up, ran in the direction of her car, and shouted, "Oh! You don't know who you fuckin' wit'!" Producing a long, black object from the trunk of her car, she screamed, "Don't put yo' mutha fuckin' hands on me!"

Jumping into her car, she threatened, "I'll be back!"

~~~~

Tookie is my first cousin. Our mothers are sisters. She and I, along with our other cousins, were raised more like we were siblings than cousins. Our mothers gave birth to us as teenagers, so we were all raised in my maternal grandparents' home for a short period of time. As children, our grandfather instilled in us the blessing of family and the importance of being supportive of one another.

As much as I wanted to be somewhere else, doing something else, my convictions would not allow me to be anywhere but where I was.

When I took my mind off of her story, I realized we were not going in the direction of where the altercation took place. Unbeknownst to me, Tookie had already assembled a retinue of sorts. "Where are we going?" I queried.

"Over to Angela's. I told her what happened and she said she wanted to come, too."

All hell, it's about to be some shit! Angela was a childhood friend of ours. As children, Angela had a reputation as being something of a fighter. I instinctively knew that if these two hot-tempered women got together all hell would break loose. *What in the world am I getting myself?*

After getting Angela, we headed to Maumee Street where Tookie said the altercation took place, and, incidentally, where the guy supposedly lived. Turning onto Maumee, we parked on the side of a red building. "How do you know this is where the White boy is?" I asked.

"'Cause this is the house his girlfriend walked to after he

pushed me," Tookie replied, matter-of-factly.

Leaving Lolita, Tookie's daughter, in the car, the three of us walked to the back of the house where about ten White people congregated on the back porch. "Tookie, you see the dude who pushed you?" I asked.

"Uhn-unh…he ain't up there."

I continued to walk toward the house. Like most homes in South Toledo, the house was a bit decrepit. Originally white in color, the one-level house had become discolored, and was now smoke-gray. The porch floorboards looked fragile under the weight of its occupants. Far off in a corner of the porch, a pile of wooden 2x4s lay, as if someone had recently finished a project of some sort. The backyard was littered with debris; empty beer and wine bottles lay scattered about the patchy grass.

Tookie and Angela followed behind me, as I approached the fence of the backyard. I looked at the faces of the White people sitting on the porch: none of them looked friendly; though, none of them looked particularly menacing, either. A tall, heavy-set White guy sat on the porch banister. Directing my question to no one in particular, I asked, "A, can I speak with the dude who pushed my cousin?"

The heavy-set guy responded in a cool, non-threatening manner, "He went to the liquor store around the corner. He'll be right back."

"All right, thanks."

We turned to leave. *Hmm, that went pretty well.*

~~~

The three of us got back into Tookie's car. Tookie drove the short distance to her apartment, not too far from where we were. She had just moved to the neighborhood. The south side of Toledo was an area largely populated by poor White people. It was well known by most Blacks that racist Whites inhabited the neighborhood. My grandmother tried to discourage Tookie from moving to the area, yet she still chose to move there.

Walking up the stairs and into Tookie's two-bedroom apartment, I immediately began unpacking and organizing her possessions. She still had many of her things in boxes. I was tremendously proud of her. Between Tookie and her sister, I thought Tookie was less likely to do well for herself. She was the younger of the two. As a child, Tookie was spoiled and irresponsible, however, as a young adult, she was the complete opposite.

Despite having given birth to Lolita at the age of sixteen, Tookie continued her education and later achieved her G.E.D. Tookie's father, Raymond, rewarded her accomplishments by helping her to buy her first vehicle. Tookie acquired work as a sales clerk at Sears and Roebuck; working over-time to be in the position where she was now able to furnish her own apartment and to live independently of her parents.

Lolita's father was in prison; while, he loved Tookie deeply and was a truly good person, he had not really contributed to the accomplishments Tookie had achieved.

After fifteen or twenty minutes of being at Tookie's apartment, she announced, "Okay, y'all ready to go back over there?"

I was secretly hoping that she had moved pass the ordeal, yet I still got up from my place on the sofa and walked out of the front door behind her.

As we were walking toward Tookie's car, her mother and brother, Kim and Booger, drove by and stopped beside Tookie's car.

Kim is one of my mother's younger sisters. My mother and Kim are separated by one year in age. My cousins and I had always considered Kim to be one of our favorite aunts. We also thought she was one of our more attractive aunts. She stood 5'6 tall and had smooth, dark skin and long, black "Indian" hair, as we Black folks called kink-free hair.

In addition to Kim's beauty, she was cool by our standards: she could do all of the current dances; she cooked great meals and baked delicious cakes; she was far more lenient than our other aunts, including my mother; and, she possessed a way of relating to children in a peer-like manner. We were able to talk to Kim about things in which most children would be uncomfortable talking to adults. Kim encouraged her four children to see and treat her as a friend rather than a mother. Kim and her children had a unique relationship: a relationship in which they drank alcohol together; cursed at one another; and fought alongside each other. They were friends and treated each other as such.

In some ways, I imagine, mothers who longed to have friendships with their children perhaps envied Kim's relationship with her children; yet, they were abhorred at the thought of their children referring to them as bitch.

Kim and Booger apparently had been informed of the situation between Tookie and the White guy. I told them that we were on our way to the guy's house and quickly filled them in on what occurred when Tookie, Angela, and I went there.

"We gone come with y'all," Kim declared.

"Okay," I responded.

Angela placed Lolita in her car seat in the backseat of Tookie's car and sat down beside her. Tookie and I sat on the front seats. As Tookie drove to the guy's house, Kim and Booger followed behind us in Kim's Plymouth Horizon.

It only took us a couple of minutes to arrive at the guy's house. Angela opted to stay in the car with Lolita, while Tookie and I got out of the car. We waited for Kim to park her car. After parking her car in the alley behind the guy's house, the four of us (Kim, Booger, Tookie, and I) walked the short distance to the back porch of the White guy's house.

We must have looked pretty tough: four Blacks exiting two cars in a mostly White neighborhood; or, perhaps, very foolish. Booger and I were in the lead. Booger was generally a very relaxed guy. Booger's birth name was actually Raymond. His father, fond of nicknames, gave him the nickname, Booger. Why such nicknames as Tookie or Booger, was unknown to me.

Aside from my love of Booger as my cousin, I genuinely liked him as a person. Even as a child, he had radiated a confidence in himself that one rarely sees in young persons. Having no other male siblings, until several years later when his brother was born, he oftentimes played alongside his sisters with their dolls. Where most boys would be hesitant to play with dolls for fear of being teased and called names by their peers, Booger did not care. He somehow had the wherewithal to know that playing with dolls would not make him anymore gay than playing with a ball would make him heterosexual. And, so, with that inner security, he continued to play with his sisters' dolls right alongside his G.I. Joe figurines.

As the White people on the porch saw us approach, all of them, except one guy, went into the house.

Booger walked up the steps to the porch, "Can I talk wit' the dude who pushed my sister?"

Armed with a baseball bat, the White guy started to move the bat around in his hands in a batter-like fashion, as if he was about to hit Booger with the it.

Booger, sensing the guy's thoughts, raised his hand in a gesture to calm the guy, "Look, I didn't come here for no trouble. I just want a apology from the guy who pushed my sister."

The guy lowered his bat. Some inaudible words were exchanged between Booger and the guy.

"I like you. You cool," Booger said.

Booger extended his fist to the guy; a gesture known as "hit the rock." It was equivalent to shaking hands. They bumped fist. Satisfied that everything had ended happily, I turned toward the fence and began to walk back toward the gate. Without turning around, I yelled, "Come on, Booger!"

However, before I could reach the gate, I heard a loud commotion behind me. I quickly turned around to see several White people running out of the house. They were armed with baseball bats, both wooden and steel; tire irons; and, wooden 2x4s. The White people were scattered all around the small backyard.

What happened! Just moments ago, it seemed that a resolution had been reached, yet now it looked like I had been transported back in time to a place where Blacks were hosed with water and beaten with Billy clubs. I hurriedly scanned the backyard. Booger was near the center of the yard dodging as a White guy swung a baseball bat at him. Another guy stood closely behind him with his bat held high waiting for, what appeared to be, the perfect opportunity to hit Booger.

Kim and Tookie were on the right side of the yard. Tookie had one of the guys in a headlock. Tookie punched him repeatedly in his face, as the guy attempted to squirm from her strong hold.

Kim stood near Tookie and the guy, looking for a chance to hit the guy, though Tookie had things well-under control.

Several White guys began to jump over the fence into the backyard grabbing whatever weapons they could find. On the porch, a guy yelled for reinforcements.

The guys surrounded Booger, each one of them taking turns hitting him with bats. Kim, too, was now being attacked.

I was panic-stricken. *What should I do? Who should I help first?* I quickly scanned the backyard and saw an empty wine bottle lying on the grass. I grabbed it, throwing it as hard as I could. I aimed for the guy who stood on the porch who yelled for more help. I missed him. The glass hit the house and crashed to the porch.

I rushed toward my family. "Come on, y'all! We got to get out of here!"

I yelled and yelled, until, Tookie, Kim and Booger fought their way to the entrance of the backyard. They made it to where I stood. We ran through the alley and pass Kim's parked car. Miraculously, we made it to Maumee St.

We were far from being safe, however. Angry Whites lined both sides of the street. Many of them ran toward us from the direction in which we had just come. I stood in the middle of the street, watching as Kim and Tookie ran toward Tookie's car that was parked two blocks up the street. Angela had wisely moved it away from the growing mob.

Booger was the last of us to make it to the street. Two of the White guys picked up rocks from the ground, throwing them at Booger as he ran up the street. I stood motionlessly in the middle of the street making sure Kim and Tookie got along safely, while simultaneously yelling to Booger to run faster. Several of the White guys began to demolish Kim's car. Lividly, I watched as they smashed in the head and taillights and shattered the windows of the car with bats. They laughed as they banged on the doors, roof, and hood of the car. I was incensed, though there was nothing I could do.

I briefly averted my attention to the direction in which Kim and Tookie had run. They made it to Tookie's car. I inwardly rejoiced. Though, my joy was short-lived. Before I could turn to check on Booger, I felt a throbbing pain in my upper arm. I turned to see a White guy standing behind me with a tire iron.

My arm ached. It instantly began to swell. The guy missed his target. I could only guess where he intended to hit me. Luckily for me, Booger had distracted the guy just in time, possibly saving my life.

The guy turned his fury onto Booger. I ran to Tookie's car, where she stood at the trunk with a long, black object in her hand. I could not quite make out the object, but I hoped that it was something I could use to protect us against our assailants.

I continued to run. As I got closer to Tookie, I was better able to see the object in her hands. It was a shotgun. I grabbed the gun from her. I felt more comfortable with it in my care than in hers. The last thing we needed was for one of the White guys to strip it from her and use it against us.

Secretly, I was afraid of guns. The sound alone was unnerving. The deafening thunder as a bullet escaped its chamber frightened me. I knew the damage they caused. The News always headlined stories in which someone was shot: a drug deal gone deadly; a hapless child stumbling upon her father's gun; teenagers playing Russian roulette. Guns were dangerous and unpredictable.

With the exception of the time when, as a child, I was allowed to carry my grandfather's shotgun, I had never handled a gun before. Allen, my grandfather, was an expert gunman. Depending upon our behavior or who asked first, as a treat to my cousins and me, he would allow one of us to carry his gun to his truck. Many Sundays, Allen would cram my cousins and me into his van and chaperone us to the Gun Club, where he and his friends met to practice target shooting.

Those fun-loving times when we were allowed to carry Allen's gun were much different than now, though. My family's lives were not in danger and Allen's gun was safely clothed in its leather carrying case; the gun I now carried was cold and heavy, naked and unprotected.

I ran toward the growing crowd of Whites. I stopped in the middle of the street, holding the gun up high, hoping the mob would see the gun and disperse. Though, they did not. Booger finally ran pass me, taking a position behind me. I ran toward them, again. Still, they did not retreat. I continued to run toward the mob, closing the gap between us with each step that I took. They still ran in our direction. If I had failed to realize it before, I knew at that moment that my family and I were dealing with a gang of crazed people. Had a guy run toward me with a gun, common sense would tell me to run in the opposite direction; yet, these people persisted.

I ran toward them. Booger trailed a short distance behind me. I ran until, finally, when I was approximately seven to ten yards from them, the mob decided to turn in the other direction and flee.

I gave chase. I wanted them as far from my family and me as possible. They scattered in different directions. Several of them turned down a small street, running between a white house and a red building. I followed.

It was suddenly dark. The building blocked the sun's brilliant rays, making it dark and eerie where I ran. I shouted angrily as I ran, "I told y'all to stop fuckin' wit us!"

It was so dark and cold. Everything began to move as though in slow motion. A lone guy ran in front of me. He pushed open a gate. I pursued.

I reached the gate, stopping just after I crossed the threshold. *Where am I? The tree in front of me; the fence to my left; the grass all looked familiar, though how?* My mind whirled. I felt like I was in a dream. Everything was quiet. A sudden stillness descended all around me. The knowledge of where I was hit me like a freight train into a car. I knew where I was…

Chapter Two

I gathered my bearings. I stood completely still. *How did I end here? I chased the mob between a meticulous white house and a red building. Surely, this backyard did not belong to the house I passed. Though, it did.*

I stood in the backyard of where our altercation began. For the second time that day, it seemed like I had been transported back in time.

I heard a sound to my right. I quickly turned toward the sound. A guy stood on the porch. We startled each other. The gun I carried was held high. The guy on the porch jumped. I jumped. The butt of the gun hit the fence behind me. It discharged. I felt the air move through the gun as its projectile escaped the barrel. Swoosh! My heart fluttered in my chest. My stomach did somersaults. Everything around me stood still. Without warning, an orange-reddish color exploded from the rifle. It temporarily blinded me.

My vision returned fractions of a second later; I turned on my heels, running back between the house and the building. My legs felt heavier. The gun felt heavier. I felt drained, like every ounce of energy had suddenly been depleted from my body. I continued to run.

As I passed a window on the side of the house, I heard a woman scream, "Oh, my God! Oh, my God…I think Adam's been shot!"

I continued to run. Booger stood at the end of the walkway. I ran pass him without saying a word to him. He followed behind me. I ran to Maumee Street, and then to Walbridge, where Tookie lived a couple of blocks away.

On Walbridge, several White people stood outside of their homes. I ran pass them. Booger was close on my heels, running behind me. I could see Tookie standing outside of the three-story apartment building in which she lived. She was frantic.

"What happened?" She asked.

"I don't know," I said, breathing laboriously. "I think I shot somebody!" I replied, frantically.

"You and Booger, go upstairs! Take the gun with you!" She instructed. Tookie ran back to the White guy's house where the guy was possibly shot. Obediently, Booger and I ran up the stairs to her apartment. Booger took the gun from me and placed it in a gym bag.

I nervously paced the hallway of the small apartment. I walked up and down the length of the corridor, until I could not take it anymore. I had to leave.

"Booger, I'm about to go."

"Where you going?"

"Over to Mymomme's," I declared.

"I'm going with you."

I looked at him, searching his face for a clue as to why he wanted to go with me. He had done no wrong. He had not shot anyone. Why? Why did he further want to involve himself in a situation that was not his? I studied his face. I found nothing there, but the same things I saw before: love and a deep concern.

I acquiesced, "Okay."

Booger grabbed the gym bag with the gun in it. "I'ma hide this," he expressed. We went to the front door, opened it, and ran down the long staircase of Tookie's apartment building. As we stepped out on the porch, we noticed that no one was outside. No one was in sight. No neighbors. No Tookie. No Kim. No vicious White people. Booger rushed across the street to Tookie's car, crouching down, he pushed the gym bag under the car.

After concealing the gun, Booger joined me across the street. We ran down the unfamiliar streets in the direction of, what I hoped was, my mother's house. As we ran, we passed a White father instructing his young son as how to ride a bike. The boy wobbly rode his bicycle, as his father protectively walked close behind him, ready to catch him should he fall.

Booger and I slowed our pace to allow the father and son to pass by us. As we did, Booger and I simultaneously spoke to the duo, "Hi." The little boy smiled brightly, as if to say, "Look at me! I'm riding all by myself!"

The proud father looked on, "Hi," he gushed.

Oddly, not even two blocks from where we were beaten with bats and chased for a block and a half, we experienced no hatred from this White father and his son. No color lines separated us. No ugly words. No mean looks. It was as if the horrid events of thirty minutes ago did not exist. We were simply four human beings crossing paths on this journey called life.

As we continued to run, I heard sirens in the distance. Was it the ambulance? Had the guy indeed been shot? Maybe it was the police, and, if so, were they looking for me?

Booger and I ran down small, narrow streets, until we reached the Anthony Wayne Trail, a major highway in South Toledo.

Safety, of sorts, was on the other side of the thoroughfare. Mymomme lived just a short distance from the highway. Once we were there, Mymomme would make everything better. She would hug away my fears; chasing away this nightmare.

Booger and I cautiously crossed the wide highway. Traffic

was heavy. We bobbed and weaved through the cars, safely making it across the street without being hit or detected by the police.

~~~

Booger and I had finally reached my mother's small two-bedroom house. The old house had always reminded me of "Little House on the Prairie." It was shabby: the windows and doors were in disrepair; the once green shingles on the roof were weather worn and falling off in some places; the chipped paint uncovered the house's wooden frame.

The inside of the house, however, was warm, cozy, and inviting. The small rooms were beautifully decorated with tasteful furniture Mymomme had acquired from family members and friends. The living room walls, painted a soft peach, adorned two large brass picture-mirrors that were separated by an ornate brass clock. Pictures of our family were meticulously hung on the surrounding walls.

I walked up the cracked, concrete stairs, onto the loose, creaky floorboards, and opened the aluminum screen door. The old door groaned as I opened it. Stepping into the living room, I was engulfed by the smell of food. My mouth watered; the aroma of fried pork chops filled the room.

My mother was home from work and preparing dinner. I walked through the living and dining room and into the kitchen. Mymomme, still in her work clothes, stood at the stove flipping the pork chops, stirring the mashed potatoes, and checking on the fried corn—seemingly simultaneously.

"Hi, Mymomme," I greeted.

"Hey, bae," she responded without looking up.

I went to the refrigerator, grabbed the Kool-Aid, and poured me a glass of it. I looked over at Mymomme. I needed to tell her what happened. Yet, I could not. I looked away, finishing my drink. I walked to the sink and rinsed out my glass, placing it in the dishwater. I opened my mouth to speak, though no words came out. I could not do it. Where would I begin? How does someone tell his mother that he may have shot someone?

She looked tired. Her white uniform pants, unbuttoned and slightly unzipped, hung loosely from her waist. It was a habit of hers to unbutton her pants immediately after she came home from work.

She was still a very attractive woman. My dad had always told me I looked like her. In many ways, it was true: my egg-shaped head; the way my nose and mouth were situated on my face; it all belonged to her. Her dark, ebony-colored skin was one of the few things I had not inherited from her. Instead, I had my dad's brown, paper bag-colored skin.

I could not tell her. It would be too much for her to handle; many of her hopes and dreams were dependent upon me succeeding in life. I was the older of her two children; the one she depended on most. My brother, Jeremiah, and I were eleven years apart in age. At ten years old, he and I were clearly very different persons. In many ways, Miah-Miah, as I called him, was more like Mymomme in temperament: he was hot-tempered and seemed to love fighting; I was mild-mannered, and, though I fought, I did so as a last resort; I was an honor roll student, he struggled in school; I loved being indoors and anywhere near Mymomme, he was happiest outside playing with his friends.

I did not tell her. Instead, I looked at her standing in her work uniform as she cooked and burned the image of her deep in my memory. I walked out of the kitchen and into the bedroom Miah-Miah and I shared. I quickly took off my bell-bottom Guess Jeans and black leather vest, laying them across the bed.

I loved this outfit. I had just bought it a few weeks ago. Bell-bottomed pants were making a come-back from the 1960s and 70s, and I intended to bring them in with style. I wore a pair of thick-soled black shoes, a wide black belt, and a black, leather vest, with no shirt on beneath it.

I slipped on a Girbaud jean suit. I neatly folded the clothes I had just taken off, and walked into the living room. Booger looked calm as he sat on the sofa. He rose as I entered the room.

"I need to leave. I can't stay here," I stated.

"Where you going? Did you tell Lawanda?" He asked. Lawanda is my mother's first name.

"Naw, I didn't tell her. I don't want her worrying," I said, adamantly. "I don't know where I'm going. I guess I'll go over Mama's," I said, looking perplexed.

"Okay. Well, I'ma go over Niecy's house, then," Booger stated.

"Mymomme," I yelled from the living room, "I'll be back!"

"Boy, you know this food will be ready in a minute," she yelled from the kitchen.

"I know. I'll be back." I knew that I would not be back by the time dinner would be ready, but, other than the hard truth, what could I tell her?

"All right, Booger, I'll call you later." I gave him a hug.

"Bye, Lawanda!" He yelled.

"Boy, I didn't know you was out here. You leavin, too?" She asked, standing in the doorwell of the kitchen.

"Yeah, I'm going over Niecy's," he said.

"Okay. I'll see y'all later," she said, before returning back into the kitchen.

Booger and I walked out of the house. I started jogging as soon as I left Mymomme's front yard. Booger jogged beside me. We jogged a little less than half a block before we reached the street where Niecy lived. Niecy was Booger's girlfriend. They had been together for about two years. She was a pretty girl; light brown-skinned and petite. She complemented Booger well; she had the same easy-going kind of personality as him, and they were in love.

"All right, Booger, I'll see you."

"Okay. Be careful," he encouraged.

"I will."

I continued my jog. I jogged along the few short streets until I reached City Park Avenue. I walk-ran down most of City Park, slowing only when I reached Nebraska Street. I slowed down as I approached a stop light at City Park and Nebraska. As I waited for the light to change, an ex-girlfriend of mine, Amber, stopped beside me in her car.

"Hey, Chris! You need a ride?"

Ugh! I cringed inwardly. I had hoped that I would not see anyone I knew. I was sweating profusely, but I did not want to seem rude.

"Yeah," I opened the car door and got in.

"Where are you going?" She asked.

"Over my grandmother's house on Wells. You remember where she lives?"

"Uhn-huh. So, how have you been? What you been up to?" Amber inquired.

I did not know what to say. Clearly, I could not tell her what had just happened.

"Not too much...I just left Mymomme's house and...was headed to Mama's house," I stammered.

"Oh, okay," she smiled.

We rode the remainder of the short distance in virtual silence. At the corner of Dorr Street and City Park, I decided that I could jog to Mama's house from where we were.

"You can let me off here. I can jog the rest of the way." We hugged before I exited the car.

"Thank you!" I yelled as she drove off.

I ran the last couple of blocks to my maternal grandmother's house. Mama, as our family called her, was, in many ways, like a second mother to me. She, in fact, loved and cared for me as if she had birthed me.

Upset with my mother because of her relationship with her new boyfriend, Jackson, I asked Mama if I could live with her when I was only eleven years old. Mama happily obliged and, the next day, I moved in with Allen and her. That was nearly ten years ago. Although I had moved into my own apartment when I was nineteen, Mama's house still felt like home to me.

Her home was a quaint, brick house. There were a total of five bedrooms, four upstairs and one downstairs; two bathrooms and a full basement. The house was not lavish, but it was clean and nicely furnished.

I opened the screen door and turned the door knob of the front door. As usual, the door was unlocked. I stepped inside. The living room was dark. Without turning on the lights, I made my way to the staircase that led to the bedrooms. I climbed the stairs, and looked in all four bedrooms. No one was home. I walked back down stairs and out the front door.

~~~~

It was dark outside, nine o'clock already; still very early in the evening for a late spring day. Mama was probably still at work, and my cousins, whom lived with her, were God knows where. The night air was refreshing. It was just what I needed to clear my head.

I did not know what to do or where to go. I knew that I could not stay at Mama's. If the police were looking for me, her home would be one of the first places that they would look.

I was tired. The day's events were finally wearing me down; emotionally, mentally, and now physically. I needed to go someplace where
I could rest and decide what to do next. Before I consciously knew where I was going, I began walking in the direction of my friend's house, Ms. Maple.

Ms. Maple and I had become friends almost by default. She was the mother of one of my best friends, Leonard. Ms. Maple was originally from Lakeland, Florida. She was one of the kindest, most southern women I knew.

Ms. Maple lived in the Old West End section of Toledo. It was a beautiful neighborhood. Many of the homes in the area were old mansions and refurbished duplexes. The duplex Ms. Maple occupied was picturesque; gorgeous hardwood floors, French doors, and an ornate fireplace completed the décor.

I knocked on the backdoor. No one answered. I turned the knob. As with the door of Mama's house, Ms. Maple's backdoor was left unlocked. I walked in, stepping into the kitchen. I quickly looked around the two-bedroom apartment. Just as I suspected, no one was home. I grabbed a blanket from the linen closet, walked into the sunroom, and laid down on the sofa. I placed the phone beside me, should someone call while I slept.

She stood in the corner of the room. Her voluptuous body was just visible in the small, dark bedroom. I could feel her anticipation. I lifted the mattress from the frame and quietly laid it on the floor. I looked at her. She looked exquisite standing there in the nude. Her body was truly a work of art. I rushed to her, gently cupping her face in my hands, kissing her parted lips. I licked her earlobes, mildly sucking her neck. Her knees buckled. I reached for her hand, escorting her to our pallet on the floor.

She lay there with her legs spread invitingly. I slid down beside her. I licked her inner thighs, caressing them as I did; she squealed in delight. I worked my way up to her abdomen and then her huge tits. I circled her areola with my tongue, blowing cool air on her nipples. She moaned in pleasure.

The soft glow of the moon was the only light illuminating the room. Its rays shone brilliantly against her smooth, honey-colored skin. I kissed her; my tongue moved deeply and passionately in her mouth. I slowly parted her legs; my fingers found their way to the hairs covering her already moist opening. I navigated my penis to her vagina, slowly entering her. She held her breath. I moved deeper within her. She inhaled short, quick breaths of air. I called her name in my deepest, most sensual voice, "Karen." She squirmed beneath me at the mentioning of her name; the sound of my voice in her ear. "Yes..." She softly, passionately replied. The sound of her beautiful, melodic voice heightened my desire for her. I entered her more deeply. I moved my penis in circular motions, allowing the shaft of my penis to rub slowly and gently against her vaginal walls. I increased my intensity. I moaned in ecstasy; trying desperately not to awaken anyone.

I slid out of her. She breathed in deeply. I moved my mouth to her breast, to her abdomen, and then her inner thighs; teasing her with the power of my tongue. She moaned. I inserted my finger in her, gently playing with her clitoris. A quick, short yelp escaped her lips. She pulled me to her, kissing me wildly. She grabbed my penis,
badly wanting me to re-enter her. I held out. Playfully, teasing her. She whispered in my ear, "I love you, Chris...I love you...I love you." I felt her warm breath on my ear; her tongue moving freely in my ear, on my neck.

I placed the head of my penis on her vulva; holding the

length of my penis, I moved the head of it along her vaginal lips. She arched her back, as if pleading for me to enter her. Finally, I acquiesced; I entered her. She tensed, grabbing my back as she did. Her vaginal walls tightened and then relaxed; tightened and relaxed. She held her breath and arched her back. She opened her mouth sensually, until finally...finally...

Ring... ring...ring! I awoke with a start at the sound of the ringing phone. I raised my head from the sofa too quickly. I felt dizzy. I looked around me. I was in the sunroom of Ms. Maple's duplex.

A dream; it was all just a dream. It seemed so real. I could still feel Karen's touch; the taste of her tongue; the passion between us.

Ring...ring...ring! The sound of the phone disrupted my reverie, quickly bringing me to the here and now.

Karen was my on-again-off-again girlfriend of the past three years. We had other partners during the break ups, but we always seemed to reconcile. She was just in Toledo the previous week. We consummated our love for one another; vowing to repair our damaged relationship.

Karen and I met during my freshmen year at Central State University in Wilberforce, Ohio. We hit it off immediately. We spent long hours talking about everything imaginable, studying together, and spending long nights in each other's dorm rooms making passionate love. She was a great girl; pretty, beautiful body, intelligent, and personable, but like many of us, she battled her share of personal issues.

As a child, Karen was molested by her mother's boyfriend. After gathering the courage to tell her mother, Ms. Carter, she did not believe her.

"Girl, you are lying! He did not do those awful things to you!" Waving her small, slender finger in Karen's face, "You stop telling these horrible stories! You hear me?!"

Karen nodded her head up and down, wiping her tear-stained face.

"You are so dramatic! It never ceases to amaze me what you will do for attention!" Ms. Carter shouted.

Karen was wounded. Her mother's lack of support destroyed an innocence and vulnerability in her that would never return. The molestation in itself would have been traumatizing enough for most anyone to accept; yet, the scars of molestation were far deeper than only being physically violated. The violation was psychologically and spiritually mutilating as well. Yet, for Karen, the abuse did not end there. She felt that her mother's actions were equally as inexcusable as the monster's who stole her innocence.

My own issues did not make her situation any easier. For years, I had been practicing bi-sexuality. Although, Karen knew about my sexuality, the knowledge did not make our relationship any better. She was already insecure as to my love and commitment to her; she now felt she had to compete with both women and men. I spent endless hours trying to ease her insecurities.

"Listen, Karen, it's you who I love and only you. I don't care who comes along, if I'm with you, it is you I am faithful to."

"I know, Chris. I know how you are…I know that you wouldn't cheat on me, but I can't help it! It's just that when I see you around other women, or now men, I just think that'd you'd rather be with them than with me."

"Karen, you can't compete with a man; no woman can compete with a man, just as a man can't compete with a woman. If I'm going to be with a man, I'm going to be with a man…if I'm going to be with a woman, I'm going to be with a woman. What I'm telling you is that you don't have to worry about either one of them, man or woman. I don't care if Janet

Jackson or Denzel Washington comes along, if I'm with you, I'm with you, and no one can take me away from you. No one!"

She smiled at me through tear-filled eyes. I hugged her, but no amount of talking seemed to totally comfort her. There always seemed to be a voice in the back of her head telling her that I would eventually leave her for another woman or for a man.

It pained me deeply. I understood what it felt like to be insecure in a person or a relationship. I never wanted anyone that I was in a relationship with to feel that they had to compete with someone else for my attention or love. My agony was further compounded by the knowledge that, in some ways, I believed my bi-sexuality heightened her insecurities. No matter what I told her, subconsciously she would always feel that she was not good enough or woman enough to completely capture me.

Ring…ring…ring! I hurriedly picked up the phone receiver. It was Booger. "Did you see the News?" He asked.

The events of the previous evening were a blur; slowly they began filtering their way into my consciousness.

"No. Why?" I asked.

"That boy was shot and killed," he stated, matter-of-factly.

I sat up quickly, "What!" I exclaimed.

"That boy you shot died," he expressed.

I raised my hand to my head, massaging my temples. "Oh…my…God," I said, slowly.

I hung up the phone without saying anymore. I sat on Ms. Maple's sofa in her sunroom trying to grasp the fullness of what Booger had just said.

How? How? How? How did he die? How did I shoot him? I never directly aimed the gun at him? I never pulled the trigger…did I? Oh, my God? Did I intentionally shoot that guy?

I could not remember. I sat there holding my head in my hands as I rocked back and forth trying to remember everything that happened; praying that the events were all a nightmare that would soon end.

After sitting on the sofa for several minutes, I finally pulled myself together and walked to Ms. Maple's bedroom to see if she was home. I knocked on the door.

"Yeah," she responded in a hoarse voice.

"It's me. Can I come in?"

"Come on, chile."

I opened the door. She lay there with the covers pulled up high under her chin. Though, her hair was tossed about her head in every possible direction, she still looked very beautiful. Her skin was pecan-brown in color. She was five feet nine inches tall and thick-boned. She looked great. She had always reminded me of a cross between Tina Turner and Patti Labelle; she had Tina's great legs and amazing beauty; and Patti's pizzazz.

Ms. Maple would not leave her home without having her hair being immaculately styled and her make-up applied perfectly. She drove nothing but the best in American-made cars; Cadillac Deville and Lincoln Town Cars. Her exquisite home was decorated with Victorian-styled furniture, set in soft pastel colors.

"I've got something to tell you." I said in a barely audible voice.

"What is it, chile?" She said, sitting up.

"I shot and killed somebody," I mumbled, looking down at the floor.

"What! What happened?! You and that Kevon been fighting again?"

Kevon was a guy I had been seeing romantically. Our

relationship was as dysfunctional as relationships get. We were always arguing and, of late, fighting with one another. We called it quits three months ago, but I guess the horrible effects of our doomed relationship remained with Ms. Maple.

"No!" I said, a little too passionately.

"Well, chile, how am I supposed to know? You know how you and that boy stayed at each other! Well, who was it then?"

I looked at her. I was ashamed. Was our dysfunctional relationship that bad? Did others think that it was so volatile that we would eventually kill one another? I cared for Kevon and, though our relationship was abusive, I would never do anything to seriously hurt him.

"No. Me, Tookie, Booger, and Kim got into it with some White people."

"What! What did they do to y'all?!"

Ms. Maple immediately assumed that we were the victims and the Whites were the perpetrators. Although her home state of Florida is a beautiful, tropical paradise, it is still a southern state; a state where racism is not a thing of the past. Ms. Maple would oftentimes tell me of the racist Whites that she dealt with while living there.

I told her what happened as quickly and as detailed as I could. "See, dat's what I say about dem damn peckerwoods!" Ms. Maple raged, "Dem damn honkies wouldn't have got dat shit off in Flo'da...dey crazy as hell down dere, but we keep 'em in dey place!"

Ms. Maple was livid. She hated to hear of any injustice, but particularly racial injustice. I told her that it was in part our fault, too, for having gone over there, but she would not hear of it.

"Ah don't care. He ain't have no business puttin' his hands on her no way. And, what she come roundin' y'all up fo'?"

She asked one question after the other so quickly that I did not have an opportunity to answer any of her questions.

"See, I'm tellin' you, that's why I don't keep a bunch of women up under me…they keep shit started. Now why couldn't she have dealt with the situation by herself?! She got into it by herself!"

There was much truth to what Ms. Maple said; yet, I did not blame anyone, but myself. As wrong as the White guy may have been for pushing Tookie, he was not to blame; as ill-tempered as Tookie may have been, the blame was not hers. I chose to go with her. She did not force me to go. I was a grown man; one month from my twenty-first birthday, and two years older than her. No. The blame rested on me.

I quietly stood in the doorwell of Ms. Maple's bedroom feeling very foolish. How had I allowed this to happen? I was an honor roll student, a prolific speaker, and a writer.

Most of my life I had heard people speak highly of me, "Oh, he smart…he gone go somewhere." Yet, there I was; going nowhere fast, except to prison. I was ashamed of myself. I felt that I had disappointed everyone: God and my ancestors; my mother and father; and, my family and friends.

I could not believe I was in that situation. I shot and killed someone. Me! Christopher LaKeith Price had killed someone. Someone died at my hands. No good; no degree of intellect; no amount of remorse; nothing would ever change that fact. I killed someone.

Ms. Maple interrupted my thoughts, "So, what you wanna do? You wanna go to Flo'da or Detroit until thangs die down?"

Sadly, although the year was nineteen-ninety four, Blacks understood that, whenever there was a situation between Blacks and Whites, rarely was justice on the side of Blacks.

"No, I can't just leave. I have Booger and Tookie to consider, too."

"Okay. Well, chile you let me know if you change yo' mind. I am here. You hear me?!" Ms. Maple said, emphatically.

"Yes. Thank you," I said, hugging her. "I'm going to go to my dad's to see if he has any advice he can offer me. I'll call you when I can."

"Okay, chile. I love you, hear?" Ms. Maple assured me.

"I love you, too." I quickly walked out of her room before I started to cry.

I exited her home through the back door. The News reported that the police were looking for Booger and me as suspects to the murder of Adam Faulkner. They also reported that Tookie and Kim were arrested the previous night in connection with the murder. I walked to Islington Street and made a left on Collingwood Boulevard. This was not a wise choice on my part. Collingwood Boulevard was a large street. Although, it was still early in the day, anybody could see me and notify the police. I really could not risk being arrested without having spoken to my daddy first. I continued to walk on Collingwood Boulevard, anyway, despite my better judgment.

Chapter Three

My cousin, James, owned a barbershop on Collingwood Boulevard, not far from where Ms. Maple lived. Once there, I hoped to call my daddy. The only drawback was that someone in the barbershop was sure to have seen the News. I did not want to take any chances of being recognized, though what choice did I have? I needed to speak with my daddy and I could not use Ms. Maple's phone for fear that it might be tapped. I decided to continue with my original plan of calling my daddy at the barbershop.

I arrived at the barbershop in just a few short minutes. As I opened the door, I looked around the barbershop. For a Saturday morning, the barbershop was relatively empty; a true rarity. I scanned the faces of the people waiting to get their hair cut. I did not recognize anyone; more importantly, no one seemed to recognize me.

I walked over to one of the barbers, "A, what's up? Can I use the phone?"

David, the barber, looked up from a guy's hair he was cutting, "A, what's up, Chris? Yeah, man, of course, you can use the phone."

"Thanks," I replied.

Picking up the phone receiver, I dialed my daddy's cell number. In 1994, cell phones were quickly gaining in popularity. Though at that time, they were not quite accessible to everyone. Usually one had to be either wealthy or very important, or both, to own one. My daddy was neither by society's standards, though he was a gadgets man. Whatever new technological gadget there was, he was sure to acquire it, no matter the cost.

My daddy had recently moved back to Toledo from Washington, D.C. He, Sara, and Tiana (my step-mother and sister) moved in with Mother, my paternal grandmother, until they found a place of their own.

My daddy was employed as director of the Rescue Crisis Center's drug rehabilitation program. A few years prior, he had earned a Master's degree in social work from Howard University, making him more marketable in the field of social work. He had been employed in quite a few areas of social work already: from child abuse and neglect to mental health and drug rehabilitation.

Sara worked as an elementary school teacher, while achieving her Master's in education from the University of Toledo. She and my dad met in Bowling Green, Ohio, where they both earned their Bachelor's degrees. They had been together for sixteen years; since I was five years old.

"Hello, this is Andrew," my dad said, answering the phone in his usual professional manner.

"Hi. Are you busy?" I asked.

I never called him by a name, as in dad or daddy, or even by his first name. In fact, I had called him dad only twice in my life. The first time was when I was ten years old; the second time I was twelve.

My reluctance to call him dad was puzzling to me. The only factor that seemed to make sense was that he had not raised me. As such, I did not share enough of an intimate relationship with him to feel comfortable in calling him dad. However,
I knew other kids, particularly my cousins, who had far less personal relationships with their fathers than I had with mine,

though they did not share in my dilemma. They effortlessly called their fathers "dad."

I originally thought of calling him daddy, which was how I usually referred to him, but the word seemed too long and drawn out to call him to his face, so I decided against it. If I was going to call him anything, it would have to dad.

I was ten years old and attending summer-day camp when I first called him dad. He was in the bathroom showering, with the bathroom door slightly ajar. Had I thought better, I could have simply knocked on the door and waited for him to answer, but I did not. Instead, I nervously called to him in a voice just above a whisper, "Dad."

The word felt foreign in my mouth. Although, my daddy was a figure in my life, he was not a constant, everyday figure. Prior to that summer, I had never lived with him; and, though he visited, his visits were typically infrequent and short-lived.

My daddy did not hear me call him. I, once again, mustered the courage to call to him. "Dad," I said a little more forcefully. Although he did not hear me say the word dad, he did hear something.

"Is someone out there?" He asked.

"Yes. It's me. Can I have some money for lunch?"

"Sara doesn't have any?"

"I don't know. She told me to come in here and ask you for some." I replied in a small ten year-old voice.

"Go look in my wallet on the dresser," he said.

"Okay. Thank you."

I ran into his bedroom and retrieved five dollars from his wallet, "I got it. Thank you."

I yelled into the bathroom, over the noise of the shower.

I excitedly ran from the apartment and into Sara's car where she and her nephew, Darryl, waited for me to return. I did it! I called him dad. I was immensely proud of myself. I was not quite sure why, but I felt that I had just achieved some sort of victory.

I did not live up to my accomplishment, however. After my initial achievement, I did not call him dad again for years.

I was twelve years old at the time. My daddy, Sara, and I were visiting our relatives in North Carolina. While there, we went to Red Lobster—one of my favorite restaurants—for dinner. My cousin, Joe, had accompanied us.

The table water was placed closest to my daddy. I asked him if he would pass it to me; though, as usual, I did not call him "dad." Either he did not hear me ask him to pass the water or he feigned as if he did not.

"Can you, please, pass me the water?" I asked a second time. He did not look in my direction, nor did he pass me the water.

"Are you talking to me?" He asked in a tone of irritation.

I replied, "Yes, can you pass me the water?"

I did not know that his irritation was about me not calling him dad.

"What?" He asked. "Is that all you're going to say?"

I looked at him bewildered. I did not know what to say. *Did he want me to say please, again?*

The waitress arrived with our order. She expertly placed our food before us, remembering who ordered what.

"Is there anything else I can get you?" She asked before leaving.

My daddy responded in his usual polite manner, "No, I think we're fine. Thank you," he smiled, brightly.

The waitress turned to leave. No sooner than her back was to us and she had walked not quite two steps away, my daddy's irritation returned. He seemed like a chameleon: one moment, he was nice and courteous; the next, he was mean and cantankerous.

"We are not going to eat until you refer to me as something," he said, seething.

Sara tried to smooth over things. "It's okay, Andrew. I'll give him the water."

Sara reached for the water container, but my daddy stopped her, motioning with his hand for her to put down the pitcher, "No, until he calls me something, we are not going to eat." Redirecting his glare toward me, "I don't care what it is. It doesn't have to be dad or daddy. It can be Andrew, but you are going to call me something!"

I stared at him, unable to speak. My throat tightened; unshed tears threatened to fall, singeing my eyelids. I was upset. A part of me understood his irritation. How could I refer to him as my daddy, yet when it involved calling him dad or anything at all, I could not. Though, in part, I blamed him. I felt that had he been a permanent fixture in my life, maybe I would not feel so uncomfortable calling him dad. Giving in, I mumbled, "Dad, can you pass me the water?"

Eight years later, and at the age of twenty, I still did not call him anything. I simply stated what was on my mind. "I need to talk with you. Are you at home?" I asked.

"Yes, I'm here getting dressed," he replied.

"Okay. I'll be there in a few minutes."

"How are you getting here?"

"I'm going to walk."

"All right, I'll see you when you get here."

I placed the phone in its cradle.

"Thanks for letting me use the phone," I said to David.

"Aw. No problem, man," he said. I cautiously walked out of the barbershop. I walked back down Collingwood Boulevard to Bancroft Street. I walked swiftly, though not too fast as to attract attention. I did not want to look like I was running from something.

As I approached Bancroft Street, I saw Kim at the stop light, driving Tookie's car. I was incredibly excited to see her. I had not seen her since the previous day; although, it was less than twelve hours ago, it felt like months. I raised my hand to get her attention, yet, before I could wave to her, I saw her shaking her head as vehemently as possible, without her shaking being overly noticeable. I understood her gesture. I quickly lowered my hand to my head, as if I was scratching it. I looked at the car behind Kim's. It appeared she was being followed by a female officer in an unmarked car. I looked away, waiting for the traffic light to change.

I crossed the street, continuing my gait. I needed to walk on another street, other than Collingwood. The boulevard was too big; someone else was bound to recognize me.

I made a right on one of the side streets leading to Parkwood Avenue. The street was less congested, making my chances of being seen more unlikely. I took Parkwood to the Toledo Art Museum and walked a short block to Mama's house to see if my Uncle Al was there, so that I could borrow some money.

I opened the door of Mama's house. As soon as I walked into the living room, my younger cousin bombarded me.

"Man, dude, they looking for y'all, man!" Dae-Dae squealed in delight.

He was excited. I imagine our being on the News had to be like a movie-turned-reality show for him. The only problem was that I did not share in his enthusiasm. This was my reality, and I did not like it. Someone was dead because of me.

"Man, they thought I was you! I walked to the store and the police stopped me! They pulled out a picture of you! I told them it wasn't me...that you was my cousin!"

Dae-Dae and I looked a lot alike. It was not the first time that we had been confused with one another.

"Who's here?" I asked, ignoring his glee.

"Al upstairs," he said.

I walked up the stairs to find Al. Dae-Dae followed close behind me like a puppy dog. Al was my mother's younger and only brother.

"Hey, Al, you got some money I can hold?" I said as I rounded the corner of the upstairs hallway.

"Now, Chris, why y'all do that? Boy, I'm telling you. Y'all go get enough of messin' with the law. These White folks ain't playin'!" Al ranted.

'Messin' with the law!' I was livid. What was he talking about? He acted as if I was a criminal with an extensive history.

"Al, you don't even know what happened. You don't even know what those White people did to us!" I said in an even tone.

I was disgusted with him. He did not know all of the facts, yet he had already tried and convicted us. I turned on my heels and walked back downstairs.

"Man, you better be careful, Chris. Man, I'm tellin' you, the police sittin' right down the street waitin' to see if y'all go come over here," Dae-Dae cautioned.

Hearing Dae-Dae's warning, Al's disposition changed. His voice softened; his words were less accusatory.

"You need anything? I got a little money I can give you." The money did not seem important anymore. I exited the house, without responding to his offer. Once outside, I turned toward Norwood Street. Al yelled from the front door, "Chris, where you gone go? You know they lookin everywhere for y'all!"

I continued my gait, though looking at him. I shook my head in disbelief. *Didn't he just hear Dae-Dae tell me that the police were right down the street, and that they were in the neighborhood looking for me? Did he not know that his yelling could draw their attention to me?*

Dae-Dae nudged him, "Al, man, what you doin'? The police might hear you." Al looked stupefied; it had never crossed his mind that the police might be able to hear him.

I walked down Norwood Avenue and through the parking lot of Warren A.M.E. Church. I had many memories of the church; specifically, the parking lot. Early weekday mornings, my cousin, Andre, and I would walk through the lot on the way to Martin Luther King Jr., Elementary School where we were students. At other times, Andre and I, along with several of our cousins, would pass through the lot en route to Smith Park, where we would play for hours.

Those pleasant thoughts seemed like a lifetime ago. We were young, innocent children then, void of a care in the world. Who would have thought that one day we would be suspects to murder? Or that, the parking lot, next to the huge church with the big stein-glassed window of Jesus, where we ran and jumped and learned how to ride our bicycles, would also become a part of my voyage into the unknown?

I reached my paternal grandmother's house in little time. Mother, as most everyone called her, lived just a few blocks from Mama's house. I approached Mother's house with the same uneasy feeling that had plagued me throughout the day; a nagging feeling of impending doom.

I could not shake the feeling. I walked up the green-carpeted stairs to the porch. I rang the doorbell and listened for the familiar chime. As I waited for someone to open the door, I peered over the railing to look at the driveway.

Mother had the driveway painted a bright green to match the color of the carpet on the porch. It was pretty, but it was strange to see someone's driveway painted. At eighty-years of age, she had not driven a car in over twenty years. I assumed that she felt she could paint it, since it was unlikely that a car of her own would be parked there.

After a minute or so, Mother finally swung open the huge white door. She looked at me through the window of the security door. I waved to her. Unlocking the security door, she smiled,

"Hey, doll! I ain't seen you in a while."

"I know," I responded sheepishly. I bent down to kiss her on the cheek.

Mother was an even five feet, three inches tall and somewhat stout. She had a beautiful personality; quick-witted, humorous, and feisty.

"I've been staying over my friend, Ms. Maple's house." I said in response to her statement about not having seen me in a while.

Without missing a beat, "And, I guess, that kept you from coming over here to see me?"

I looked away. What could I say? Obviously, I could have come to see her, regardless of where I lived or with whom I lived.

"You want something to eat?" Mother asked, having already moved passed my neglect and on to being "Mother."

The house smelled wonderful, as usual. I walked through the living and dining room, and into the kitchen where the aroma was strongest. Several pound cakes were placed on the kitchen table. A lemon and chocolate cake lay on the counter, alongside a dish of roast beef and potato salad. Since Mother had retired, five short years ago, she began to bake and sell cakes full-time.

Mother prepared big meals, as though she had a large family to feed. When, in truth, prior to my daddy and his family's move to Toledo, she had lived alone. She would oftentimes give much of the food she cooked to homeless persons and drug addicts in the neighborhood. She had a beautiful, warm and giving spirit.

"No, I'm fine," I said.

As much as I wanted to have a slice of cake, I did not have the appetite to eat anything, which was highly unusual for me. I usually could eat under any circumstances, especially something sweet. But, these circumstances were different, something of which I was not accustomed.

"You lookin' for your dad?" Mother asked.

"Yes, is he here?" I knew he was there. I saw his truck parked outside as I walked to the house. I felt awkward and at a loss of words.

"He's upstairs."

"Okay." I walked up the stairs, turning into the first bedroom on the right. I knocked on the door.

"What's up, son? How's it going?" He asked as he sat on the bed putting his socks on his feet.

I looked around the small room. It was the room where he slept as a child. *It was hard to imagine my daddy as a young boy sleeping in this room. The young mind could not quite fathom a time when his parents were anything other than his parents.*

I searched my mind trying to find the right words to tell him the reason I had come there. How does a person tell his father that he not only shot someone, but that this same someone was now dead as well? He looked at me expectantly; waiting for me to say why I had come there.

"I shot somebody."

The words spilled from me. I looked at him, waiting to see what he would say. His countenance remained unchanged, as if I had just told him that I was going around the corner to the store to buy a Snicker's candy bar.

"What happened?" He calmly asked.

Now, that was strange. It was as though we were a family of mobsters or gang bangers, and me telling him that I had killed someone was an everyday occurrence. But we were not mobsters or gang members, and I had never told him that I had killed someone. I continued to look at him, trying to find a clue as to his nonchalance. I found none, so I began telling him what happened.

After I finished telling him the story, he asked me, "What do you want to do?"

"Huh?" I asked.

"Do you want to flee the city; go to Detroit?" My daddy was by no stretch of the imagination street-wise, so it was strange for me to hear him suggest anything other than to obey the law. In his younger years, he had a brush or two with the crime, but, by most accounts, he was a "square," as Mymomme called him.

I had expected him to suggest something else or to advise me differently. Though, despite his education and professionalism, he was still a Black man in America. He, like Ms. Maple, understood, better than I, what I was facing. They had obviously lived longer than me. They knew too well the blatant racism of the sixties; the discrimination of the seventies; the struggle of the eighties; and the injustices of the nineties. In their minds, nothing had changed; White folks were still White folks, and Black folks were still the underdogs.

"No, I'm going to stay here and fight the case," I said.

"Well, what do you want to do?"

It was strange. Technically, I was a month and a half from being twenty-one, thereby a "legal" adult, but seemingly overnight I had been transformed from a child to an adult.

"I need to get an attorney. I have a little money I saved to get a car. I should also turn
myself in to the police soon."

I still could not believe what my life had become; that I was having a conversation with my father about submitting myself to the authorities and acquiring an attorney.

"Let's get an attorney first, before you turn yourself in. We need to see what he says. You need to lay low for a while until we find someone, though."

"Okay."

"It really sounds like self-defense to me, but let's see what the attorney says. Have you told your mother?"

"No," I said, shaking my head from left to right.

"Let's go downstairs and tell your grandmother, and then I'll take you over to Carol's until you turn yourself in to the authorities."

Carol was my daddy's older sister. Mother had four children: two girls and two boys. My Uncle Phillip passed away when I was seven years old. My dad was the baby of the four, with fourteen and sixteen years between him and his sisters.

We walked downstairs and into the den where Mother sat watching television. "Mother, Chris has something he wants to tell you," my daddy said.

I stood looking at her. I did not want to share the news with her. It pained me that I had taken someone's life, though I was deeply saddened for having to tell my family that I had killed someone. I was ashamed. I felt that I had let down them all, even without them having expressed it. In the same solemn voice, I repeated the still unfamiliar words, "I shot somebody."

Chapter Four

The days leading up to my arrest went by far too fast. My daddy and I left Mother's house and went directly to Aunt Carol's.

It was a beautiful, sunny day; much too beautiful to be stuck in the house with the weight of the world on my shoulders. Aunt Carol's daughter, Brandy, was there to let us in the house. Brandy was not just my first cousin, but she was also one of my closest friends.

Brandy had a very calm, reassuring manner about herself that made talking to her easy and comfortable. She was also one of the few people I knew who practiced thorough, sound judgment. I could go to her with a problem and trust that she would give me honest, unbiased feedback. To me, her ability to impart her knowledge and understanding of things was invaluable.

I had noticed that too often many people had friends who gave them partial advice or opinions; either the friends simply did not know how to decipher between what was right from what was wrong, or they said what one wanted to hear, rather than what one needed to hear. Brandy told me the truth. She shared her candor with me in a gentle manner, thereby protecting my sensitive feelings, while still conveying the truth. I felt that everyone needed someone like Brandy in their lives.

The front door of Aunt Carol's house was unlocked. Brandy came downstairs as I walked into the living room. Our eyes met for an instant.

A warmth of empathy radiated from her green-colored eyes. She walked to me and hugged me close; firm and loving. I relaxed a bit in her embrace, relishing the moment. I seldom had someone to comfort me while I had experienced the woes of life. I was raised to be independent and a leader. More times than not, I was the person consoling and offering words of knowledge and wisdom to those in distress. Brandy's extension of comfort felt good, yet unsettling for me. I disengaged from her embrace. I simply could allow myself to get used to be comforted.

I did not know what lay ahead of me, but I felt in my spirit that there would be times when there would be no one to console me. It was better for me that I become acquainted with standing on my own two feet without the support of others.

"Hey, you," she smiled, looking up at me. Brandy was exactly five feet in height.

Stepping back to look at her more closely, I returned her smile, "Hey."

She held my hand reassuringly for a moment, then turned to my dad, giving him a hug. Brandy and my daddy conversed for several minutes until he announced that he was leaving.

"Son, I'm going to head out. I'll be back some time tomorrow. I don't want people to see me coming here too often and guess that you are here. Make sure that you don't tell anyone where you are and stay off the phone as much as possible."

"Okay," I replied as I hugged him. He kissed me on the cheek, "You're going to be all right. We'll get through this."

I nodded affirmatively, accepting his words of encouragement.

The days and nights at Aunt Carol's passed without incident. I spent the bulk of my days watching television or talking to Brandy. It seemed that no sooner than I had arrived at Aunt Carol's, it was time to go. It was Monday, and I was being whisked away to Aunt Rachel's.

The days appeared to run into one another. It was another beautiful day; sunny and refreshingly warm. Yet, to me, it felt overcast and cold, like a rainy, winter day. I was disconnected from the things around me. Each night I slept with a huge weight on my mind that prevented me from sleeping soundly; I awoke and went through my day with the same feeling. Though, I did not know the person I had shot, I carried with me the loss of his life. I mourned his passing, as if he were a close relative of mine. Nothing could brighten my days; not the radiant sun outside; not the love and support of my family; not the hope of a better day.

I inconspicuously opened the passenger door and stepped into my dad's jeep. I should have been nervous about being seen, but I was not. Nothing seemed to matter; not even the threat of being identified or apprehended. A boy's life was taken away at my hands; a life that could not be brought back. No amount of praying could change the course of events that had occurred. I had committed an irreversible act: I had killed someone.

"Son, how are you?" My dad asked, as he turned the ignition of the car.

I looked out the window of the car, "I'm fine." I could feel him looking at me. I did not want to look at him. I did not want to face him, or anyone for that matter. I wanted to sit by myself and sulk in the void of nothingness that had come to occupy my mind.

"We're going to meet with a few attorneys today. I scheduled an appointment to meet one of them at the Red Roof, near Westgate Mall."

"Okay," I said flatly.

We arrived at the designated place. The restaurant looked like a country-western saloon. It had once been a Ponderosa's Restaurant. I used to work there as a waiter for a brief time. I quit after about a month. Kevon and I had begun to date, and I could not bear to be away from him. I foolishly quit the job, so that we could spend more time together.

My daddy and I looked around the restaurant; neither he nor I knew what the attorney looked like. To the far right of the room, I saw an older heavy-set, White guy sitting by himself. He looked directly at us. If he was the attorney, he did not seem very interested in getting our attention.

My daddy and I walked over to his table.

"Excuse me," my daddy said. "Are you Robert Mead?" The guy nodded his head affirmatively. My dad extended his hand, "My name is Andrew Richardson, and this is my son, Christopher." The guy shook my daddy's hand nonchalantly.

"Hi," I said. I did not feel comfortable with this guy. There was something about him that was unsettling.

"May we?" My daddy asked before sitting down to join the man at the table.

"Sure," he said with his mouth filled with food.

We sat down.

"As I expressed over the phone, my son needs an attorney. Son, you want to tell him what happened?"

I really did not want to talk to this guy, but I felt that it was in my best interest to do so. I felt uneasy in his presence. I could not quite put my finger on what disturbed me about him, but there was something. I told him the story, as he inhaled the meat from the bones of his Bar-B-Que ribs.

I was not a mean-spirited person. Generally, I did not talk negatively about anyone, though, as I looked at Mr. Mead, I could not help to think of Boss Hogg from the show, "The Dukes of Hazzard." Mr. Mead's mannerisms were nearly identical to Boss Hogg's: the way he ate his ribs; how his napkin was tucked between the collars of his shirt; his weight; not to mention, he was not particularly a pleasant person—another one of Boss Hogg's less than flattering traits.

After I finished the story, Mr. Mead took the time to grab his napkin from the collars of his shirt to wipe his greasy mouth.

"Well, it sounds to me like he committed murder," he said, flatly. "I'll take the case for fifty-thousand dollars, but he'll probably be found guilty of first degree murder."

I looked at him across the table from me with unbelieving eyes. *Was this man serious? Had he heard what I told him?* I do not know what sort of time that I expected to receive, but I knew that I had not committed first-degree murder.

"What do you think, son?" My dad asked.

I shook my head, "No, I think we should find someone else."

My demeanor toward Mr. Mead was not rude, but it was not particularly pleasant either.

We stood to leave.

"Thank you, sir, for your time," my daddy said.

"Thank you," I mumbled.

My dad was obviously far more of a gentleman than I. He knew how to be polite and cordial, even in the worst of situations.

We stopped at one additional restaurant where we met another attorney. He, too, was middle-aged and White. Although, he was more pleasant than the other attorney and his fee was slightly less, he echoed the same sentiments as the first attorney.

"I can represent Christopher for twenty-five thousand. If we take it to trial, the jury will find him guilty of murder."

"Murder?" My daddy asked. "Even given the circumstances

and the fact that he did not pull the trigger?"

"Yes," the attorney said.

"How much time does a murder conviction carry?" My daddy asked him.

"Anywhere from twenty-five years to life."

This time my daddy did not need to ask what I thought. We politely got up from the table, thanking the attorney as we left.

Our next stop was to the office of Tim Bradley, a brilliant, African American attorney. My daddy had spoken with Mymomme, and both of my parents agreed that we should see how much Bradley, as most people called him, would charge to represent me. My daddy parked his Jeep in front of Bradley's office building in downtown Toledo; a risky move, considering I was wanted for murder.

Toledo's police department was located downtown. There was sure to be police everywhere. I did not voice my thoughts to my daddy; instead, I walked alongside him into the three-story building to Bradley's office.

The receptionist greeted us at the front desk. My daddy introduced us, explaining that we had an appointment with Bradley. She, in turn, picked up the phone, notifying Bradley of our presence. Shortly thereafter, Bradley walked into the room. He was tall and slender; medium-brown-complected, the color of sun-dried dirt. He appeared mature and sophisticated in his well-fitted, double-breasted suit. His short, dark, silver-streaked hair was neatly combed to the back. His demeanor and carriage made him look foreign in Toledo. In a city like Washington, D.C., or Atlanta, where there were so many Black professionals, he would have fit in easily; yet, in Toledo, where there were so few African American professionals, he stood out.

Bradley smiled brightly at us, revealing beautifully-lined, white teeth. After we all had shook hands, my dad and I followed him to his office. Bradley offered us two chairs across from his desk. His office was sparsely furnished: an average-sized desk and two chairs for clients; no pictures of family member sat on his desk; no framed degrees adorned the walls.

"What can I do for you, gentlemen?" Bradley asked, as he smiled.

"Timmie, as I said on the telephone, my son had an altercation with some White people on the south side of Toledo. Son, why don't you explain to Timmie what occurred?"

My daddy and Bradley were about the same
age. Apparently, they knew one another, which was the reason that my daddy referred to him as 'Timmie.'

Once again, I shared the details of the unfortunate day of June 3rd. Bradley listened intently as I told him what transpired. After I finished telling him the story, Bradley said, "I think we should take it to trial and let the jury decide the outcome."

My daddy and I looked at one another, not quite sure how to take what Bradley had expressed.

"So, do you think we can beat it?" My daddy asked.

"Well, I don't know, but there is a possibility," Bradley replied.

"I won't be convicted of murder?" I interjected.

"I can't guarantee you that, but, considering the circumstances, I don't think so. I'm going to fight for an acquittal."

Wow! He had already delegated himself as my attorney, and he felt that we could win the case!

I felt a glimmer of hope. "How much would you charge us?" My daddy asked.

"Ten thousand; four thousand now, and the remaining six

after the trial," Bradley stated.

Ten thousand dollars! That was a lot of money, though in comparison to the figure the other attorneys quoted, and the fact that the other attorneys said that I would be found guilty of murder, made ten thousand dollars seem like pennies!

"What do you think, son?" Again, as with the previous attorneys, there was something about
Bradley that caused me to feel a little trepidation. I innately sensed something, yet I could not say what it was. He was intelligent, handsome, and charismatic, however, something was amiss. My daddy had shared with me that Bradley had been involved in some illegal drug activities some years ago, yet that was not the reason for my concern. I could not determine the exact cause for my feelings, so I disregarded them.

Despite my apprehension, for the first time since all of this had occurred, I had to admit that I felt there was some light at the end of the tunnel.

"I like what he said, especially after encountering those other attorneys!" I said.

My daddy laughed, "I agree, son!"

Bradley looked puzzled. My daddy filled him in on our experience with the previous attorneys. Bradley laughed, understanding all too well how we must have felt.

~~~~

The challenge of acquiring a quality attorney was one of the many hurdles I would have to overcome. Despite Bradley's willingness to accept my case, a feeling of loss still surrounded me. I was enveloped by a sense of foreboding. I grieved Adam's passing. I constantly played over and over in my mind Booger's words of doom, 'That boy was shot and killed.'

I could not get the events of that fateful evening out of my mind. *How did he die???* I questioned repeatedly in my mind. I understood how he died, of course. More specifically, I wondered how I had shot him.

I had never in my life had an accurate aim. I could not throw a ball, a rock, or any other object with accuracy. As a child when I threw a softball, it always veered to the left or right by several feet of the intended catcher. At other times, my cousins and I would throw rocks at stop signs; their rocks would hit the target. Mine? I would be lucky if the rock came within ten feet of the sign.

How then, I agonizingly questioned within myself, could I have successfully shot someone with a gun? Although the gun was held in the direction of Adam, it was never directly aimed at him. How, then, could a small projectile have hit him?

In my mind's eye, I saw where Adam and I were positioned: he was on the porch and I was on ground-level looking up at him from several feet away. The gun was pointed upward, though not directly at Adam. It simply made no sense to me. It was as if some unseen forces were at work plotting my destruction.

How could this happen? I am not a murderer. I did not like to kill pesky houseflies, because I felt that, in a spiritual sense, they deserved the right to live. I was not an evil-minded person. I simply did not have what it entailed to kill someone; that being, the mentality or the athleticism. Yet, I was wanted for murder, and was very likely looking at time in jail, to expect the least.

~~~~

My dad and I arrived at Aunt Rachel's minutes after we left Bradley's office. We entered Aunt Rachel's backyard through the alley behind her house to avoid detection. Her petite, 4'10 frame could be seen in the doorwell, as we approached the house. I opened the screen door, and bent down to hug her. She patted me on my back and quickly ushered me into the house away from the possible gaze of onlookers.

Aunt Rachel's small, two bedroom house was nice. It reminded me of Mother's house, only smaller. I walked in the kitchen where I waited for my daddy and her. After entering the kitchen, she gave me a quick tour of the house, as though it was my first time being there.

She talked quietly and moved around with the efficiency of a lion stalking its prey. I suddenly understood the enormity of her actions. I was a suspect to murder; she was hiding a fugitive of the law in her home. This was monumental for this seventy-plus year old woman.

She took me to her second bedroom, removing a rug that concealed a trap door. I peered down the opening. The room was large enough for a twin-sized bed. I felt like I was experiencing a piece of history. *Was this how it felt to be a run-away slave? Was I being shown a hiding place in the home of a courageous abolitionist?*

Ironically, while the house did not exist during the time of slavery, there was a historical legacy to the room. Aunt Rachel was the first of Mother's siblings to arrive to Toledo from their hometown of Bessemer, Alabama. As family members of ours made the pilgrimage to the industrious North and its lure of factory work, many of them lived with Aunt Rachel and her husband until they found homes of their own. It was not uncommon for twelve to fifteen people to occupy this small house, including the hide-away room into which I peered.

After my tour of the house, Aunt Rachel instructed me not to use the phones. Like my dad, she feared that the phone lines may have been tapped. I could go anywhere in the house that I wanted, but in case of an emergency, I was to go into the hide-away room.

I nodded affirmatively to her instructions. Once again, my dad bid me farewell. "Son, I'll see you in a couple days. I'll meet with Timmie to discuss when he thinks it would be best for you to turn yourself in."

"Okay," I said. We hugged and he was gone. I quickly began to miss his presence. My dad had a take-charge manner that made me feel comforted, even in the midst of my circumstances. With him gone, I felt alone and vulnerable.

~~~

I could not resist. I had to get on the phone. I needed to speak with someone. Aunt Rachel was gone to work, and I was left in the house by myself. As a cosmetologist, she worked from eight o'clock in the morning to six o'clock every evening.

I called Mymomme. I had not spoken to her since the night of June third. I had wanted to call her many times before, but my father's admonishment regarding the phone stayed with me. I could not wait any longer, though. I needed to hear her voice. I picked up the phone receiver with little trepidation.

"Hello, Mymomme?" I said into the phone.

"Huh?" Her voice sounded strange. She had a naturally low voice, but even still the voice on the other end of the call did not sound like hers at all. It was lower and gravelly, as if someone had scraped her vocal chords with sandpaper.

"What's wrong with your voice?" As soon as I asked the question, I knew the answer. She had been crying, and apparently a lot. The sound of her voice was a remnant of the pain she felt because of the situation in which I had gotten myself. My heart began to beat erratically; my stomach quivered.

"Nothing," she responded solemnly. She did not want me

to know that she had been crying.

"Oh," I said, at a loss for words. A brief moment of silence developed between us before anything was said.

"How come you didn't tell me?" Mymomme finally asked.

"Mhm mmm...I didn't want you to worry."

A mother's love is truly a blessing. Many times we, as children, take for granted the blessing we have been given. My mother and I had always enjoyed a particularly close relationship. Although, it was not free of issues, she was still my mother. She had not done everything right as a mother, but she did what she could or what she knew to do. She loved me deeply, and I loved and cherished her in my soul. I was appreciative that God chose her to be the vessel in which I came into the world.

"You know they got Booger, don't you?" she asked.

"They? They who?" I questioned.

"The police. Him and Todd was out at Raymond's house and they caught him out there." Todd was Booger's best friend. They had been friends since they were young kids. People oftentimes referred to them as brothers, although Todd was White.

"What?!" Oh, no! I had hoped this would not happen. I did not know what the plan was, but I did not want Booger to go to jail for something that I did.

"Yeah, he been there since last night."

"Does he have an attorney? Have you spoken to Tookie or Kim?" I asked.

"I don't think so. I don't know if Raymond got the money to get him a attorney. Tookie and Kim out. They let them go the next day."

Raymond was Tookie and Booger's father. After Kim and Raymond separated, unlike some father's, Raymond maintained an active part in the lives of his children.

"Yeah, I saw Kim the day after all of this happened. I was walking down Collingwood and I saw her driving Tookie's car. There was a police car behind her."

"Was it?! Did they see you?"

"Uhn huh. Kim did, but not the police officer. It was because of Kim that I knew there was a police car following her. I was about to wave at her, but she started shaking her head. When I looked behind her, I saw a woman driving a vehicle that looked like an unmarked police car."

"Hmm, it's a good thing she did that, otherwise you'd be locked-up already."

"I know."

"So you and your daddy got Bradley, huh?" She asked, changing the subject. She and my daddy had been communicating a lot, lately. They separated when I was a young kid, and they completely called it quits when I was five. They had little to say to one another, except when it concerned me.

"Yes, we did. He seems like a good attorney," I said, not really knowing what else to say. I was in a garrulous mood when I initially called her, but, after hearing the sadness and hurt in her voice, I no longer wanted to talk. Again, I wondered how I had gotten myself into all of this trouble.

"Yeah, he is. They say, he one of the best in the city," she replied.

"That's what my daddy told me, too," I responded.

"Mmm hmm, he is…well, I'ma get off this phone. You ain't supposed to be on it, is you?" Mymomme asked.

"No, but I needed to talk to you. I love you," I said. My throat ached; my tears were stuck there, or so it seemed. I would have liked to have let them out, if for no other reason than to release the tension in my throat, but none would fall.

"I know. I'm glad you did. I love you, my son."

"I love you, too, Mymomme. Bye-bye," I said, as I swallowed through the lump in my throat.

"Bye, bae," she said in her deep voice.

I put the phone in the cradle, thinking about the mess in which I had gotten my family and myself.

~~~

The following day I was scheduled to submit myself to the authorities. My daddy arrived at Aunt Rachel's house shortly before noon. As I approached his truck, I could see the silhouette of a person through the slightly tinted windows of his Jeep. Mymomme sat in the front passenger seat. My heart leapt with joy. It seemed like forever since I had last seen her. I opened the back passenger door, climbing inside.

"Hey there!" I chirped.

"Hey, bae," she smiled, looking back at me. She was trying to be strong, though I could see the sadness and hurt in her eyes. She looked as if her world was truly falling apart. I remained upbeat. I had to be strong for both of us. If I fell weak, her world would undoubtedly crumble.

"Are you hungry, junior?" my daddy asked.

"No, I'm fine...thank you," I replied.

"Are you sure you don't want any Wendy's or McDonald's before we head downtown?" He asked.

"No, I'm okay."

If I had known what was good for me, I would have taken his offer and eaten something before turning in myself, but I did not know any better.

"Okay, well, we are headed downtown to the Safety Building," he said.

The Safety Building is a division of the police department.

Amongst other things, I assumed, it was where fugitives turned in themselves when a warrant was issued for their arrest. Bradley told the authorities that I would be voluntarily submitting myself to avoid being arrested as a wanted suspect to murder. Being arrested involuntarily did not look good for a wanted fugitive. It appeared as though the person was evading the law.

When we arrived at the Safety Building several reporters and cameramen stood outside of the building awaiting my arrival. Someone had apparently told them that I was turning in myself. Like vultures circling over freshly killed prey, the reporters patiently awaited my arrival.

"Are you ready, son?" My daddy asked.

"Yes, I'm ready," I said in a strong, confident voice.

I hugged Mymomme before exiting my daddy's truck.

"Come on, let's go," he said as we climbed out of the truck.

He and I walked beside one another, passing the reporters and cameramen, and entered the Safety Building. Fortunately, certainly to their dismay, we went undetected by the reporters. With my processed hair cut short, and my daddy dressed in his usual garb of a suit and tie, they must have mistaken us for typical citizens, rather than a father accompanying his son—a suspect to murder.

~~~

As my daddy and I passed through the glass doors of the Safety Building, we saw Bradley standing off to the side waiting for us. Bradley smiled at us and shook our hands. My dad and I turned to one another. It was time for us to part ways. My daddy's face wore a look of pain, as though he had lost something precious.

"Well, son, take care of yourself and be strong. Everything

will work out fine."

His soft, light-brown eyes filled with tears.

"Okay. I'll be all right," I said, speaking through the ever-present lump in my throat. I felt like crying, but as usual nothing would fall from my eyes. I was not afraid of what lie ahead of me. Though, I was concerned for my family. One catastrophic event had forever changed the lives of so many people.

I hugged my daddy. We embraced each other strong and long, kissing one another on the cheeks as we parted.

"I love you, my boy," he said, regaining his composure and smiling brightly through even, pearly white teeth.

"I love you, too," I smiled back.

I looked over my daddy's shoulder to where Bradley stood. He smiled as he walked over to where I stood.

"Are you ready?" He asked in a gentle, friendly manner.

"Yes." I said, nodding my head affirmatively.

"I'll be right back," Bradley said to my daddy.

Bradley and I walked over to a desk where a police officer sat. The officer smiled at me, as he stood up and came from behind the desk.

"He has to handcuff you before he takes you into custody. It's standard procedure." Bradley informed me.

"Okay." I said.

I placed my arms behind my back and turned my back to the officer as he approached me. I felt the cold steel encircling my wrist, and then with a click, I was bound.

"Okay. Is that too tight?" The officer asked, turning me in the direction in which we would be walking.

"No, it's okay," I said.

I was surprised by his concern. I had expected him to be rude or mean, but he was neither. I quickly turned to my daddy before the officer led me away, "Bye!"

I was taken to a small room with a table and several chairs. I sat there until a civilian-clothed officer and Bradley walked into the room. The officer, who identified himself as Detective Sinclair, asked me a few perfunctory questions: my name, address, etc. He then read to me the Miranda Warning. Bradley expressed to him that I would not be answering any questions regarding the case. Detective Sinclair accepted my right not to discuss the case.

He smiled politely at me, "an officer will escort you to booking."

I smiled back, nodding my head to him. I was appreciative of his kindness. He was nothing like television shows had portrayed detectives to be: there was no loud talking; no threats of ensuing punishments; no demeaning names were being thrown at me. Had I not been handcuffed and sitting in an interrogation room, one could have easily mistaken our verbal exchange as simply a conversation amongst men.

I was quickly booked: mug shot taken, fingerprinted, and my valuables were securely locked away until my release; although, save a little change, I did not bring anything of real value with me. I had prepared myself for the impending moment days ago. It was inevitable.

After being booked, I was taken to the bull-pen. The bull-pen served as a holding cell for inmates being transferred upstairs to the pods or dormitories. Generally, arrested persons remained in the bull-pen for three to five days, unless they were released from jail sooner than that time.

Booger was only in the bull-pen for two days. I assumed that he was transferred upstairs because of my arrest. It was well-known by both laypersons and law enforcement that we were jailed for the same offense. The circumstances of our incarceration were heavily televised; our photos had been taken from our homes and aired on the local News stations.

Whenever possible, the authorities tried to keep inmates who were arrested for the same crime separate from one another to lessen the likelihood of violence ensuing between them, and to prevent co-defendants from sharing pertinent information related to the case with each other.

After being booked and escorted to the bull-pen, I was given a thick, brown, wool blanket and a plastic pillow. A county correctional officer escorted me to a barred-room. Upon his hand signal, the huge gate unlocked, and began clanking open. I looked pass the doorwell and into the bullpen. Men, both young and old, were lying everywhere: some were on green, plastic-covered mattresses; others were lying in fetal positions on the hard concrete floors, wrapped in cocoons of blankets similar to the one I had been issued.

The walls of the bull-pen were heavily stained. The original color appeared to be white at one time. Though now, they were a pale mustard color. I walked into the room carrying my blanket and pillow close to me for fear that they would brush up against the soiled walls, while also being careful not to step on anyone lying on the floor.

The first area I entered was an entry way of sorts to another room further in the back. I walked to the second room, passing two locked cells to my right. I later learned that the cells were used as total-confinement rooms for the inmates who were severely disruptive.

The room in the back was in no better condition than the entryway/room that I had first entered. In fact, it appeared to be worse. Three bunk beds and a couple of cots were placed in the small, over-crowded area. An exposed toilet was positioned in the left corner of the room; there was no stall or walls to surround the stainless steel commode. It simply sat in the corner of the room for all to use, without a hint of privacy.

I knew for certain that I would not defecate in the toilet, not only was there no privacy, but it was beyond nasty: dried feces were caked on and around the bowl; urine was scattered everywhere, including on the floor surrounding the toilet. Unbelievably, there were people, snuggly encased in their state-issued blankets just a mere three feet from the foul-smelling waste-hole.

I stood transfixed with my back close to a wall, though careful not to rest on it. I did not know what to do or where to go. All of the beds were taken, and I was by no means going to lie, sit, or squat on the floor. I was doubtful that I could remain standing for three days, but I was determined to do so, if I must.

Thankfully, however, after a few short minutes of standing, a guard shouted through the gate, "Jones, bunk and junk!"

I did not know what he meant, but, before I could ponder any longer, a guy who was asleep on one of the bunk beds quickly raised his head, grabbed his blankets, and rushed for the gate.

"Jones?" The officer barked, as he looked at a photo in his hand.

"Yeah," the half-asleep guy responded.

"Somebody must love you," the officer stated sarcastically, "you've been released."

The guard signaled for the gate to be opened, and the guy was gone. I looked around to see if anyone would claim the guy's spot on the bunk bed. When no one moved, I walked to it, hoisted myself, and climbed to the top bunk.

I sat on the bunk bed, contemplating what lay ahead of me. *What would I do next? How long will I have to be in the atrocious place?* I looked around at the men assembled in the room. I sat amongst what most considered the derelicts of society: drug addicts, homeless persons, thieves; those of whom family and friends had relinquished all hope of positive change. Many of the inmates were clothed in near rags, unkempt, and in need of showering. I wondered what their individual stories were; what happened in their lives for them to be in the county jail?

"Chow!" A male officer shouted through the steel bars.

Mayhem suddenly broke loose. The dead had risen. Those that were, at one time, sound asleep were awake and rushing to the gate. I had no idea what the commotion was about. I stayed on my bunk bed waiting to see what would be revealed. Soon, one by one, the men began to enter the room with brown, paper bags. The men hurriedly reached into the bag, unveiling the treasured contents—food. I looked down from my position on the bunk bed at the meal that was being served: a carton of milk, two slices of bread, some sort of deli meat, and a small cup of fruit. The miniscule servings did not seem hardly worth the commotion they caused; though, perhaps for many of the jailed men, the meal was better than no meal.

"A, man, you better go get yo' bag. They ain't go serve nothin' else until the morning," a guy in the bunk bed next to me professed.

"Naw, I'm okay. I'm not hungry," I responded.

"Well, can you get it and give it to me?" He asked, sheepishly.

"Yeah," I looked down from the bed to make sure my feet would not hit anyone in the head as I jumped down from the bed. I walked to the gate and grabbed a bag from the slot. I walked back to my bunk bed, handing the bag to the guy before I jumped up to the bed.

"Man, thanks! Thanks, man! You sho you don't want none of this?" He asked, earnestly. "Naw, I'm cool." I replied.

"I'm telling you, man, you oughtta take something. It's gone be a long time before they feed us again"

"It's okay." I said, as I smiled, "Go ahead and enjoy

yourself. I'll be alright."

"Alright, well, thanks, man."

The guy was truly appreciative. It was funny, in an interesting way rather than an amusing one, how so many of us take small things, like a sandwich, for granted. Many of us are so accustomed to going to the refrigerator, the grocery store, or a restaurant to get what we want that we forget how fortunate we really are.

Although, I had never had a weak stomach, I really did not think I could eat anything while I was in the bullpen. The stench alone was vomit-inducing, not to mention the sight of the toilet or the grimy walls and floor.

"Hey, man, what's yo' name?" The older Black man to whom I had given my food asked.

"Chris." I said.

"Chris, my name is Willy. It's good to meet you," Willy replied, enthusiastically.

I liked him, without knowing wholly why, though something about him told me that he was all right. I was usually a good judge of character.

"It's nice to meet you too, Willy." I said, smiling.

I did not mean to smile; it was my way. My daddy always said, 'Son, shake a person's hand firmly, look them in the eyes, and smile'. I do not think that my daddy meant that I should extend the same courtesy in situations where I would be meeting someone for the very first time in jail. As an inmate in a correctional institution, something as innocent as a smile could be taken as a sign of weakness or flirtatiousness. I was not weak, and I definitely was not flirting with Willy. Although, I liked Willy and felt that he was a cool guy, I did not know him well enough to let my guard completely down.

"How old are you, Chris?" Willy asked. He appeared to be about fifty-five years of age.

"I'm twenty. I'll be twenty-one next month," I said.

"Twenty?! You still a baby! You aint got no business in here!"

I smiled again…I could not help myself; his dramatic response was funny to me.

"I know." I said, again contemplating my circumstances. Willy dared not ask me the reason I was in the jail. It was an unspoken rule amongst inmates that you never ask someone the circumstances of his incarceration. Although some inmates went against the unspoken rule and inquired anyway, Willy did not have the gall to do such a thing.

He was an old-timer, or con, as they preferred to call themselves. In fact, it was an insult to refer to someone like Willy as an inmate; a man who had been in the criminal justice system for most of his life. The term inmate represented the new order; a group of young incarcerates who did not know or understand the unofficial rules of prison life. Willy was definitely not an "inmate". Not only did he respect a person's right to privacy, he also associated with a select few. Old-timers were very particular about with whom they shared their time.

"Well, I hope you get out soon. Prison ain't no place for a guy like you," Willy responded, wisely.

"Thank you," I said, both accepting his intended compliment, as well as his hope of good fortune.

Chapter Five

All things considered, the hours into the days in the bullpen went by rather quickly. I still had not eaten a full meal; although, I did manage to eat a couple of apples, and I drank some juice. I just could not bring myself to eat the food.

The food itself was not my issue. I was in jail; realistically, I did not expect a gourmet meal. The bigger issue for me was the smell of the bullpen. I did not like to breathe in the stench of the place, much less breathe in the odor while trying to eat and simultaneously keep the food from erupting from my stomach. It took too much effort. I ate only what was necessary to maintain my strength and health. And, just when I thought I could no longer take being in the bullpen.

"Price!" an officer shouted after I had been there for three days.

"Yeah," I responded.

"Grab your stuff. You're moving upstairs." Although I was still in jail, I was happy to get out of the bullpen. Willy left for home a day earlier, though, before he left, he educated me on how to conduct myself while incarcerated.

"Just stick to yourself, youngster. Don't gamble, and most of all, stay away from them fags. They ain't nothing, but trouble. I know you a man and got needs, but jack yo' meat. It'll keep you out of trouble. I'm tellin' you them fags ain't the route to go. I done seen all sorts of fights and thangs because of them," he stated adamantly.

While I had always been a self-directed person, I listened

intently to what Willy said. In part, because he was older and he had experienced a part of life that I had never imagined would be my life, but also because I felt that you can always learn something from anyone. Sometimes people will only listen to certain individuals; they discount and disregard the words of those who do not fit their image of educators. Though, life has shown me that true knowledge can come from anyone: from an alcoholic on a street-corner to a felon to substance users to children. Knowledge and wisdom are indiscriminate, regarding the vessels in which they employ.

While I did not like that Willy referred to homosexuals as fags, I understood the message he conveyed, without wholly understanding how I understood it. Though, later, Willy's advice would prove helpful to me.

The following day after Willy's release, I was escorted from the bullpen through long and winding corridors to Common Pleas Court where I was arraigned. The arraignment process was uneventful.

"Mr. Price, how do you plea?" the judge asked me.

"Not guilty," I responded, as I looked up. My wrists, clasped in handcuffs, ached under the weight of the metal.

"Very well, then. I see that you have acquired counsel."

Bradley stood beside me in an impeccable, double breasted suit and tie. He smiled at the judge.

"Yes, I have," I responded.

"Very well, Mr. Price, you will be assigned another judge to preside over your case, as I only handle arraignments."

"Thank you," I replied, not really knowing why I was thanking him, but I did so anyway.

After the arraignment, I was taken back to the bullpen, though not for long. Within an hour of my return a correctional officer instructed me to grab my things. I grabbed the pillow and blanket I was given and passed through the steel gates.

"Stand right here," the officer instructed me, along with three other guys who were also being transferred upstairs. We stood to the right of the officer as he grabbed a clipboard with papers attached to it.

"Follow me," the officer commanded.

One by one, the four of us followed the officer into a room. "Drop your blanket in the basket over there. Take your clothes off, and place them in one of these bags."

We obeyed his orders. The four of us stood naked in the cold room awaiting our next command.

"Jones!" The officer's voice boomed.

"Yes, sir," the guy standing next to me replied.

"Turn around, spread your cheeks, and cough," the officer commanded.

The guy complied. I thought that the whole routine was a bit invasive, but I did not voice my opinion. The officers had to do what was necessary to ensure that drugs and weapons were not being taken upstairs to the dorms.

After the four of us had been screened, the officer instructed us to find jumpsuits in our sizes amongst the hundreds of brown jumpsuits shelved along a wall. Having found our correct sizes, we once again marched behind the officer to the elevator. Two of the guys got off on the third floor, which was the floor where primarily younger offenders were held.

On the fourth floor, the elevator stopped. After the doors of the elevator opened, the officer told the guy and me to exit the elevator. Standing on the other side of the open elevator doors were two correctional officers. A big, beefy White officer told the other inmate to follow him.

The other officer, a very pretty, Black female officer, directed me to follow her. The officer looked out of place in the jail. She appeared to be in her mid-thirties. She had beautiful, graham cracker-colored skin, and small dainty features. Her body looked amazing in her grey uniform. She was very curvaceous; filling in the uniform in all the right places.

The officer led me to a beige-colored gate, with the words 4NW painted above it. She signaled for the officer in an encased bullet-proof booth to open the gates. The gate slid open. We stepped inside, standing before another gate. As one gate behind us closed, another one in front of us slid open. We walked inside the dorm. I quickly scanned the room. Four steel picnic tables were bolted to the cement floors. A television was mounted to the wall. Twelve doors with numbers above them lined the far wall. The officer and I stepped further into the dorm, rounding a corner. We stopped in front of a door with the number three painted above it. The door to the room slid open.

"This is your cell," the officer expressed.

I walked into the room: a stainless steel sink and toilet were positioned near the far end of the cell; a steel desk was mounted to the wall, and a small, steel stool was bolted to the floor. On the right side of the 6X9 room, a small twin-sized bed, with a thin green mattress lying on top of it, was welded to the wall.

"I'll have a trustee bring you some sheets and an extra blanket. It gets really cold in here. He'll also bring you some soap and toilet tissue. The shower is to the right of your cell," she stated as she turned to leave.

"Okay. Thank you."

"You're welcome," the officer said as she walked away.

I sat down on the stool in my cell surveying the cell. The room was not as horrible as I thought it would be. In fact, it was not really that bad at all. Everything in the room, save the stainless steel sink and toilet, were painted beige. The concrete floors were in need of sweeping and mopping, but that could be easily remedied. The CO (correctional officer) told me that cleaning supplies were always accessible; one merely had to ask, and he could clean his cell whenever he wanted.

At the far end of the room was a small window that was made of what appeared to be bullet-proof glass. I tried to look out the window, though the windows were darkly tinted making it difficult to see much of anything through them. I sat back down on the stool planning my next move. *I need to clean this room and then shower.* I stood up, walking out of the room and into the area where the other inmates congregated.

Many of the eight or nine inmates sat at the tables watching television. A guy who appeared to be in his mid-to-late twenties walked around the perimeter of the dorm, as he listened to music on his walkman. He looked strange walking around the small, caged area, though, I guess, one had to do what he must to stay in shape while confined.

Another guy was in a corner of the dorm doing push-ups with a deck of cards resting beside him. I would later learn that he used the cards to count how many push-ups he did in a set. If he pulled a face card (a king, queen, or jack) from the deck, he would have to do ten push-ups; an ace required that he do fifteen push-ups; the numbered cards involved him doing the number on the card. I was impressed with the lengths the guys went through to stay healthy.

I wanted to get some cleaning supplies to clean my cell, but I did not know how to acquire them. One of the guys watching television saw me looking around.

"What's up, man?" He asked.

"Not much… a, you know how I can get some stuff to clean my room?" I asked him.

"Yeah, you got to go over there and press that button," he

said pointing to what looked like a support beam. "When the CO pick up, tell 'em you need some stuff to clean your cell."

"Ok. Thanks." I said as I walked over to the support beam. I pushed the silver button. A few seconds later, I heard a male voice through the speaker that was mounted to the ceiling.

"Yeah, what you need?" The CO asked in a gruff tone.

I turned to face the camera that was also mounted on the ceiling, "Can I get some cleaning supplies for my cell?" I asked.

I was a little irritated from the manner in which he spoke.

"I'll have the trustee to bring it around there," he said as I heard the crackle of the speaker, an indication that our communication was over. I did not like rudeness. I think civility is the least action that two people can extend to one another. Ordinarily, I would have thanked anyone who helped me, though the CO's tone and mannerism made any attempt at common courtesy difficult for me.

I stood at the gate waiting for the inmate-trustee to arrive with the cleaning supplies. Within a couple of minutes, the gates of the dorm clanked open. A young, nice looking guy wearing an orange jumpsuit rolled in a mop bucket, with a broom and dust pan attached to it.

"What's up?" He asked, as he nodded his head at me and passed the mop and bucket.

"What's up," I responded, accepting the mop from him, along with some paper towels.

"It's a disinfectant in one of those bottles, a deodorizer in the other, and window cleaner in the other one. They got labels on them saying which one is which."

"All right, thanks," I said as I turned to leave to clean the cell.

I did not waste any time cleaning. I swept the floor, wiped down the mattress, desk, and the stool with the disinfectant. I

poured some sort of orange powder into the toilet stool, which turned the water green. I did not know what kind of cleanser it was, but it smelled good, similar to Pine-Sol. I used the same cleanser on the sink. I figured if was strong enough to clean the toilet; it had to be good enough to clean the residue from the sink. Lastly, I mopped the floor. It was not
too dirty, but I mopped it twice, anyway, just to be certain that it was clean.

Having thoroughly cleaned the room, I removed the linen from the laundry bag the trustee gave me. The sheets were discolored, but they smelled fresh. I put them on the bed, laying the wool blanket across them. I needed to shower badly. I felt grimy after having been in the bullpen for three days without a shower. I hung the cleaning supplies back on the outside of mop bucket and pushed it to the gate. I walked to my cell. I grabbed the bath towel, wash cloth, and soap I was given and walked to the shower. It was a single-person shower, for which I was grateful; it gave me a sense of privacy, especially after having to urinate in a room full in men in the bullpen, and then being stripped searched as if I was a slave on an auction block. It felt good to be able to wash myself without feeling like I was being watched.

Surprisingly, I had not had a bowel movement since I had turned myself in to the authorities. Ordinarily, I would be concerned about going days without defecating, though, because I had not eaten much while in the bullpen, I was not alarmed. Once I resumed a healthy diet, things would return to normal.

I was not a hypochondriac, though I was very in-tuned with my body. If something was physically amiss, I was well aware of it long before it became an issue, and I did not hesitate to go to the doctor. I would much rather catch a possible problem early on, rather than to put off an ailment, allowing it to escalate into something else because of my neglect.

I lathered myself with the soap I was given by the CO. The soap was harsh, but it would have to suffice until I was able to buy my own through commissary. As I dried myself, I smiled inwardly. It is amazing how truly the little things in life can bring us pleasure, if we allow them. I felt like a million dollars; just from the blessing of being able to take a shower!

After I dried myself, I put on the jumpsuit I was given. I walked to my cell. The CO's would soon be conducting count. I was told that they counted the inmates after every shift change. It was already after three o'clock in the afternoon. I needed to call home before Count started to let them know that I was doing fine. I had not talked to anyone since I had been jailed. I noticed that there were three pay phones located on a wall near the gate of the dorm. I picked up the receiver of the phone farthest to the left. I dialed Mama's number. An automated operator directed me to speak my name into the receiver. I did as I was instructed. After a series of clicks, the call was connected. Like clock-work, Mama answered the phone on the third ring as she always did.

"Hello," she said in her southern tone.

"You have a collect call from 'Chris'," the automated operator said. It continued, "to accept the call, please say, yes; if you do not wish to accept the call, simply hang up."

I waited for Mama to accept the call. Before long, I heard her say, yes into the receiver.

"Hi, Mama," I said, once we were connected.

"Hey, baby... how you doin, baby?" Mama asked in a concerned voice.

"I'm okay." There was a short pause, then...

"Aww, baby, why'd you have to go over there with that girl?" She asked.

"I don't know, Mama. I felt like she needed

my help, so I went over there. I didn't know all of this was going to happen." I said, feeling very foolish for going with Tookie.

"I know you didn't know, baby. I sure wish you wouldna went. I told Tookie she shouldn't move over there with them damn honkies, but she had to move over there, anyway. And now look what happened," she expressed.

"Yeah, but that boy had no right putting his hands on her and calling her a "B", Mama." I said, empathetically.

"Baby, that's the same mess Tookie said. Do you know how many times I been called a bitch," she asked, rhetorically, "Tookie shoulda just left that shit alone! Then, she gone call y'all and involve y'all in it. I just wished you woulda done like these other boys when she called."

"Huh," I asked confusingly, "what other boys?"

"Derrick and Andre. She came over here asking them to go with her, but they told her, no...I sure wished you woulda said the same thing," she repeated, again.

Hmm, Tookie asked Derrick and Andre to go with her before she came to get me, but they had refused. I felt stupid, like I had been duped. *If I had said no as well, I would not have been in jail. The guy would still have been alive.* I felt awful. *Was I wrong for going with her?* Should I have done as my other cousins did and not involved myself in her mess? I was conflicted; a part of me felt that I needed to be there to support Tookie. I was raised believing that family stuck together and supported one another. But, my support had cost someone his life, and Booger and me our freedom.

"Yeah, I wish I hadn't gone, too," I said in a solemn voice into the receiver.

"Everybody's been asking about you. They all worried about you. How you feeling?"

"I'm fine," I said, but, in truth, I was not. I felt horrible. I had killed someone. My actions had led to someone's demise; my cousin's and my incarceration; and, my family's pain. How could I have been so foolish? Why did I not simply insist that we leave the situation alone when Tookie suggested that we go back to the White people's house?

"Chris?" Mama said in her southern tone.

"Yes?" I replied.

"Baby, you gone be all right?" Mama asked in a concerned voice.

Mama had always been like a second mother to me. When I moved in with her and Allen, she and I would spend countless hours talking about everything of which my young, inquisitive mind could think. I learned how to be a more compassionate and loving person because of Mama. There were countless times when I witnessed her give her last dollar to any one of her seven children. She virtually raised many of my cousins and me during our mothers' drug-addicted years. Tired, after having worked fourteen and fifteen hours, she would come home late in the evening and cook us dinner. In the early mornings before school, it was Mama who we asked and received lunch money for school. She was my special love: a consistent love; a love that I knew would always be there, no matter what adversities may have come.

"Yes, ma'am," I said. Though, in truth, I really did not know that I would be.

"Okay, baby. You know, I love you very, very much, don't you, Christopher?"

"Yes, I know you do, Mama," I replied, earnestly.

"You have one minute remaining," an automated operator stated. Wow! An in entire thirty minutes had passed so fast! It seemed that we had just got on the phone.

"Okay, Mama, this phone is about to hang up. I'll call you tomorrow, okay?"

"Okay, baby. I love you, baby, and don't you ever forget that, baby."

"I love you, too, Mama, and I won't forg…" Int…Int…Int. The busy signal of the phone reverberated in my ear; our phone call had been disconnected. I did not like timed phone calls. They seemed a little too impersonal. I put the phone back in its cradle and walked to my cell. A few short minutes later, count was announced. We were instructed to close the doors to our cells. After doing so, I sat down on my bed. I felt saddened by my conversation with Mama. I had hoped that the conversation would cheer me some, but instead it added to my feelings of despair.

I could have dealt with my incarceration better had my being in jail not affected so many other people, with the most detrimental effect being to the Faulkner family; for it was they whom had lost a loved one. Though, my remorse did not end there, as my family was tremendously affected by my incarceration as well. The pain I felt of having hurt so many people was severe. I wanted it to end. I did not know how much more I could take. In the blink of an eye my entire world had changed: I had shot and killed someone; hid out for several days after the incident; and, was now incarcerated in the county jail as a suspect to murder. I was horrified. I would have never imagined that I would be incarcerated, let alone for murder. I was disappointed in myself. How could a person who was so positively directed as I was, who had wanted to do so much for humanity, be incarcerated for taking the life of another? I felt that I had disappointed God; that I had failed Him.

Count ended. Within seconds, I could hear the clamor of the other inmates as they exited their cells. "Chow!" I heard a male voice yell.

It was dinner time. I did not have an appetite. I remained

in bed, having no intentions on getting up to get the meal. After a few minutes, I heard a soft rap on the door of my cell. I looked up from beneath the blankets covering me. A guy stood at the door. "Yeah?" I called out.

"Chow," he stated.

"Yeah, I heard him. I'm not going. I'm not hungry," I said.

"Can I get your tray, then?" He asked.

I really did not feel like getting up. I just wanted to lie where I was and think. I needed to make sense of the events of the past few days.

"Yeah, here I come," I said, rising from the bed.

I pushed a red button that opened the door of the cell. As I stepped outside of my cell, many of the other inmates were sitting down eating already. I walked pass them to the gate where the trays of food were being handed to the inmates by a trustee, with a CO standing closely by watching him as he did so. A couple of guys stood in front of me awaiting their turn to get their trays. I grabbed my tray when my turn came, and walked back inside the dorm. I gave the tray to the guy as soon as I entered the dorm, walking away from him to my cell as I did.

"A, man, you don't want none of this?" He asked.

"Naw, I'm cool." I said, continuing my gait. I walked into the cell, closing the door behind me. Though, before I could lie back down, I heard a soft tap on the door. It was the same guy whom I had given my tray.

"A, man, I just wanted to thank you for yo' tray," the medium-brown complexioned guy expressed.

"You're welcome," I said, as I stood at the door of the cell. The guy looked as if he had more to say. I stood at the door a moment longer.

"I'm Dashon," the guy said with his hand extended.

Dashon looked like he was a couple of years older than me.

His hair was cut short, and had not been brushed in a while, it seemed. His brown jumpsuit was disheveled, though not malodorous. He appeared to be a pleasant guy, but I was not interested in making friends. I could not be rude, though.

"I'm Chris," I said accepting his extended hand and shaking it. We stood at the door. Again, he looked as if he had more to say. I waited patiently for him to say whatever was on his mind. I had heard countless stories of how young, weak men had been raped or either forced into being another inmates "woman," as they called them. Dashon did not look like the type to take advantage of someone in that manner, nor would I have allowed him to take advantage of me, regardless of whether he looked like it or not. I had already resolved in my mind before I submitted myself to the authorities that I would defend myself at all cost.

I could not help wondering what Dashon's intentions were, though. He simply stood outside of my cell unable to say what he was thinking. I really hoped that it was not anything of a sexual nature. I did not want to have to say anything mean to anyone already.

"Um, man, if you don't eat your food, they gone move you downstairs to the Psyc floor and make you eat." The words had finally spilled from his mouth.

"Huh?" I asked with a confused expression on my face.

"If you don't eat, the CO's will transfer you to the second floor where they keep the crazy dudes, and make you eat."

I looked in Dashon's eyes searching them for truth. He did not flinch under my gaze; he did not look away.

"How can they force someone to eat?" I asked.

"Cause, you are a ward of the state; they are like your parents now. They can do whatever they want to ensure your safety," he said.

I was livid. I was not trying to starve myself. I simply was not hungry. It angered me that these people had so much control of our lives. If I did not want to eat, I should not be forced to eat. It was one thing to be confined to a small room and told when to wake up and when to go to sleep, but to be made to eat seemed outlandish to me.

"Okay, thanks, man." I said to Dashon in an appreciative manner, albeit gruff tone.

"No problem," he said as he walked away.

I closed the door to the cell. I sat down on the bed, thinking about what Dashon had just told me. I felt violated for some reason. I had always valued my autonomy; to be told what to do, when to do it, and how to do it bothered me. *I am not going to allow them to tell me what to do*, I thought obstinately.

I lay back down on the bed. I drifted off to sleep. A few hours later, there was another rap on the door. I awakened.

"Snack time," I heard the now familiar voice of Dashon say.

With our previous conversation still fresh on my mind, I stubbornly yelled out, "I don't want it!"

Again, I was not hungry, though my defiance came in being told that I had to eat what and when I did not want to eat. Years later, I would learn the error of stubbornness.

"Can I have it?" Dashon asked.

"Yeah," I responded through the closed door.

I lay my head back down on the pillow.

I wish I would get up from bed for a stale cookie and a small carton of milk! I will not allow these people to reduce me to what they had reduced these other inmates to...they can jump up like yard dogs to the bark of a CO's call of 'chow' if they wanted to, but I would not!

Eventually, I drifted off to sleep. I awakened during the middle of night with my circumstances firmly on my mind. I thought of the guy I had killed; I thought of my conversation

with Mymomme days ago and the sound of despair in her voice; the look of sadness on my daddy's face, as I was led into custody by the police
officer. I replayed in my mind the conversation between Mama and me earlier that day. I felt hopeless. All of the positive things I had accomplished seemed for naught.

I was an honor roll student. I went to church faithfully; and read the Bible religiously. I had practiced the teachings of Jesus Christ; I loved everyone and anyone with every fiber of my being. I helped anyone and everyone that I could, without prejudice or expectation of anything in return. I spoke at various schools and churches trying to educate and inspire people through love. Yet, in comparison to my transgression, all of these qualities--my spiritual convictions, my love of creation, and my educational achievements, seemed miniscule.

A malevolent voice whispered to me, "You're nothing! You are unworthy of the love and blessings of God." I listened to the voice. "If you are truly a child of God's, how could you kill one of His children?" The voice asked. I began to question my virtue. Continuing the voice said, "No, you are one of mine! Anyone who takes the life of another belongs to me. Besides, God can't really love you, or He wouldn't have allowed any of this to happen...you wouldn't be here. Adam wouldn't be dead, but He doesn't love you. That's why you are here. You need to give up. All you're doing is hurting your family!"

I considered the words of the voice. I thought of every wrong deed I had ever done: every fight; every argument; every curse word. It, the malevolent voice, was right; I was not worthy of the calling I thought God had bestowed upon me. I could not be one of God's chosen ones. How could I be one of His? I had killed someone.

I did not want to continue living. I did not want to continue hurting those that I loved more than life itself. I could not bear the responsibility of my actions--I had killed someone. I had committed the unforgivable sin by taking someone's life; a life that was not given to me to take. I prayed to God, hoping that He would forgive me for my actions, both past and present. I thought of my family and hoped that the Creator would comfort and protect them in my demise.

As I lay on the hard mattress, I consciously willed myself to die. There is a realm that exist between life and death; a void of nothingness that is akin to deep space. In my pursuit to end the pain and suffering I had caused, I forced my spirit to travel to that realm; to the unknown. Although I was conscious of lying down, I could not physically feel the mattress beneath me. I felt light, weightless, as my spirit traveled into a void of darkness. The mental, emotional, and physical stresses of living were absent from my being. I was no longer encumbered with the worries of being physically bound in my body. My spirit soared to an unknown dimension.

"I could reside in this place forever," I thought within myself.

Continuing to drift, I thought of all the damage I had caused; the life I took and the pain of my family. I continued to drift...on...and...on...and...on. My spirit relished in the worry-free dimension it had found. I felt at peace; free of everything: heartache, loneliness, desire.

Suddenly, I felt a tugging, a yanking of sorts: the feeling of being nudged awake. My mother's face flashed before me; I saw Miah, my younger brother; Mama; Allen; my daddy; my Aunt Sherry; Brandy...a collage of my family's faces. I heard a voice that sounded much like my own, though it was not mine, "It is not yet time, Chris! You cannot die. You are special to me, one of my chosen vessels. Your work is not yet done." It became clear to me to whom the

Voice belonged. I began to cry, heaving uncontrollably.
 "But I failed you! I killed someone!" I cried.
 "Everything happens for a reason, Chris...your transgressions are forgiven!"

Without notice, my spirit leapt back into my body. I was discombobulated. I looked around the dark room. The blankets were tossed about the bed. I sweated profusely. I had no idea what time it was. I got up from the bed, walked to the door and looked through the narrow glass window. I did not see anyone, only the steel picnic tables. I walked back over to the bed and sat down. My mind whirled. I felt physically drained, yet spiritually invigorated at the same time. My experience with near-death was crystal clear to me. I could still feel the weightlessness of my spirit as it traveled. I could not believe that I had almost died. The thought was strange to me; I was a hair from being gone from the earthly realm forever! I stood up, again; pacing the floor as I began to think.

I felt renewed, like I could conquer the world. My previous doubts and insecurities were of the past. I was me, again; the confident, directed Chris that I was before all of the current events happened. I forced myself to lie down to get some sleep. I had a long journey before me. I had to be well-rested before I could tackle the work I had to do.

Chapter Six

I awakened the following morning with the night's experience vivid in my mind. I said a prayer of thanksgiving to God. I thanked Him for saving me; for encouraging and inspiring me to live; I thanked Him for loving me, wholly and unconditionally.

I viewed my being jailed differently after the previous night's experience. I better understood the circumstances of my incarceration. *'Everything happens for a reason'*. I could not say that I fully understood why things had happened as they had, though, because of my spiritual experience, I was better equipped to deal with the fact that I had killed someone and the aftermath of Adam's death.

The cumbersome responsibility of my actions and the truth of those actions no longer weighed on my spirit in the same manner as they had before. I no longer allowed myself to wallow in the misery of my actions. I had killed someone, whether intentional or not. Someone's life was lost at my hands; that fact was inescapable. Although, I still grieved for Adam, and I still hurt for the loss that I am sure his family and friends must have felt, I had to go on with living. I had to fulfill the will of God.

At times, my mentality seemed selfish. How very easy of me to pick of the sticks, per se, and go on with living when I had taken that right from someone else; when I had denied a human being the ability to go on with living by taking his life.

I had no retort. I simply felt deep in my soul that it was not meant for me to give in to my circumstances; to continue berating myself; to die. I felt that I had to continue living, if not for my family and myself, then because it was expected of me by the Creator. My work was not yet done. God had saved, protected, and poured His spirit into me for a reason. I had to fulfill His will. I had to continue with the good work I had started before Adam's death.

Although, I could not see the clock on the wall in the dorm, I knew that breakfast would be served soon. I paced the small cell as I thought about what lie ahead of me.

Then, like clockwork, "Chow!" The CO announced.

It was 5:30, as breakfast was severed at the same time every day. I determined that I would have to start eating. I did not know how long I would be confined in the county jail, though I knew that I had to stay healthy. I refused to allow the devil to defeat me. I would not wallow in my misery any longer. I had to be strong for my family and myself. A very tragic event had occurred; a life had been lost at my hands. As much as I wanted to, I could not change that fact. For reasons that were unknown to me, the Creator had purposed that I should live. I graciously accepted the blessing of life that had been given to me with renewed enthusiasm.

I exited my cell, walking toward the line of inmates that had congregated at the gate, awaiting their trays of food. I stood in line behind the guy that I saw walking around the dorm exercising when I first arrived.

"Hey, what's up?" He asked, smiling.

The guy was slender in build and about 5'9 tall. He was medium-brown complected. His smile surprised me. Looking at him yesterday as he walked, he looked mean and unapproachable. However, seeing him in close proximity and smiling, he was the exact opposite. I detected a sensitivity and warmth in him.

"Hey. Good morning," I responded, smiling back at him. We grabbed our trays from the trustee and sat down at one of the picnic tables to eat.

"What's your name, man?" The guy asked.

"Chris," I said, looking up from my tray.

We were served bowls of grits, two slices of white bread, a small carton of milk, and an apple. The food was identical to what we were served in the bullpen, but it seemed a little more appealing on the dorm than it did in the bullpen. I concluded that its appeal had to do with the environment. It was much cleaner on the dorm; making it more conducive for eating.

"Cool, Chris. I'm Andre, but everybody calls me Dre."

"Nice to meet you, Dre," I said, shaking his hand. As I began eating my breakfast, I started to think of what I needed to do to assist Bradley in defending me. I first had to familiarize myself with the charges against Booger and me.

"A, Dre, do we have access to a library here?"

"Aw! Yeah, man! We go to the library every Wednesday," Dre said. Continuing, "It's a law library here, too."

"Huh? A law library?" I asked.

"Yeah, you know, so if you want to learn more about your charges, you can go there and read the law books."

I could not believe what I heard! It was as if Dre was reading my mind. My dad had always told me that "our steps are ordered...everything is as it should be-nothing happens by chance." My meeting Dre was proof of that assertion. It seemed to me that Dre and I were meant to meet and have that conversation. I made a mental note of the day and time of the library's hours.

Someone turned on the television that was mounted to the wall. As I finished my breakfast, I heard my name being spoken on the News. I was surprised. It felt strange to hear my name on television. The newscaster detailed the events of our case. Pictures of Booger and me were shown on the television screen. Everyone in the room turned at once in my direction. I ignored the gazes of the others, as I continued to listen to the report.

I sat flabbergasted as I listened to the News' account of what transpired. The newscaster stated that my family and I were members of the Bloods, a notorious Black gang. I could not believe what I heard. I had never been a member of any gang. I deplored the actions of gangs; people committing acts of violence, including deaths, against one another, because of the color one wears or where he lives.

The newscaster did not mention anything about the White people's negative involvement in the situation: no mention of the weapons they used against us, nor did they mention that a mob of them chased us as we attempted to flee.

I was outraged. Such false-reporting was so typical of the media. I determined that I would not allow the local media to report such misleading information about my family and me.

"Dre, where can I get some paper and a pen?" I asked.

Dre turned his attention from the News. The News' report about my ordeal was over. The News team had moved on with other stories.

"You can buy some from commissary. The COs will hand out the list of what you can buy today. If you have money on your books, they'll deliver what you order tomorrow. If you don't want to wait until then, you can ask the counselor for some," he said.

Commissary was important in jail. We inmates were allowed to buy anything from stationary products to toiletries to snack foods. Though, of primary interest to most of the inmates were the snacks, because the food we were served was so unfulfilling.

"Okay. Thanks," I replied.

As soon as the counselor's shift began at eight o'clock, I pushed the button to the control booth.

"Yes," a CO asked into the intercom.

"May I speak with a counselor?" I asked directing my voice to the speaker on the ceiling."

The counselor, Ms. Johnson, was a short, thickly built woman. She had beautiful almond-colored skin. While she was not particularly warm as a person, she was pleasant and very helpful.

"Sure. I'll give her a call now." Although there were quite a few COs that had horrible dispositions, there were some that were actually quite kind. The CO working in the control booth was one such example of the kinder COs.

Ms. Johnson arrived a few short minutes later. "Hi. I was wondering if I could have some writing paper and a pen or pencil, please," I asked as she approached me. She and I had never met before, though I presume she was given a report on all the new inmates.

"Yes, you can," she replied. "How are you adjusting? Is there anything else I can help you with?"

"I'm getting along okay. Thank you," I said.

"Well, if you need to talk, let me know. I'm going to also give you a list of the rules here, so that you aware of them."

"Okay. Thanks.

"I'll be right back with your paper and pen," Ms. Johnson said before speaking with a few more inmates, and then exiting the dorm.

Fifteen minutes later the gate to the dorm slid open. Ms. Johnson walked in with paper and pen in hand. I watched her as she walked. Her walk amused me. She walked with purpose; sort of like Sophia from the movie, "The Color Purple."

I, too, had begun to walk around the perimeter of the dorm. It was not only great exercise, but it also helped to me think more clearly. I was better able to process my thoughts while in motion. Usually, when I was at home, I would pace back and forth from room to room as I talked on the phone or did schoolwork. Mama would always playfully chide me, "Chris, you gone wear a hole in that carpet, if you keep pacing like that." I would look up from what I was doing and smile at her, continuing my gait.

I walked over to Ms. Johnson. She handed me a yellow-papered legal pad and ink pen. Before I walked away, I thanked her. I took the paper to my cell, and, then, exited the cell to continue walking. I needed to do a little more thinking before I started to write. I was excited. I was anxious to do something productive. My first order of business, I concluded, was to write the judge assigned to our case. Because the media had falsely accused my family and me of being gang members, I felt that I needed to convey to the judge who we really were, rather than who we were portrayed to be.

I walked back into my cell and retrieved the paper and pen. I sat down at the desk and began to write a letter to the judge. My writing started off well, though, as I proof-read it midway through, it seemed more like a poem than an actual letter. I continued to write; yet the more I wrote, the more its structure became that of a poem. I wrote fervently. The words and thoughts seemed to leap from my mind and onto the paper. When I looked up fifteen or twenty minutes later, the letter-poem was complete:

To Know Me

Is to know my history
It is knowing that I am the descendants of great kings and queens
The product of strong willed, self-determined, God-fearing Black, brown, and high-yellow slaves.

To Know Me

Is to know those who represent me
It is the ability to listen to Maya, while also hearing her,
It is watching Oprah, but also seeing her.
It is the ability to sing in unison with Whitney, but it is also achieving a togetherness in harmony,
It is walking alongside Dr. Martin Luther King, Jr., but it is also comprehending the significance of his March.

To Know Me

Is to see me
It is seeing my black wooly hair,
My cappuccino-colored eyes
Cherokee-high cheek bones
Wide nostrils
and Full lips

It is taking note of my big hands
My broad bosom
My back of steel
And my archless foundations

To Know Me

Is to lose your smirk of contempt and hate
And to replace it with a smile of respect and adoration

To Know Me

Is to see me, to understand me…to love me unconditionally.

As I looked up from reading the poem, I thanked God. I was pleased. It was not the letter that I set out to write, but I knew that the poem was the work of Him through me. The words flowed too easily; the message conveyed too clearly. I entitled the poem, "To Know Me." The poem was more a reflection of black people as a whole, than it was about me as an individual, or even my family for that matter. In that regard, "To Know Me" actually meant, "To Know Us."

The message of the poem was directed to Whites, as well as African Americans. It was written to educate Whites about who we Blacks were as a people, though it was also intended to educate Blacks about ourselves.

The system of slavery had deprived many African Americans of such self-knowledge, thereby robbing many of us of our identity. Our self-perception was rooted in America and its perception of us. We came to view dark skin as unattractive; too kinky hair as unappealing; anything White was considered right. Many of us did not know our value historically or presently.

In the first stanza of "To Know Me," the poem establishes that African Americans have a history that extends beyond the horrors of slavery. We, Blacks, are the descendants of great African kings and queens: Cleopatra, Tutankhamen (Tut), Nefertiti, and Shako Zulu. Such monarchs successfully ruled thriving civilizations for thousands of years before the colonization of Africa by Whites.

While many African Americans, understandably, deplore the institution of slavery, its use showed the true fortitude of a people who were treated with no more respect than a common alley cat. The multi-hued people rose above the degradation of a system designed to misuse them. From the trenches of debasement came the unyielding spirits of Harriet Tubman, Nat Turner, and Sojourner Truth.

Although everyone is special to the Creator, some of us come to Earth with a unique purpose to fulfill. Persons such as Maya Angelou, Oprah Winfrey, Whitney Houston, and Dr. Martin Luther King, Jr., not only had the giftedness to unite people who were similar to them in race, but God blessed them with the ability, through their respective talents, to bring together people who were different from them as well.

Maya Angelou in her autobiographies expressed the truth of race relations, and, in doing so, she educated and inspired countless people of all races and ethnicities.

Oprah Winfrey reigned as queen of daytime television for over twenty years. In tuning in to the Oprah Winfrey show, it was important for the African American to see that the highly successful woman is of African descent just as they are. She is dark in skin complexion, endowed with thick, coarse hair, and a curvaceous body like many African American women. While watching the charismatic, intelligent woman, the Black person ought to see that the same attributes with which the Creator blessed Oprah reside in them as well.

Whitney Houston had long been considered "The Voice." Her beautiful singing voice and impressive vocal range left many stupefied as she sang with the grace of a flamingo in flight and with the ease and fluidity of a butterfly. As a multi-platinum recording artist, she sold millions of albums worldwide. Yet, perhaps at no other time was her vocal giftedness made more apparent than when she sang the Star

Spangled Banner at the XXV Super Bowl. Millions of viewers watched as the young woman united Americans of varied races, ethnicities, cultures, and sexual orientations through the prowess of her voice.

Dr. King was a leader of the Civil Rights Movement. While many other persons, both African Americans and non-Blacks, had contributed to the fair and equal treatment of people, no other person in America had been quite capable of leading people for a single cause as Dr. Martin Luther King, Jr.

The next two stanzas of "To Know Me" spoke of the physicalities of African Americans. Because we Blacks were oftentimes made to feel less than proud of our physical features, the poem communicated an acceptance and love of our outward beauty, as well as a demand of respect.

I lay down on the bed after finishing the poem. I was exhausted. I needed to take a nap, but I could not seem to find any solace. I had so much to do. I got up from the bed and entered the dorm. The Blade, Toledo's newspaper, had already arrived.

I rarely read the newspaper, though since my family and I were a topic of interest, of late, I decided to read it. I thumbed through the paper until I located the story of my case. As I sat reading the paper, I became more and more incensed. The Blade reported the same story that the News had. I did not like being a topic of something as horrific as murder, but I especially did not like that the events were distorted and falsified. I left the day room and went into my cell.

Picking up my pen and paper, I began to write. I felt that I needed to counter the inaccurate depiction that Toledo's media had cast of my family and me. I sat for hours writing persons of influence: talk show hosts Oprah Winfrey, Ricki Lake, Maury Povich; Naim Akbar, a well-known black psychologist, author, and prolific voice against racial injustices; Councilman

George Reynolds, who would later become Toledo's first Black mayor; and, a host of local Toledo judges.

I detailed the circumstances of my being jailed, hoping that one or all of them would bring light to our story. It was a shot in the dark, but I could not just sit back and let Toledo's biased media portray us as something that we were not. They would unfairly influence their audience, destroying any chance of our having a fair trial.

~~~

The days and weeks quickly passed into months. I was still in jail. Although, I had tried to be released on bail, my efforts were in vain. I needed to be free to successfully fight my case. None of the talk show hosts had responded to my letters. While both Naim Akbar and George Reynolds had responded, neither of them could extend any support. In a letter to me, Mr. Akbar stated that, although he was empathic of my situation, he lacked the resources to assist me. Each year, he included, that he received hundreds of letters from incarcerated persons requesting his help. Yet, because of financial reasons, he was unable to do anything to assist them.

I understood his position. I knew how popular he was in the African American community. While his support would have helped greatly, I had to accept that he could not assist me.

Councilman Reynolds's letter expressed similar sentiments, in that, although he was empathic of my incarceration, there was not anything that he could do. However, Mr. Reynolds's did offer several useful pieces of information for me: the persons who attacked my family and me were members of a white supremacy gang, known as TK (True Keepers, Triple K, Klu Klux Klan). Mr. Reynolds's, along with law enforcement officers, was aware of the racists acts of the gang; and, that actions were being taken to stop them from further committing such acts.

I could not believe what I read! The persons involved in our case were a known white supremacy gang! While I was ecstatic about the possibilities of the information for our case, I was appalled that nothing had been done to stop them from terrorizing people. Perhaps had actions been taken to disjoin the gang, my family and I would not be entangled in this ordeal.

I needed to get out of jail, though how? Booger's and my bail had been set at one hundred thousand dollars. We did not know of anyone who had that much money. Though, if I could get two hundred thousand dollars in property, I could be bailed out. I decided to turn to my family. I implored my grandmothers, mother, and aunts to post their houses as bail. They had all agreed, yet, just as I thought I would finally be released, my daddy convinced them not to post their homes as collateral.

"You told Mother and them not to use their homes for my bail?" I blurted out over the phone to my daddy.

"Yes, I did," he replied nonchalantly.

Although Mymomme had already told me that he convinced Mother and my aunts not to post their homes as bail for me, his actions still came as a shock to me.

"Why?" I asked, bewildered.

"Because I don't know that you'll return for your court hearings. You've never been in this kind of situation. If the case doesn't go in your favor, you may try to skip town. These women had worked hard to own their homes, and I couldn't jeopardize them losing them, if you decide to skip your court hearing."

I was astounded. I could not believe what I heard. I stood with the phone receiver firmly held against my ear. *Was he serious?!* I would never do anything as foolish, thoughtless, and insensitive as what he suggested.

"What?!" I asked, trying hard to control my voice and my mounting anger, "It is because of the reasons you mentioned that I would not do anything so selfish...I know that these women have worked their entire lives to acquire their homes! If I were so stupid to even slightly entertain running, I wouldn't do it!"

"Well, I don't know that, Chris," he said, as if we were talking about something as miniscule as whether a particular shoe that was in season.

I absolutely could not believe what I heard. Yet I knew my daddy, if he held a certain belief about someone, it would take the second coming of Jesus for him to move from his position. I did not have the energy or the desire to argue my stand with him.

"Okay. I'll talk with you later." I said, hanging up the phone.

I stood at the pay phone on the dorm for several seconds, digesting our conversation. "Skip town?!" I was flabbergasted. Of course, I did not like being in jail, though I could not bring myself to do something as heartless as evade my punishment at the risk of my family losing their homes. It was my decision to turn in myself to the authorities. If I were so afraid of being jailed, I would have never made the decision to voluntarily submit to the authorities.

I grabbed my walk-man, placing the headphones over my ears. I began walking around the dorm, quickly pushing the conversation between my father and me out of my mind. It hurt me that he would think that I would commit such a selfish act, but I could not worry about it now. I learned that one of the ways to survive being incarcerated was by not allowing everything to upset me. If one cannot do anything about a situation, the best way of handling the situation was by leaving it alone. Worrying over something that one cannot do anything about did far more harm than it did good.

Chapter Seven

I walked around the dorm exercising; doing my usual laps when he walked into the dorm. His head was slightly lowered, an indication of defeat. He was a big guy: six feet, six inches tall; three hundred pounds. He had strong, handsome Latino features: dark, straight hair; round face, and slightly slanted eyes.

The brown state uniform he wore snuggly hugged his large body. There was nothing particularly unique about him. He looked like any of the other inmates that flowed in and out of the dorm every week. Though, he was not by any means an ordinary inmate. Unbeknownst to me, he held the key to my family's and my exoneration.

I continued walking around the dorm, eyeing him carefully. He followed closely behind the CO as he was escorted to his cell. His personal belongings were wrapped in his linen, which he carried over his shoulder. He walked into the room that would become his cell. Minutes later he re-emerged, found an empty picnic table, and began looking at a show on the television. I continued walking, though watching him closely.

Bernie, a young, Black guy, opened the cell to his door. He nearly bumped into me as he exited his room, but I moved out of his way before we collided into one another.

Bernie pardoned himself, "Aww...mmmmy fault, Chris, mmmman."

Bernie stood in front of his cell. He yawned loudly as he stretched. His dark, full lips were white and cracked from dehydration. He smacked his lips, scanning the dorm to see who was present. Bernie peered at the new guy, walking in his direction as he did so.

"Aaaaa, maaaan, what's yoooo name?" Bernie stuttered loudly as he spoke to the new guy. The guy looked up slowly as Bernie approached him. "A, maaan, I thiiink I knnnooow you!" Bernie yelled before the guy could respond.

The new guy continued looking at Bernie, waiting for him to say more.

"A, dddon't you ssstay on the sssssouth ssssside?"

"Yeah," the guy said in a soft, low voice.

"Yyyyeah! I thththought I knnnew yyyou!" Bernie walked over to the guy, taking long strides as he did. "MMMan, whwhwhat's yo' name?" Bernie stammered, standing in front of the guy.

"Alonzo," the guy said in a cool, soft tone.

"Awww, whwhwhat's up, mmman? I'm Bbbbernie!" Bernie smiled broadly revealing a missing front tooth.

"What's up?" Alonzo responded quietly.

"Mmman, Aaahhh, uuuseta be over that wwwway all the tttttime!" Bernie said loudly, "Yyyou know MMMike and Jjjjames, and, uhh, damn what's that nnniggas nnnname?" Bernie concentrated earnestly to remember the third guy's name.

"Tito?" Alonzo asked.

"Yyyyeah, ththat's ththat nigga's name!" Bernie said excitedly.

"Yeah, I know them," Alonzo said, slowly smiling.

The two of them began to converse. Bernie continued to stand, talking animatedly while Alonzo chimed in every so often. Alonzo appeared comfortable talking with Bernie. I wondered if it was because of the way Bernie looked or behaved, which made him appear non-threatening. Generally a person had to warm up to Bernie. His loudness and over-the-top energy caused some people to be skeptical of him. Though, despite his rough exterior, he was a cool, personable guy.

After talking for quite some time, the two of them walked into Alonzo's cell. They were in the cell for several minutes when Bernie rushed out of the cell, shouting my name, "Chchchchris! A, Chchchchris!" He yelled.

"Bernie, why don't you walk over to him and get his attention?" Herbert asked. Herbert was one of the older guys on the dorm. Though, Herbert liked Bernie as a person, Bernie's uncouth behavior sometimes unnerved him.

"Oh, okkkkay, Herb. Mmmmy ffffault, man." Bernie apologized, making his way toward me. "A Chrrrris, ccccome here, mmmmaan," Bernie asked excitedly.

I stopped my exercise and followed him. He led me to Alonzo's cell. Inside the room, Alonzo sat on the bed, looking solemn.

"Chrrrris, ththis is Aaalllozzzo," Bernie introduced us. "Ttttell him whhhat yyyyou told mmme," Berniee said, directing his statement to Alonzo.

I looked over pass Bernie to where Alonzo sat.

"Hey, what's up?" I said by way of a salutation.

"What's up, man" Alonzo responded.

He looked down for a moment, as if he was gathering his thoughts. "You caught your case on the south side?" Alonzo asked, still looking down.

I tried to meet his eyes, but he refused to look up; when he did look up, he avoided my eyes. I did not know what prompted his question. Bernie had not told me anything, he simply urged me to follow him. Despite my reservations about disclosing information about my case, I replied to his question.

"Yeah, I did," I said, waiting for him to say more.

"Some dudes in a gang named TK?" He asked, continuing

to avoid my eyes.

"Yeah," I replied hesitantly.

I did not like being asked questions without knowing why the questions were being asked, especially about my case. I never knew with whom I came in contact. He could have had associations with the gang for all I knew. "Why, what's up?" I asked, unable to continue with the game of charades.

"I shot one of the dudes in the gang," Alonzo replied.

I did not know how to read him. He looked like he was both ashamed and saddened by his actions, but I could not tell. I did not know how to respond to the information. I did not know what his revelation meant to me, so I simply stood there waiting for him to say more.

"Yyyy'all nnnneed tttto ttttalk!" Bernie said unexpectedly. He was unable to hold his peace any longer. "Ttttthhhhe ssssame ddddudes ttthat fffffucked wit yyyy'allll fffucked wit AAAlonzo!" he continued. I felt foolish. I finally understood why Bernie felt that it was so important for me to meet Alonzo.

I turned to Alonzo, "What happened?"

"Well, me and my girl was at home when Steve Drummond knocked on our door."

Steve Drummond... Steve Drummond? Why did that name sound so familiar to me? I searched my memory trying to recall where I had heard the name before, when suddenly I remembered. The name was mentioned in my police report. Steve Drummond was reportedly the head of the TK gang. Wow! So this guy was involved in both of our cases. I turned my attention back to Alonzo and his story.

"My girl went to the door with the baby. When she answered the door there was a bunch of people outside in our yard with bats and sticks and shit," Alonzo said in his soft tone.

As he told his story, he continued to avoid my face. Instead, he opted to look down at the floor. After carefully studying him, I finally deduced that he was shy. His failure to look me in the eyes meant nothing more. Sometimes a person's reluctance to avoid a person's gaze meant that he was possibly lying, or that perhaps he had something to hide. That was not the case with Alonzo. He was simply uncomfortable talking to people whom he did not know.

It seemed strange to me that a guy as big as Alonzo would be shy. I had always assumed that big guys were assertive and outgoing, though not Alonzo. In fact, I would later learn that he was the antithesis of my assumption; he was a gentle giant.

Alonzo continued, "I heard Steve yelling and talking shit, telling me to bring my fat ass outside. So, I got up from the sofa, grabbed my piece, and walked over to the door where my girl stood."

"A piece? You had a gun?" I asked, interrupting him.

"Yeah, I wasn't taking any more chances this time," he said, looking up at me for just a moment before looking down to the floor again.

"What do you mean 'this time'? Did you have run-ins with him before?" I asked.

"Yeah, a few days before this happened," Alonzo said, referring to the events that led to his being jailed. "Steve and a bunch of the others came to our house and pointed a gun to my baby's face."

"What! Are you serious?!" I exclaimed. I could not believe what I heard.

"Yeah," he responded sadly. I looked over to where he sat on the bed. I felt sorry for him. His shoulders hung low and his face held the look of a wounded warrior.

"Did you call the police?" I asked. Ever since my altercation with the gang, I had wracked my brain trying to think of what I could have done to avoid the catastrophe that occurred. The only thing of which I could think was to have called the police, rather than going to the gang members' home.

"Yeah."

"Well, what did they do?"

"Nothing, except come to our house and wrote a report."

"That's it?! They didn't arrest the guys; investigate the situation, or anything?" I asked incredulously.

"Naw. They just took down the names of the people who were involved," Alonzo replied.

I was shocked. Well, there went my assumption that the police would have handled things responsibly.

"I'm sorry…I interrupted you. Finish what you were saying, please."

"It's cool," he said. "Man, you should be a lawyer…the way you ask questions!" He said smiling.

I laughed at his remark. It was not the first time I had heard the statement.

"So, I goes to the door and just like last time, there are about fifteen or twenty people in my front yard. I say, 'what's up?' And Steve says, 'Why don't yo Spic ass find a girl of your own kind?'"

I did not understand. "Huh? What did he mean?"

"Spic? That's a racist word used toward Mexicans. Kinda like the N-word toward Blacks."

"Yeah, I heard of the word. I mean, what did he mean by 'find a girl of your own kind?'" I asked, naively.

"My girl is White." Alonzo said, matter-of-factly.

"Oh! My fault, I didn't know." Everything suddenly all made sense to me. The reason for the gang's animosity toward Alonzo and his family had as much to do with Alonzo's race, as it did the fact that his girlfriend was White.

"Yeah, that's why they kept bothering us. They didn't like that we were together," he said, mirroring my own previous conclusion. "So, I say to them 'just leave us alone.' Steve started hollering and shit at me. They start to throw shit at my house. Some guy starts to bang on my car with a bat, man."

Alonzo looked really sad at the mention of his car. Latinos were in many ways like Blacks to me: they were drawn to colorful clothes; were very family-oriented; and, truly valued their cars.

"So, I pulled the piece out of my pocket and moved my girl out of the way. She started screaming for me to forget about it, but I'm pissed that these guys keep bothering us for no reason," he sighed deeply before continuing.

I was empathetic of Alonzo's situation. I thoroughly understood his fears and frustrations. As my family and I were being chased by the mob on Maumee Street, I kept thinking over and over *just leave us alone*, yet, obviously, they did not. I believe they would have persisted in their chase until one of my family members or I was seriously hurt or killed.

Alonzo's face conveyed a look that his whole life had come to a drastic end—I guess, in some ways it had.

"So, all hell really broke loose when they saw the gun, but shit, it wasn't nothing but a twenty-two," he said, continuing his story.

"A twenty-two?" I asked, looking perplexed. Alonzo looked up, smiling at my ignorance.

"Yeah, that's a small hand gun," he replied.

"Oh," I replied innocently.

"Yeah, so I take the gun and just start to shoot into the crowd, not really aiming at anyone. I just wanted to get them away from my house and family," he stopped talking, as if he was finished with his story.

I looked to Bernie and then back at Alonzo waiting for more details. Neither one of them said anything.

"Okay, so what happened next? Did you shoot someone?" I asked.

"Yeah, one of the guys got hit with one of the pellets, and it traveled."

"Huh?" I was confused.

Pellets? Traveling? I did not know what he was talking about.

"There are two basic kinds of bullets: a single projectile and a bullet that sprays pellets. The gun you used in your case sprayed pellets." Bernie must have shared specific details with him about my case.

"Oh." I said, still confused. My knowledge of guns and bullets was very limited. I knew that an assortment of guns were manufactured, though I was clueless as to their various purposes. I definitely did not know that there were different kinds of bullets, the exception being with shotguns. I knew from Allen's guns that the bullets used in shotguns were humongous and filled with tiny black balls. I involuntarily winced. It was horrifying to think that I had shot someone with such a projectile.

"The bullet you used sprayed, hitting the guy in more than one place," I winced, again. In my mind's eye, I could see these small black objects piercing Adam's small frame with lightning speed and the force of a locomotive. I could not believe that I had caused that sort of pain. I had always felt that I was far too sensitive to hurt someone in the manner that I had hurt Adam, yet I had.

"The bullets in my gun were similar to the bullets in yours, because they spray."

It was strange hearing Alonzo refer to the bullets as mine. By giving me ownership of the bullets, I felt worse about Adam's death; more responsible for his demise. Knowing that the gun did not belong to me allowed me to subconsciously avert some of the blame away from myself; though, listening to Alonzo forced me to take full responsibility for his death.

"When I shot into the crowd one of the bullets hit this guy...because he was running the pellets traveled through his body until they hit something that caused him to collapse and die."

"Wow!" I exclaimed.

I stood in the same place in the room transfixed by the information I had just learned. It was truly amazing how little I knew about guns and the destruction they caused.

"Man, I'm sorry to hear that. So what did they charge you with?" I asked.

"Aggravated Murder." He said solemnly.

"What! But your situation was self-defense!"

"Yeah, I know. That's what I think, too." Alonzo said, dejectedly.

"No! I know that it's self-defense. I researched the self-defense law in Ohio. There are four statutes or guidelines that must be present for the offense to be considered self-defense, and your circumstances fulfills each guideline. You have to fight your case. You can't let them convict you of a crime when you were the victim." I said adamantly.

In the few months that I had been in the county jail, I had become something of a jail-house lawyer. I did not ask for the title, nor was it entirely true. I knew little to nothing about the law. I simply felt that all too often guys would come to jail with exaggerated charges.

Prosecutors would intimidate guys into accepting plea bargains and lengthy sentences for offenses that they did not commit. Although many times the offenders had committed an offense, more often than not, they did not commit the offense for which they were convicted. I stood by the truth. If I did not commit a particular offense, I would not "cop-out" and say that I had. Because I openly spoke out against such unfair practices of the prosecution, many of the guys would seek my advice regarding their cases.

"I don't know, man. I don't know if I can win." Alonzo said doubtfully.

It seemed that he had already considered accepting a plea bargain.

"What! I'm telling you, man, your case falls under the guidelines for self-defense. You can't allow them to give you a bunch of time for something that you did not do. You have to think about your family, your girlfriend. You need to think of your young daughter who needs her father to be present in her life, and not present while being confined. I'll testify on your behalf as to what happened in my case, and perhaps you can testify during my trial. The jury will see that the actions of the gang are not random. We can help each other."

Something that I said struck a chord in Alonzo. His face changed; it brightened. "Okay, man. I'll fight my case and take it to trial."

I smiled. I was pleased for him. I knew in just the couple of hours of conversing with him that he was a cool dude. He did not deserve to be in jail, especially for protecting himself and his family.

~~~

I watched through the foggy, tempered glass window of the county jail as the summer season blended into autumn. My twenty-first birthday had come and gone. I had cried profusely. It felt
like all of the pain and disappointment of my actions that led me to being incarcerated came rushing in with the force of a mighty hurricane.

I recalled that fateful day of June third and its aftermath with exact clarity: the fight; Adam's death; the hurt I caused my family; and, my subsequent jailing. I could not believe that I was spending my twenty-first birthday in jail for murder. Gone were the dreams of a precocious young child whose soul's desire was to help people.

Tookie, who was originally charged with a minor offense of disorderly conduct, was now jailed as well. The prosecution, after months of investigation, felt that Tookie, too, was responsible for the death of Adam. During Tookie's hearing for the disorderly conduct charge, she was bamboozled by the prosecution and charged with murder. She was arrested on the premises of the court room, and detained in the county jail with Booger and me.

The news came as a shock to our family. It was bad enough that Booger and I were incarcerated; now they had to add Tookie to their list of worries. Though strangely, my aunt, Kim, was not indicted. Kim was, after all, involved in as much of the altercation as any one of us. The only factor that set Kim apart from us was her age; she was thirty-seven.

My belief was that Kim did not fit the media or the prosecution's theory of young, Black, gang-affiliated delinquents attacking and killing a White guy. Although, I did not want Kim to share in our misery, it was very peculiar that she was not placed in jail. Or, at the very least, I would have expected the prosecutors to file charges against her, though none were. For me, the prosecutions' inaction was additional confirmation that our case was not simply about the death of Adam; my cousins and I were also battling the criminal justice system and its' centuries old practice of racism.

~~~

Karen, my on-again, off-again girlfriend, moved in with my family in Toledo shortly after she had heard of my incarceration. She visited me at least once a week and we spoke on the phone as often as we could until the phone bills became too outrageous.

She lived with my mother for a short period, then Ms. Maple, then Mama, and finally with Kim. At each of the places she lived, she or the other person would grow tired of the other. None of them seemed able to get along with Karen. They bickered with one another until Karen had moved from one home to the next. Rumors began to abound about Karen's behavior.

"Chris, I just don't like the way she act around other men…she too flirty… I went over Mama's house and she got her legs and feet up in the chair with her legs spread apart…I don't know, maybe I'm old-fashioned, but a lady ain't got no business sittin' like that, especially when a bunch a boys runnin' around. And, she had on some short, hoochie-mama shorts, too. It just don't look right," she continued. "And, she be all up on Dae-Dae and Andre, in they faces and stuff…she come down stairs with her house dress on and nothing on underneath. Mama eventually had to tell her to go upstairs and put some clothes on!"

I listened intently to what Mymomme said. She had been holding in what she told me for quite some time. I understood what she meant about Karen, but I also knew Karen. Some of it was just Karen's way, particularly her presumed flirtatiousness. Much of Karen's flirty behavior had to do with her having being molested as a child. Her sexually suggestive manner was an extension of her abuse; she did not mean any harm. Though, soon her behavior became deliberate and no longer innocent.

"Hey. Who is this?" I asked after my call was accepted.

"This Dae-Dae. What's up, Chris?!"

"Not much, cousin. What's up with you? What's going on

over Kim's?"

"Nuttin', man. Just chillin'. They bar-b-qued and shit, so I just stopped through...man, what's up wit yo' girl?!"

"Who?" My stomach did somersaults. I knew who he was talking about, but I feigned as though I did not.

"Karen, man! That girl off the hook! She was all in Rodney face...she let him kiss her! Ain't no tellin' what else they done did...and, you know she workin' downtown at that strip joint, don't you?"

I didn't know what to say. I knew that Karen was strip dancing to support herself while she was in Toledo. She maintained that she was not doing anything inappropriate with the clientele, but I was not there, so I could not say one way or the other. Karen also told me about the guy Rodney. Apparently, he was someone who lived in the neighborhood. They were playing a card game
and he unexpectedly kissed her. I asked her if she was attracted to the guy and she admitted to me that she was.

"Yeah, she told me. Is she there? I want to talk to her."

"Yeah, man. She out there with Kim and 'nem getting fucked up...drinking and smoking and shit. Hold on."

I heard him yell for Karen to come to the phone. Seconds later, she was on the line.

"Hello?" She said, winded.

"Hey. What's up?"

"Hey, baby...I miss youuuuu!"

Just as Dae-Dae had said, Karen had been drinking and doing God knows what else.

"Karen, I need to talk to you...I can't do this anymore..."

"What?! What they say about me now?!"

"It doesn't matter, Karen. I love you, but I can't deal with a relationship now. I'm in here fighting for my life. I'm doing all I can to win this case; to show this judge who my cousins and I really are. I can't worry about whether or not you're out there being faithful."

"Chris, this shit ain't fair! They lying on me! They just don't want us to be together! I came all the way up here to be with you…" She started to cry.

I felt torn. I loved Karen, but I knew that I could not remain in the relationship. My mental and emotional health depended on me severing our ties. I could not express with absolute certainty that everything I heard was the truth, but I knew that much of it was, particularly anything that Mymomme and Mama said. Not only were they truthful persons, but they also wanted me to
be with a woman. They would not contrive a story and risk me leaving the one woman who I truly loved.

I also understood the seriousness of my offense. I did not know how the jury would view the events leading to Adam's death. My prayer was that my family and I would not be found guilty, though there was no way of knowing. Karen was young. She had needs that I could not fulfill. It would have been selfish of me to hold on to her knowing that I could not be the man that she needed.

~~~~

Autumn all too soon gave way, ushering in the brisk chill of winter. I watched from the window in my cell as the beautiful crystal flakes cascaded from the sky, accumulating into a thick blanket covering the streets. I anxiously awaited our trial, which had been set for the twenty-first of January.

"Price," I heard my name called over the loud speaker in the dorm.

I emerged from my cell, "Yes?"

"You have a visitor outside the dorm in the cubicles," the

CO stated.

"Okay, thank you."

I had no idea who the visitor could be. I searched my memory trying to recall if anyone had mentioned to me that they would be visiting. The visitor had to be a professional person; otherwise our visit would be held downstairs in the visiting room, not in the cubicle designated for special visitors. As I exited the dorm and rounded the corner, I saw an older White man sitting in a chair.

"Hi," I said, looking at the guy quizzically.

The guy stood up, extending his hand, "Hi, Christopher, I'm John Davis. I'm a private investigator. Your family retained me," he explained.

Oh, that's right! At Bradley's suggestion and my urging, Mama hired him. He was a retired police officer who worked as an investigator to supplement his income. Bradley had informed me that he had used John's services in previous cases. He felt that his help would be invaluable in gathering information about the case, specifically the details about the gang.

Bradley and I had had a heated exchange a few weeks prior, in which he all but accused me of wrong doing in the altercation between the gang and my family. I was livid.

"What?!" I said, leaning forward in my chair.

"Admit it: you guys are members of the Bloods. You heard about the gang and wanted to show them whose gang was the baddest!"

I did not know if he was employing some sort of strategy to ascertain if I could handle the pressures of a trial by jury, or if he simply did not believe what I had told him when we first retained him. Whatever the case, I did not like it.

"Listen, I don't have to lie to you or anybody else about anything!" I said angrily, "First of all, I don't find any integrity in being in a gang; I can handle the woes of life on my own. I don't need a gang to validate me, or to give me courage! Secondly, if I were in gang, believe me, I'd let you know. I don't have anything to hide. Had you come down here to visit me, like a good attorney is supposed to do, you would have known this, instead of accusing me of doing something and being someone that I am not!" I hissed.

He smiled at me sheepishly. "Well, what is it that you want me to know, Chris?"

His demeanor indicated that he was relinquishing his accusations, but I was still irritated. He had successfully dodged me for weeks. I told my daddy about his behavior, though he appeared to be so impressed with Bradley as a person that my words fell on deaf ears.

"You should have returned my phone calls and come to visit me like I asked you. I'm in here for murder, not a minor traffic violation—just in case you didn't know!" I responded hotly.

"I apologize, Mr. Price." He said in a professional manner.

It unnerved me that some people had to experience a less than pleasant side of a person in order to gain his respect. Sitting back in my chair, I eyed him carefully. I could not believe that he had avoided me for so long. Each time he visited the county jail, which was a couple times a day and several days a week, I was informed. Although, it was against the rules of the jail for the COs and counselors to divulge such information, many of them still shared with me when Bradley was in the facility.

"I've learned that the people who were involved in me and my family's altercation are members of a white supremacy gang. There's a Latino guy in here whose family was threatened and harassed by the same gang. I agreed to testify at his trial as to what occurred in my situation, and he agreed to testify at my trial," I said evenly.

The legitimacy of the gang and Alonzo's desire to testify at our trial was great news to me; though, because of Bradley's lack of support, my enthusiasm was curbed.

"Okay. I'll see what I can find out. Perhaps you can have your family hire an investigator. I've worked with this one in particular on several cases before. The information he gathers can prove invaluable."

Nearly two weeks later. I found myself standing across from John Davis, the investigator.

"Hey. How are you?" I asked, shaking his outstretched hand. No one had mentioned to me that an investigator had actually been acquired. As a result, I was surprised by his visit. I think that I subconsciously expected him to Black. Quite honestly, I felt uncomfortable sharing the details of my case to a former police officer, though specifically a White police officer. I had been instructed so often by so many people not to discuss my case that it seemed strange to openly discuss my case with anyone, let alone this guy.

He told me a little about himself, much of which I already knew. Although he seemed like a nice, sincere guy, I did not know if I could trust him.

"So you want to tell me a little about your case?" He asked.

I really did not want to, but I did so anyway. I told him the gist of the case, including the information that Alonzo had shared with me. He looked at me intently as I spoke. His demeanor was completely different than Bradley's. John seemed sincerely interested in what I had to say. Bradley always made me feel like he simply listened to what I had to say, because he had to.

"Very interesting stuff, Christopher. I'll make sure I check into it and see what I can come up with," John replied to me, before standing and extending his hand for me to shake.

"Okay. Thank you for your help. I appreciate you," I said, shaking his hand.

I had to admit that my assumptions about him proved to be false. It was a relief having someone on the outside that was willing to put forth the necessary energies to help me. He seemed trustworthy and genuine.

~~~

Three weeks later I received a letter from Karen. Truthfully, I had to admit, I was pleased to see her familiar script. As soon as the CO handed the letter to me, I rushed to my cell to read the contents in private. I opened the letter in a flurry. Karen's penmanship was beautiful as usual. I hurriedly began to read the letter…and then stopped. I could not believe it. I put the letter aside, placing it on the bed. I raised my hands to my head, holding it tightly…no…no…no. It could not be true!

I sat on the bed for a long moment until I had composed myself well enough to continue reading the letter. I started over from the beginning, stopped at my previous place, and then continued. When I finished reading the letter, I neatly placed it back into the envelope. I sat on the bed with my back against the wall, staring at the adjacent wall as I absorbed the contents of the letter.

Karen was pregnant. As I read the letter, I secretly hoped that the baby was mine. Though, the next sentence quietly put that thought out of my mind, a pregnancy test revealed that she was three months pregnant, making it impossible that the child could be mine since I had been incarcerated for six months already.

After I had severed our relationship, Karen went to work that evening at the strip club. She entertained the advances of one of the regular clients at the strip club. He invited her to spend the evening with him, she obliged.

The two of them went to a motel, where they drank alcohol, and had sex throughout the night. One month later, she learned that she was pregnant.

Eventually, I got up from the bed and put the letter with the other mail I had received over the previous few months of my incarceration. I could not do anything about the pregnancy and so I pushed it from my mind, concentrating instead on what lie ahead of me.

Chapter Eight

The New Year brought with it a wealth of hope for me. John, the private investigator, had returned with more news about the gang. Not only did the gang have their personal insignias, but the deceased, Adam Faulkner, also had the insignia tattooed on his ankle, which solidified the gang's legitimacy and Adam's membership in the gang as well. The gang had also left their stamp on buildings in south Toledo. Perhaps not so ironic, the letters "TK" and the word "Nigger" were spray painted on the door and hood of Tookie's car.

In addition, Bradley asked that I contact people who would be willing to act as character witnesses on my behalf. I chose two of my former high school instructors, Eileen Carter and Bernice Hicks. I wrote both of them detailed letters, explaining my need, and if they would represent me during my trial. They both agreed.

Bradley arranged a meeting with Tookie and Booger's attorneys. The four of us, Bradley, Alex (Tookie's attorney), Madison (Booger's attorney), and I met outside of my dorm in the cubicles. Madison and Alex were both public defenders, who had never represented someone being tried for murder. I shook their hands upon meeting them.

"Hi. How are you two?" We had seen one another dozens of times during the many court hearings we had to attend over the past several months, though we were never formally introduced.

"Great, Christopher," Alex said, smiling.

"I am well, Christopher. How are you?" Madison asked.

"I'm well, all things considering," I said, smiling at both of them. They both seemed to be in pleasant moods. I assumed from their demeanors that Bradley had informed them of the reason for our meeting.

"As Bradley may have shared with you two, I am going to testify during the trial as to the events that occurred. For you, Madison, that means I will be admitting to my guilt; that is, that I was the person handling the gun as it discharged. My hope is that by doing so, Booger will be exonerated of the murder charge against him and he will be released. I will also make it known that neither Booger nor Tookie was in the vicinity as the gun discharged."

Both Madison and Alex looked at me with relief in their eyes. They really did not have a case without my confession. All of the evidence in the police report pointed to Booger as the person who shot Adam. Each of the witnesses said that a Black guy with the bad eye (Booger's right eye was discolored as the result of a childhood accident) was the person who shot Adam. I believe they falsely identified Booger for three reasons: the first reason being that, during the time that the altercation began, it was Booger who asked for an apology from the people on the porch. Many of witnesses remembered him because of that initial meeting; the second reason is because Booger's right eye was memorable, thereby making his face easier to recall; and, the third reason is that Booger and I resembled one another (we are separated by a quarter of an inch in height, nearly the same in skin complexion, and have similar facial features), which made it difficult for some people to tell us apart from one another.

For Alex, my decision to testify removed Tookie from the

scene of the crime. Tookie had been charged with murder, because the prosecution felt that the initial situation occurred as a result of her actions (speeding; nearly hitting the White couple as they crossed the street; and then threatening the couple that she would be back after she was pushed). The prosecution, therefore, felt that Tookie acted as an accomplice to the murder.

"Well, thank you, Christopher. Your actions are commendable and courageous," Madison said. Alex smiled in appreciation. Bradley was not pleased with my decision to testify. He initially tried to have our trials separated; however, the judge would not allow us to have separate trials. After the judge's decision not to separate the trials, Bradley wanted me to allow the jury to convict Booger of murder and, then, for me to testify that it was I who had actually handled the gun as it discharged.

From a legal standpoint, Bradley's strategy sounded great, though from an ethical vantage it was blemished.

"Booger is my cousin," I reminded him. "I could not allow anyone to take the blame for something that I did, not to mention someone as near and dear to me as my cousin."

At the time that I stated my position on the matter, Bradley was not pleased; and, from the look of his face, he still was not thrilled. Yet, I had to do what I felt in my spirit was the right thing to do. Booger had already been jailed for six months for something he did not do. I simply could not allow him to be incarcerated any longer, if I could help it.

"It's not a problem at all. It's what I am supposed to do." I said, shaking each one of their hands, as they prepared to leave. A CO came to the cubicle to escort me back to the dorm. I waved good-bye to the attorneys. I felt really good spiritually, like a weight had been lifted off of me. I had always known that I would make the choice that I did, though it still felt good to do so.

~~~

Criminal trials are long and tedious. Television and film make trials look very interesting, though the truth of the matter is that they rarely are anything of the sort. In my case, the selection of jury members in itself took a whole day.

Generally expressing, dozens of constituents are pooled from across county seats. From these pools, the defense and prosecuting attorneys must choose twelve jurors and one representative. Seems simple enough; yet, it is not. Each attorney chooses or rejects a potential juror for a variety of reasons. The reasons are numerous and unique to each particular case. A perspective juror can be rejected because of lack of a formal education; while another person may be chosen because of her political views. Jury selection is an exhausting experience.

The jury members chosen for our case were unique. The United States' Constitution states that jury members should be representative of the defendant's peers; yet, all of our jurors were middle-aged, resided in the suburbs of Toledo, and, save one juror, were White. They hardly represented my cousins and me: young, Black, poor, and inner-city residents.

Despite Bradley's avid objections, the judge ruled that, because of the racial and socio-economic composition of Toledo and its surrounding cities, the jurors were a representation of our peers. The gist of Judge O'Connor's ruling meant that, because Toledo was a predominately White, middle-class city, the jurors consisted of the persons who represented the racial and socio-economic standing of the majority of Toledo's citizens. The Constitutional Amendment which stated that the jury should be reflective of the defendant's peers did not qualify, at least not to my cousins and me.

~~~

Distressing news met me at the door late one evening. I was in my cell reading when I heard the chatter of voices outside of my door. I walked to the door, pushing the button to open it. As the door slid open, I saw a glimpse of Alonzo's face as he walked to his cell. He looked as he did the first day I met him: distraught, as though his entire world had collapsed around him.

I soon learned the reasons for his downcast countenance. He had accepted the prosecutions' plea bargain. He was given a sentence of fourteen to forty years in prison. He would soon be transferred from the county jail to prison. Gone was the hope that we would testify for one another; gone was the hope that we would be acquitted on the basis of the similarities in our cases.

~~~

Our trial began the following day after jury selection. It was a particularly stressful time for me, though I was relieved to finally move forward with the trial. I was awakened early that morning to prepare for the day's proceedings.

Weeks before the start of the trial, Bradley requested that my family gather clothes for me to wear during the trial. Mymomme went through my excessive wardrobe, and chose several of my silk shirts and dress slacks to wear. Confined defendants, as my cousins and I were, were allowed to have their personal clothes to wear during their trials. Such an action was an attempt of the Court's to allow the defendants to be viewed without prejudice by the jury. If a confined defendant entered a court room donning a jail jumpsuit, he may have been considered guilty in the minds' of the jurors before being actually tried.

My personal barber was allowed to enter the jail the night before to cut my hair. During the six months of my incarceration, my hair had grown to a short afro. John, my barber, lined and trimmed my hair to perfection. It felt good to have a haircut after having gone so long without one.

I ate my breakfast alone and quietly, as I thought about the ensuing trial. Afterwards, I showered and began to get dressed. I took my outfit out of the garment bag. I recognized one of my favorite shirts and my leather pants in the bag. I pulled out the white and tan printed, long sleeve shirt, and put it on. I retrieved my tan-colored, leather pants from the garment bag. At that time, the pants were very fashionable, especially in the northern cities, like Detroit, Toledo, Chicago, and New York. Lastly, I slid my brown belt through the loops and slipped into my multi-colored brown, leather, hard-soled shoes.

I looked in the mirror. I looked like my old self. I had a moment of nostalgia: I missed getting dressed in nice clothes. I breathed in deeply and exhaled the memories of yesteryear. I said a quiet prayer to God, expressing faith in his will, and exited the counselor's office where I had changed into my clothes.

Minutes later Booger turned the corner, dressed in a navy blue suit. We smiled at each other. The CO handcuffed us. After boarding the elevator, we stopped on the second floor. Tookie entered the elevator, dressed in a floral print dress. It was good to see them both. I only saw Tookie when we had court hearings, though I saw Booger regularly, as we were housed on the same floor.

We took underground tunnels to the court house. We were escorted to our seats at the defendants' table in the courtroom. As the bailiff took off our handcuffs, he reminded us not to talk to anyone in the courtroom. I looked around the courtroom. Seated behind us, I saw several of our family members and friends. I smiled at them, remembering the bailiff's admonishment.

Before I turned back around, I scanned the faces of those who had come to support us. I looked and looked, though to no avail, she was not there.

A week prior, Mymomme and I had a heated conversation. She had begun to use drugs, again; specifically alcohol and crack-cocaine. As disheartening as the news of her substance use was, it did not come as a surprise. She had several failed attempts at sobriety over the years. No matter how often she tried, her moments of abstinence were short-lived.

This time, however, Mymomme's drug usage was different. In times past she had maintained a functional lifestyle; in that, our family did not suffer as a result of her drug use. She continued to work, she cooked dinner every evening, and she made certain that her bills were paid. She appeared to be a recreational drug user, yet her usage had escalated. She began to spend the money I left in her care to support her addiction.

"Mymomme, I thought you were going to send me some of my money?" I asked over the phone.

"I was, but I had to pay the phone and light bills…I thought Mama was going to send you some money," she said, with a hint of irritation in her voice.

"She was, but I told her not to, because you said you were

going to send me some of my money...well, what happened to your check from work?"

"What?!" Her irritation was more apparent.

"What happened to the money from your check from work? Why didn't you pay your bills with your money?"

"None of yo' damn business!"

"Huh?! You use my money to pay your bills and it's none of my business?!"

"That's right!"

"Hmmpf," I scoffed. "So, what am I supposed to do about commissary? You know they don't feed us much of nothing in here. Plus, I need some more toiletries..."

"Some what?"

"Some toiletries; some soap and lotion and stuff..."

"Ask Mama or yo' daddy for some!"

"What?! Why should I ask them for some money when I have my own?! Plus, they've done a lot by paying for my private investigator and Bradley's fees!"

"Well, I don't know what to tell you, then!"

"Okay... just give the rest of the money to Mama, and I'll have her send it to me."

"I ain't got it..."

"What? Are you using, again?"

"It ain't none of yo' damn business what I'm doing...You just worry about yourself!"

"How can I worry about myself when you are out there using and spending my money on drugs, when I need every cent to either fight this case or survive in here!"

"You shouldna left it with me, then!" She hung up the phone without saying good-bye to me.

I stared at the phone, shocked by her behavior. I could not believe that she had talked to me as she had. The woman I was on the phone with was new to me; she did not behave like Mymomme at all. Our relationship was not perfect, primarily because of her drug abuse, but we had always been close and maintained a level of respect for one another.

She was my mother and I loved her, chemically dependent or not; yet, it pained me that she allowed drugs to take hold of her life the way she did. Though, such was case with life, I surmised. Some of us were not able to deal with the hardships that sometimes came with living without the reprieve that substances offered.

She was such a strong, fearless woman when I was a child. I surmised that life had finally taken its toll on her.

While I realized that she used drugs before my incarceration, I shared the blame for the severity of her current substance use. Her life was filled with so much misery, heartache, and disappointment that much of her hope of a better life was dependent upon my success as a person. When I had fallen as prey to the vices of life, so, too, did her strong-hold on life. My incarceration was the "straw that broke the camel's back," as went the adage.

I turned around in my seat. Moments later our attorneys and the prosecution walked into the courtroom. Within minutes after our attorneys arrived, the bailiff told us all to stand as Judge O'Connor entered the courtroom. Judge O'Connor gave a brief outline of the case, instructed the jury as to their role, and reminded the audience on courtroom etiquettes.

Both sides, the prosecution and defense, presented their opening arguments. The prosecution, of course, made us appear to be a bunch of heartless hooligans. Alex and Madison made a valiant attempt at a strong opening statement, though their inexperience showed. Bradley, however, was at his finest. He seemed at his best when he was in the courtroom with everyone's eyes on him. He spoke well, moved about the courtroom regally, as if it were his throne, and he made it a point to look each juror in the eye, establishing an intimate connection with them from the start.

Both sides presented their witnesses. The state's primary witnesses were the state coroner and Angela Horn, our childhood friend who accompanied Tookie and me to the house where the altercation took place. Both of their testimonies were brief and revealed nothing other than what was already known.

The coroner stated that the deceased, Adam Faulkner, was shot on the left side of his abdomen, and killed with what appeared to be a shot-gun. The prosecutor presented several photos of Adam prior to and after his death. The photos were passed around to the jurors, and then to my cousins and me.

I looked at the first photo for a long moment. My stomach quivered. Seeing the photo further brought home the realization that I had taken someone's life. I quickly flipped through the other photos until I reached the final one. It was a photo of Adam while he was alive. He was very nice looking: his blondish-brown hair hung low to his shoulders; his smooth, sun-kissed skin looked radiant; his smile was soft and innocent.

After the coroner's testimony was complete, Angela took the stand. She looked terrified as the prosecutor interrogated her. Angela relayed the events as they occurred, she neither incriminated the gang, nor did she offer any new details to the case. I wondered what she had initially told the prosecution for them to use her as a witness. Apparently she must have shared something with him that he thought would make her a viable witness. Though whatever it was, if there was anything, it was not expressed during his interrogation of her.

As Bradley stood up to cross-examine Angela, all eyes were on him. Angela seemed even more afraid of Bradley than she had with the prosecutor. She cried as she detailed the events of what transpired, making known that we had not planned for any of the event to happen. Bradley concluded his examination, and Angela was dismissed.

Danielle and Matthew Faulkner, brothers of the deceased, were both called as the state's witnesses. Danielle was actually the person who pushed Tookie, igniting the series of events that led to Adam's demise; Matthew was the person who stood on the back porch of whom Booger asked an apology on that fateful day of June 3rd.

It was strange seeing them. I had read their names many times in the police report, though I could not remember what either of them looked like.

Danielle sat timidly in the witness' chair, as he gave his account of what happened. When Matthew took the stand he was just as cocky in the witness' chair as he was when we first encountered him. Their testimonies revealed nothing; no new information; nothing that was particularly damaging to my cousins and me.

After the prosecution presented their case, Bradley presented his witnesses. Ms. Carter and Ms. Hicks took the stand first. As character witnesses, they both testified that I was a kind, intelligent, and loving person. Although they were my instructors in high school, I had developed a genuine friendship with them after I graduated.

In fact, as a college freshman, Ms. Carter asked me to speak to her students about the joys and perils of college-life. I enthusiastically accepted her request. I loved educating, and the students responded well to what I shared. I spoke about a number of things, including safe sex/abstinence, the importance of self-love, and the need for a college education.

Ms. Carter and Ms. Hicks' testimonies were very helpful, in that they showed who I was and not what the charges against me depicted me to be. Before dismissing them, Bradley asked them if they could see me murdering anyone. They both replied that they could not.

A gang task force officer also testified as Bradley's witness. His testimony was invaluable, because it solidified the legitimacy of the gang and characterized the gang from the vantage of a law enforcement officer. He stated that the task force had been tracking the gang's involvement for several years, and that their acts of violence was just as menacing as those of gangs, like the Bloods, Crips, or Folks. He shared the same facts with those in attendance for the trial that John, the private investigator, had expressed to me about the gang's graffiti being spray painted on buildings and that they had their personal insignias tattooed on themselves.

I was the last to testify. Bradley looked over to me, leaning down, "You ready?" He asked.

"Yeah, I am." I said, nodding my head affirmatively. I stood up and walked to the witness stand where the stenographer reminded me that I was in a court of law and that I should tell the truth. Afterwards, I took my seat. I looked out to the audience. The family members and supporters of Adam sat on the left side of the courtroom; my family sat on the right side. Looking out at them resembled a scene from a pre-civil rights film, in which Blacks and Whites were made to sit separately from one another.

It was good to see our family supporting us; yet, because of the circumstances, it was heart-wrenching.

"Will you please state your name for the record, please?" Bradley asked me.

"Yes, my name is Christopher Lakeith Price," I responded coolly.

I probably should have been nervous, but I was not. I felt that this was the time for our story to be heard. For the past six months, I had listened or read about the circumstances surrounding our incarceration. Now was the moment for me to tell what transpired, without the media's biased slant.

"Mr. Price, can you please tell the court what happened on the evening of June of third?" Bradley asked.

"Yes." I began telling the events as they transpired, beginning with Tookie arriving at Leslie's house.

As I relayed the events, Bradley and the court stenographer stopped me several times. Bradley stopped me to clarify a particular event; the stenographer stopped me, because I was talking too fast for her to keep pace. I apologized to her, though, all the while I was thinking, how strange it was that the pace at which I spoke was too rapid for her. On television the stenographer was always shown hitting the stenograph with the grace and efficiency of a gazelle. I surmised that this was yet another difference between reality and television drama.

I related the events in great detail, stopping at the point where Adam was shot. "Now, how was the gun held, Mr. Price?" I demonstrated how I held the gun. "And, where were you standing?" Bradley produced a diagram of 503 Knower (the house where the altercation took place) and 501 Knower (the building beside the house). I walked to the diagram. Using the pointer, I indicated where I stood on ground level between the house and the building.

"Okay. So, tell us again, Mr. Price, you are running along a walkway between 503 and 501," Bradley said, pointing to the diagram. "You stop once you reach the backyard, and what happens next, Mr. Price?" Bradley asked.

"Yes. I stopped once I reached the backyard, because I heard a sound to my right and the realization of where I was began to dawn on me," I said.

"Explain that to me, Mr. Price. The realization of where you were?" Bradley asked.

"Yes, well, as I ran behind the White guys, we entered the backyard from Knower Street. I had never been on Knower Street. The altercation occurred in the backyard. I didn't know what the front of the house looked like. So, as we ran from the front of the house to the back of the house, I was disoriented. As I stood at the gate entering the backyard, I suddenly realized that I was in the backyard of where the altercation began." I explained.

"So, you are in the backyard, you hear a sound. How much time had passed?" Bradley asked.

"Not long at all; a second, maybe a fraction of a second," I replied.

"What happens next?" Bradley continued.

"I quickly turned toward the sound. I looked..." Bradley interrupted me. "So in what direction are you facing?"

"I was facing the back porch of 503 Knower, with my back to 501 Knower."

"Okay. Continue, please."

"I looked up. There was a White guy on the porch. We startled each other. He jumped..." Bradley interrupted me again.

"You looked up, because you're on flat ground and the porch is elevated?" He asked.

"Yes."

"Okay. So, you look up, there's a guy on the porch. You both are startled."

"Yes. He jumped. I instinctively jumped backwards, and

the butt of the gun hit the fence."

"Okay. There is a fence behind you?"

"Yes. The fence surrounded the entire backyard, but it also separated 503 and 501 Knower."

"Okay. You jump backwards, hitting the fence. What happens next?"

"The gun discharged. I saw an orange-reddish color. It blinded me for a split second. Once my vision returned, I ran back between the houses."

"The gun discharges, you are blinded by the gunfire. What happens to the guy?"

"I don't know. Once my vision returned, I ran."

"Okay, so you run between the houses, then what?"

"As I ran between the houses, I heard a woman scream, 'Oh, my God! I think Adam's been shot!"

"So what do you do?" He asked.

"I kept running. I saw Booger…uh Raymond, standing in the middle of Knower Street. I ran pass him, turned left onto Maumee Street. I made a right on Walbridge Street. I saw Raylene and Kim standing outside. When I reached Raylene, she asked me what happened."

"What did you tell her?"

"I told her that I didn't know, but that I thought that I had shot someone." I continued to relate what transpired.

I told the court room how Booger and I had run to my Mymomme's house; that we separated and I ended my journey at Ms. Maple's.

"How did you learn of Adam's death?" Bradley asked.

I looked into Bradley's face and, then, out to the courtroom. I saw my aunt, Natalie; my cousin, Andre; and, my daddy seated amongst my other family members in the audience. I looked over to where Booger and Tookie sat at the defendants' table: I thought of Tookie's young daughter, Lolita, and how sad it must be for her to be without her mother; I looked into Booger's eyes and recalled the intense love he held in his eyes as he spoke of his girlfriend, Niecy. I recalled the morning Booger called me with the news that Adam had been shot and killed. I saw it in my mind's eye as clearly as I saw Bradley standing in front of me.

I remembered the beautiful, innocent look of Adam's smiling face in the photo the prosecutor presented. A life lost. A smile never to be seen again…laughter never to be heard. Suddenly, without warning, tears slowly began to trickle from my eyes.

All of our lives had been forever changed. None of us would, nor could we ever be the same. My tears began to gain momentum. I cried uncontrollably; heaving as I did.

"Mr. Price, are you alright? Would you like to take a break?" Bradley asked me. I bounced back from my reverie. Everyone in the courtroom was looking at me. I tried to blink away the tears, but they continued to spill from my eyes, cascading down my face. Bradley stood in front of me offering me a box of tissue. I grabbed several of the tissue, and apologized to no one in particular.

"No, I'm fine. Thank you," I said.

I sat up, trying to regain my composure. I breathed in deeply several times, "Booger called me the next morning and asked me if I had seen the News," I said in a shaky voice.

"I told him that I hadn't. I asked him why." My voice broke, though I continued speaking, "He said that the guy had been shot and was dead."

"Are you all right, Mr. Price?" Bradley asked, again in a soft, consoling manner.

I must have looked as though I was going to pass out or

something. My relationship with Bradley had changed drastically since I had taken the witness' chair. He was suddenly protective of me. My vulnerability had brought forth a kindness in him that I had not seen in him.

"Yes, I'm okay." I said.

"Thank you. I have no further questions, Your Honor."

Bradley smiled warmly at me before walking to the table where my cousins and their attorneys sat. Mr. Reeves, the prosecutor, stood up to cross-examine me. He was an older, White guy with a deep, gravelly voice.

"Mr. Price, you said that you and your family were chased by these guys with bats and sticks?"

I sat up in my seat, leaning forward. I was on guard, "Yes."

"And, that you were the person who shot Adam Faulkner?"

"Yes, that's what happened."

Mr. Reeve looked at me for a long moment before asking his next question. I looked back at him waiting for his question, prepared to shoot it down. Though nothing could have prepared me for what he asked.

"Mr. Price, you aren't trying to take the blame for an act your cousin committed, are you? You wouldn't have made-up this elaborate story for us just to save your cousin, would you? I mean, you're an intelligent, college-educated person. You come in here with influential, character witnesses hoping that we would buy the story and your cousin would be released. Isn't that right, Mr. Price?" Mr. Reeve asked, peering above the rim of his bi-focal glasses at me, as though he had just solved the case of the century.

I was flabbergasted. I could not believe what he had asked me. Though, what was more unbelievable was that he was serious.

"No. What I said is the truth." I said evenly.

"No further questions, Your Honor." What?! That was it? I thought that Mr. Reeve's interrogation would go on forever. Instead, the whole ordeal lasted just a few short minutes. I looked out into the audience at my family, and then to Bradley, who was smiling. I had defeated the big, bad prosecutor with the simple truth. I inwardly smiled, as I stepped down from the witness' chair to take my position beside my cousins and Bradley.

After I testified, the attorneys presented their closing arguments. One by one our group of defense attorneys took the stand. As with the trial, Madison and Alex's inexperience was apparent, though my testimony gave them the help they needed by removing Tookie and Booger from the scene of the crime.

Both Bradley and the prosecutor's closing arguments were strong and concise. Bradley encouraged the jurors to examine the evidence. Should the jurors find that the evidence does not support a conviction of murder, Bradley urged them to render a not guilty verdict.

The prosecutor still believed that I had accepted responsibility for an act that Booger committed. He urged the jurors to convict my cousins and me of murder, stating that we had all acted together in the death in Alex Faulkner.

After Mr. Reeve's closing remarks, the jurors were commissioned and court was adjourned until they reached a decision. My cousins and I were taken to a holding cell, where we waited until the verdict. It was the first time we were able to talk freely about our case. Although, we had written letters to one another over the past few months, we were cautious about what we expressed for fear that the contents of our letters would be read. We rejoiced in the blessing to be able to sit and talk face-to-face.

~~~

Hours passed by and still no word as to the jurors' verdict. Although I desperately wanted to go home to my family and friends, I was not apprehensive about the jury's verdict. My spiritual experiences in jail had renewed my faith and my trust in God. I better understood the blessing of life. I had come to know God in a way that I had not known Him before. As we sat waiting on word from the jurors, I made a personal promise that, regardless of whether or not I was released, I would not forsake the gifts I had been given.

Just as I finished my prayer, "Price, Jones, Jones!" The CO called.

The three of us stood up and began walking to the gate.

"A decision has been reached," the CO said.

We looked at one another.

"Okay. Here we go," I said, approaching the CO, so that he could handcuff me. After Tookie and Booger were handcuffed, the CO opened the gate. We walked through the underground tunnel with our ankles and wrist bound by chains and cuffs. As we entered the courtroom, our family smiled at us. I basked in the energy of their love and support.

Minutes later, the bailiff instructed the courtroom to stand, as Judge O'Connor entered the courtroom. After she entered, we waited for her permission to be seated. Once we were granted permission to take our seats, Judge O'Connor again reminded everyone of courtroom etiquette. She then directed her attention to the foreman of the jury.

"Has a verdict been reached?" She asked.

An older, White guy stood up, "Yes, Your Honor, we have made a decision."

"Please read the verdict," Judge O'Connor instructed.

Booger, Tookie, and I sat motionless. Our hands were tightly intertwined within one another's, all of us lost in our own private thoughts.

The foreman looked down at a piece of paper, "Raymond Jones, in the charge of murder, not guilty; Raylene Jones, in the charge of murder, not guilty."

Tookie, who sat in the middle of Booger and me, shook our clasped hands vigorously, pleased with the jury's decision.

"Christopher Price, in the charge of murder, not guilty." The foreman announced. I bowed my head, silently mouthing thank you to the Creator.

"Raymond Jones, guilty of the lesser included offense, involuntary manslaughter; Raylene Jones, guilty of the lesser included offense, involuntary manslaughter; Christopher Price, guilty of the lesser included offense, involuntary manslaughter."

Pandemonium erupted in the courtroom. Sobbing could be heard in the distance. My cousins and I looked at one another silently, wondering what a conviction of involuntary manslaughter entailed.

Judge O'Connor hit the gravel before her, quieting the courtroom. As the courtroom quieted, "Thank you, foreman, and thank you ladies and gentlemen of the jury."

She then directed her attention to my cousins and me, "You each have been convicted of involuntary manslaughter with a minor offense of aggravated rioting in the death of Adam Faulkner.

Your attorneys will explain the nature of the convictions. On February 17, 1995, you all will receive sentences for said convictions. In the meantime, you will be held in the county jail until such time arrives." Rapping the gravel, Judge O'Connor dismissed the jurors and adjourned court.

My cousins and I stood up quietly as the deputy sheriffs handcuffed and chained our ankles. Bradley approached me with a broad smile on his face. He shook my hand, stating that he would come to see me soon. The deputy sheriffs directed us through the crowd of people assembled: our family, family and friends of Adam, and the throngs of television reporters.

We entered the elevators that would take us to the tunnels beneath the streets leading to the county jail. I was lost in thought. Throughout my stay in the county jail and during my trial, I had prayed that God's will be done. I did not know exactly all that my prayer entailed, though I had not expected it to include involuntary manslaughter.

In my mind, I believed that I would be found guilty of either murder or acquitted of the charge. While our attorneys explained to each of us that the judge would allow lesser included offenses, such as involuntary manslaughter, to be submitted with the offense of murder, we had not expected that we would be convicted of any of them.

Lesser included offenses, as they were explained to us, consisted of a large array of possible offenses, such as involuntary manslaughter, voluntary manslaughter, or negligent homicide. Although the jury did not find that our actions were consistent with a conviction of murder, they did find that there was cause for a conviction of involuntary manslaughter, which is essentially the unintentional killing of another person.

"I can't believe they found us guilty." Tookie said, breaking the silence, as we walked through the underground tunnels. She looked defeated; her countenance revealing her disappointment.

"Yeah, I know. I didn't think that they would find us guilty, either." I said, unsure of what else to say.

"It's cool. The judge can still grant us probation. She ain't got to give us no time," Booger interjected.

He seemed optimistic and unfazed by the jury's verdict. "At least they didn't find us guilty of murder. We still have a chance of going home. It's up to the judge now," Booger added.

Tookie and I remained silent. I did not know what she thought of Booger's statement, but I was unsure of our future… Booger was right, though. Judge O'Connor could grant us super-shock probation, which was reserved to persons who were convicted of high degree felonies. I was uncertain as to whether Judge O'Connor would grant such a motion, however.

Chapter Nine

February 17th arrived quickly. Once again, Booger, Tookie, and I stood before Judge O'Connor. However, this time it was to receive our sentence. Our fate now rested in the hands of one person. Judge O'Connor had the power to reprimand us to a halfway house with time served, or she could sentence us to time in prison.

During the sentencing we, as well as the victim's family, were allowed to speak. A middle-aged woman rose to speak on behalf of the Faulkner family. Tears slid down her face as she unfolded a sheet of white notebook paper. My heart ached for her. Although my family and I had survived the events of that day, I imagined what it must feel like if one of us had been killed.

"Your Honor, my name is Diane Faulkner. I am Adam Faulkner's step-mother. Adam was a beautiful, young boy. Although, I am his step-mother, I loved him as though he was my own child." She stopped reading for a moment, as she attempted to control her emotions.

"These people, Your Honor," she said, looking at my cousins and me, "took my son's rights away from him! They sit over there without a single tear in their eyes; without a single bit of remorse. My son will never have children; we will never be able to hear his laughter."

"He didn't have a choice in this matter! He was gunned down without the right to choose whether he should live or die, because these people took that right away from him! They took my precious, beautiful son away and now they sit over there with their Bibles, laughing as though nothing has happened! Do you see what you took from me!" She screamed, holding up a picture of Adam in her hands.

"Do you see what you've taken from my family!" She yelled, as tears streamed down her face. She walked slowly to her seat where an older guy hugged her.

"Thank you, Ms. Faulkner," Judge O'Connor said. "The defendants will now be given an opportunity to speak."

Tookie and Booger both spoke briefly. They expressed their deepest, heartfelt sorrow and took their seats. It was my turn to speak next. Although I was given the opportunity to express the details of our altercation to the courtroom during our trial, Ms. Faulkner's statements ignited a fire in me that could not be easily extinguished.

"Your Honor, I cannot express how deeply sorry I am about the events that took place on June 3rd. I have spent countless days and nights agonizing over what occurred. Because of my actions, my cousins are now faced with the threat of prison, my family has endured insurmountable pain, and the Faulkner's have lost a loved one; and, although I grieve for their loss, I have to say that the fault was not ours alone."

Continuing, "I listened to Ms. Faulkner as she talked about Adam and what we did to him and their family, as if they were completely innocent in all of this. We all heard the testimony of the gang task force officer; we all heard him state that these people are members of a white supremacy gang. Everyone heard from not only my testimony, but also from the testimony of Matthew Faulkner of how these people chased us with bats and various other weapons, and that their intent was to 'whoop some ass,' as said by Matthew Faulkner."

"I have absolutely no problem expressing that my family and I were wrong for going to their house. We should not have ever gone there expecting to receive an apology. Yet, the blame is not simply ours. The Faulkner's testified that we tried to flee and that they would not let us escape. They beat us and chased us for two blocks with no indication of retreating. Their intent was to seriously injure us or to kill us, and, yet Ms. Faulkner talks of them as if they were innocent by-standers!" I opened my mouth to say more, though before I could Judge O'Connor silenced me.

"Thank you, Mr. Price. We were made aware of the events that took place during the trial. We are not here to retry the case. You will have that opportunity, if you so choose, when you file for an appeal." Moving right along, she continued. "You and your cousins are now here to be sentenced for the death of Adam Faulkner. The jury found the three of you guilty of involuntary manslaughter. I sentence you, Raylene Jones, to six to twenty-five years, during which time you will be reprimanded to an Ohio State Correctional Institution; Raymond Jones, you are sentenced to six to twenty-five years, during which time you will be reprimanded to an Ohio State Correctional Institution; and, Christopher Price, you are sentenced to nine to twenty-five years, during which time you will be reprimanded to an Ohio State Correctional Institution."

Judge O'Connor tapped her gravel, dismissing the court. My cousins and I, once again, stood motionless, as we absorbed the latest news of our lives. The bailiffs escorted us from the courtroom. As we made our way to the elevator that would lead us to the underground tunnels, we passed our family members. Many of them were openly crying. I was concerned about how they would handle our sentences. Though, as hard as I tried, I could not discern whether their tears were of joy or sorrow.

We remained in the county jail for an additional two weeks. Then, on the third of March at three o'clock in the morning, the steel gate of the dorm clanked open.

"Price, gather your things, man. You're riding out," a CO said, standing on the other side of the locked door to my cell.

I rose from the bed, slipping on my brown jumpsuit. The day was finally here. After nine months of being incarcerated in the county jail, I was now being transferred to prison. I was anxious to leave. I was ready to start doing my time. I had heard quite a bit about prison during my stay in the county jail; some of the information was good and some of it was bad. I had been told stories of rape, beatings, and extortion. Although, I was sure that there was some degree of truth to the stories, none of them frightened me. While I only stood five feet, seven inches tall, I had resolved that I would do whatever was necessary to protect myself.

The door to my cell opened. I walked out of the room, and quickly said good-bye to my friends that I was leaving behind, some of whom were crying. Many of us had become far more than just dorm mates. Together we battled the pain and the disappointment of being jailed. We had shared our joys, our fears, and our sorrows; in effect, we had become surrogate family members to one another. I suddenly felt a deep sadness.

I had become a man while in jail. The old Chris died in the six by nine feet cell. A new, re-fined Chris had been born. Gone was the child who believed that his mother or father could protect him from anything. Heartache and disappointment had given way to wisdom.

I would not miss the county jail at all, though I would miss the special people I met while in there; wonderful people whom society had written-off as junkies, unwanted and unneeded. I felt that I had been blessed with the opportunity to forge relationships with people whom I may have never met had it not been for my being jailed. I was able to see beyond their misdeeds and saw them for the gems that they were. I soon came to understand that these people were no different than anyone else in the world.

~~~

I exited the dorm. Across the hall, I could see that several inmates had already gathered at the elevator, waiting to be transported to their new home. As I walked closer, one of the inmates looked familiar. My heart leapt in my chest. It was Booger! We were being transported to the prison together.

"What's up, cousin," he said, as he looked in the direction of the CO. A separation had been placed on us while we were awaiting our trial. We did not know if it was all right for us to speak to one another now that the trial was behind us. Apparently, it was okay, because the CO did not say anything.

"Hey there!" I said.

I was so happy to see him! I wanted to give him a big bear hug!

"How have you been?" I asked as we got on the elevator.

The elevator doors closed behind us. Booger and I were so engrossed in our conversation that we not did notice that the elevator had stopped on the second floor. We talked excitedly as though we had not seen each other in years, as opposed to just two short weeks ago. We were in a world of our own; totally oblivious of those around us.

"Hey, Mr. Price!" a female voice sang. I could not believe my ears. I knew the voice could not belong to who I thought it did. I turned my head in the direction of the person's voice. To my delight, Tookie entered the elevator!

"Hey, you!" I said in an enthusiastic whisper.

I wanted to hug her. Yet, I remained cool; as cool as I could as I exposed every tooth in my mouth! I smiled so broadly! I could not have asked for a greater blessing! I did not realize how lonely I was for my family until I met up with those two. We chattered incessantly until we reached the bus that would take us to our final destinations.

~~~~

Once again, my cousins and I, along with about thirty other inmates, were cuffed at our hands and ankles, bound and chained like beast in a circus. Booger and I were chained to one another. Tookie and five other female inmates sat in the row of seats in front of us. A locked gate separated the females from the male inmates; another gate separated the female inmates from the driver and his co-driver.

Save the heavily tented, barred windows and the massive shotgun positioned next to the driver, the bus looked like a yellow school bus. We sat uncomfortably on the leather seats for several hours, riding through small hick towns, until we reached our first destination. I slept most of the way, waking periodically as the bus trod over badly paved roads.

We arrived at a small, white building with about a dozen similarly structured buildings littered across the grounds. The compound was encased within a barbed wire fence. A sign in front of the buildings identified our destination as Marysville Correctional Institution for Women. The deputy sheriff stopped the bus. His co-driver got up from his seat and unlocked the gate that separated them from the female inmates.

He signaled for the female inmates to exit the bus. One by one the female prisoners descended the stairs, until all six of them stood in front of the institution waiting for the COs direction.

"Bye, cousin…bye, brother…I love y'all!" Tookie said.

She appeared unafraid as she stepped off of the bus. I feared for her mental well-being as much as I did her physical safety. Tookie was a strong and capable, young woman, but she was entering an unfamiliar world. She was an affable person and made friends easily, but she would not have the comfort of family with which Booger and I had been blessed.

"Bye, Tookie. I love you, too. Be safe," I said, sadly.

"See you, Tookie. I'ma write you," Booger shouted.

Booger seemed unmoved by all that was going on around him. He behaved as though we were going on a field trip. Booger was in many ways like his father—very resilient and tough as nails.

"Okay. Make sure y'all write," Tookie said, looking directly at me.

I smiled at her. Although writing was a passion of mine, I was somewhat slack when it came to writing letters. Letter-writing was a tedious chore to me.

"Okay," I said, as she stepped off of the bus.

The deputy sheriff left the women in the care of a CO. He and his partner climbed back in the bus and took their previous positions. The bus slowly pulled off from the institution. Booger and I struggled to see Tookie from our seats on the bus. Just as the bus rounded a curb, we were able to catch a glimpse of her waving. We could not wave to her, because of the cuffs and chains, though I smiled in hopes that she would see me. I felt an overwhelming sadness and loss in my spirit.

We were transported to the Correctional Reception Center (C.R.C.) in southern Ohio. C.R.C., was the receiving center for many of Ohio's male inmates. Another receiving center was located in northern Ohio near Cleveland. The days at C.R.C., were monotonous. We were locked in our cells for most of the day. The only exceptions were when we were allowed out of our cells for meals and recreation. We were served three meals a day: breakfast, lunch, and dinner; during which time we had six minutes to finish eating each meal. After the six minutes elapsed we were escorted back to our cells, whether we had finished our meal or not. We were given one hour to recreate in the gym and ten minutes to shower three times a week.

Thankfully, we were housed at C.R.C., for only three months. On May 26, 1995, Booger and I, along with ten other inmates were transferred to Lima Correctional Institution.

Lima Correctional Institution was at one time the Lima State Institution for the Criminally Insane. Its massive structure was built during the years of 1907-1915. It was the one of the largest brick structures in the United States, second only to the Pentagon. In 1982, the facility became the property of the Ohio Department of Corrections. Since its opening, Lima Correctional Institution had become the home of thousands of convicted felons.

We entered the facility through the cafeteria. After exiting the bus, our shackles and cuffs were removed. We were then escorted to the quartermaster, where we were issued our state clothes: three light-blue shirts, three navy blue pants, one pack of three pair of underwear, one pack of three t-shirts, three pair of socks, and a pair of boots.

As we walked down the heavily shined, brick floors,

inmates lined the walls awaiting our arrival.

"Mmm mmm...damn, look at these mutha fuckas here!" One of the inmates indiscriminately shouted at us.

"Yeah, man, I see them! This is fine bunch of pussies, but I got my eye on this cutie right here!" Another inmate shouted.

"A, yo! Look, I found me one, too! This bitch is mine!" A third inmate yelled, pointing at one of the younger guys who had gotten off the bus with us.

I continued walking in single file with the other guys. I was unfazed and unimpressed by their antics. Some of the other guys looked afraid. They shuffled along, with their heads hung low, trying to avoid detection.

"Move out, inmates!" One of the COs yelled at our antagonizers.

The guys scowled at the CO as they walked away. One of the guys winked his eye in our direction before he strutted out of sight. After we received our clothes, we were given our dorm assignments. Booger and I looked at the small, white pieces of paper, and, to our surprise, we found that we were on the same dorm—6A. I silently thanked God for allowing us to be housed together.

As we walked to our dorm, I looked out of the windows. The facility was structured in the shape of a huge rectangle. It was divided into twenty-six dorms. The dorms were assigned letters between A-F, or numbers between 1-11. The dorms located upstairs, as was ours, had the letter "A" placed behind the number, as in 6A, 7A, or 8A.

The dorms were partitioned into five units. The units were named after Greek numbers, such as Alpha, Beta, Delta, etc. Each unit consisted of a unit manager, two counselors, and a lieutenant correctional officer. The units' staffs were responsible for handling an array of inmate concerns: from personal issues, as in mental issues or family problems; to dorm-related issues, such as bed assignments and work assignments.

Each dorm housed anywhere between seventy and one hundred twenty inmates. Like the Pentagon, Lima contained an inner court. The inner court was known as the Center Yard. It consisted of a small baseball diamond, a basketball court, and a paved sidewalk, where inmates walked or jogged around the yard.

We reached 6A, walked up the stairs that led to the dorm, and presented our white slips of paper to the CO.

"All right, you two find your bunks and get settled in," the CO pointed in the direction of what was known as the big dorm.

Booger and I walked in the direction in which the CO had pointed. As we entered the big dorm, the first thing that caught my attention was the odor. The room smelled like a locker room. It was also extremely warm. Although four huge, oscillating fans were mounted to the upper portion of the walls, the room was still stifling hot.

Dorms like 6A were divided into four rooms: a big dorm, a four-man annex, a six-man annex, and a ten-man annex. The annexes were the most desirable living quarters, because less people lived in them. The big dorm housed fifty inmates. In the big dorm, bunk beds lined both sides of the walls and the middle area of the room. To express that the room was overcrowded would be an understatement.

We looked down at the paper to see which beds we were assigned. To my dismay, my bed was located in the middle row, on the top bunk, and closest to the entrance of the dorm. Being assigned a bed in the middle row meant that the inmate had very little privacy; every movement of his was seen by everyone.

Booger was lucky, however. He was given a bottom bed along the wall and in the back of the dorm. He could not have asked for a better bed in the big dorm.

We made our beds; putting the sheets and blankets that we had been given on the beds. Afterwards we gave ourselves a tour of the dorm. Our tour started with the dayroom. The dayroom was large. Two men played pool on one side of the room, while several other men watched them; four men sat at two other tables playing spades and some other card game. In the center of the day room, twenty or so chairs were situated around a 27" television that was mounted to a wall.

I glanced at the television to see what was being watched. Just as I had suspected, the guys were watching the soap opera, "The Guiding Light." I had never known that so many men watched soap operas until I was jailed. I had no theory as to their fascination with daytime dramas. I simply observed that they were very popular amongst incarcerated men.

Booger and I left the dayroom and headed for the bathroom. The showers were located on the left side of the hallway. It was a communal shower: six persons were able to shower at one time. On the opposite side of the hallway was a washroom, where the men groomed. Five sinks lined the wall, four of which had mirrors above them. As with the county the jail, the mirrors were not made of glass.

"Booger, look at this," I said. "The mirrors are funhouse mirrors like in the County."

"Uhn huh," he laughed as he touched one of them. "Yeah, they don't bend like the mirrors in the County, though," Booger observed.

"Uhn huh. They must be of better quality than those in the County. You can better see yourself in these, but they're still not glass. They must make the mirrors of this plastic to prevent someone from breaking them and using them as a weapon," I concluded.

We exited the washroom. There were two other rooms along the hallway. The rooms contained urinals and toilets. The partition that separated the urinal from the toilet was low, offering no privacy for the person defecating. Both of the rooms reeked of urine and mildew. As I looked at the urinal, I saw that urine was splattered along the wall surrounding the urinal; small, black bugs flew around the drain of the urinal. On the far wall, clotheslines were hung with pants, shirts, yellowed-underwear, and darkly stained socks hanging from them. The air in the room was thick and stale with no circulation, which explained the stench of mildew. The clothes were not able to dry properly.

We walked back towards the big dorm. The COs had changed shifts. It was three-thirty, almost count time. The CO, a middle-aged, White guy, locked the door of the dorm. Fifteen minutes later, he blew a whistle, announcing the start of count. Inmates poured into the sleeping areas from the dayroom, showers, and bathrooms.

I hoisted myself up and sat down on my bed on the top bunk. A few of the inmates that were asleep were awakened. They woke up with a start, jumping out of their beds, looking frightened. Everyone in the dorm was eerily quiet. The day's events were finally starting to get to me. I laid my head down to rest a bit until count was over, when I suddenly felt a short, quick tap on my bed.

"A blood, you gotta stand up!" A guy who looked several years older than me said in an urgent whisper. I looked at the guy for a moment.

"What?!" I responded angrily. I could not believe this! I

had not been at the institution for a full day and already I was being tried. I pitied him. If it was a fight he was looking for, I was going to give him a fight that he would never forget. He was a big guy, about six feet tall, broad shouldered, and easily two hundred pounds. He resembled the actor Lawrence Fishburne. I looked him up and down, unmoved by his size and height.

"You gotta stand up!" The guy said with more urgency, though this time I detected a panic in his voice that previously was not apparent to me. I looked down at him with an angry scowl still on my face, but one that had begun to turn to more curiosity than anger.

"What?!" I asked.

"It's standing count, man. You gotta stand up for standing count, or the CO will put you in the hole." The guy said in the same urgent manner as he had moments ago. I looked around the dorm. Everyone, except Booger, who was fast asleep, and me, was standing up. I jumped down from my bed.

"Booger! Booger!" I said, matching the urgency in my voice with the guy's who told me to stand up.

"Huh?" He responded from across the room.

"You have to stand up! You hear me?!" I said.

Booger raised his head quizzically for a moment and then stood up. I exhaled a sigh of relief. I looked at the guy. I felt foolish.

"Thanks, man," I said, appreciatively.

The guy put his index finger to his lips, silencing me, "It's cool," he whispered.

~~~

Each CO assigned to work on a dorm was responsible for counting the inmates who resided on that particular dorm.

After the inmates on the dorms were counted, the COs called the control booth, sharing with them their individual counts of the inmates. The numbers were compared with number the control booth had tallied for the entire institution. If the numbers matched, count was cleared; if they did not, a recount was ordered until the numbers were in line with one another.

Count lasted just twenty minutes; clearing at 4:05. We were allowed to leave our sleeping areas, though the front door of the dorm remained locked until dinner was called.

"Hey, man, thanks, again, for letting me know about count," I said to the guy who rescued me.

"Aww. It's cool, man. I didn't want to see you go to the hole for some bullshit. My name is Carlos," the guy said.

"I'm Chris," I said, extending my hand.

"Yeah, I saw you and dude come in here. Where y'all coming from?" Carlos asked.

"That's my cousin, Booger. We came from C.R.C., but we're from Toledo…alright…thanks, again." I said, abruptly. "I'm going to go see what's going on with my cousin," I said, pointing in Booger's direction.

I cut the conversation short. Although I appreciated Carlos' help, I did not know him. I, honestly, did not want to make any friends. I had heard how the guys, young and old, preyed on guys that were new to the institution. I did not want to give him the opportunity to try anything.

I walked down to Booger's bed. He was fast asleep, again.

"Hey," I said, nudging him. "Are you going to dinner?"

"Yeah, is it time, yet?" He asked, opening only his left eye.

"No, they should be calling it soon. Is your eye hurting you?" I asked.

As a child, Booger was hit with a rock in his left eye. Although he had some vision in the eye, there was very little.

After several surgeries, it was now blue in color and very sensitive to light and smoke. The big dorm was filled with cigarette smoke, which explained his discomfort.

"Chow!" The CO shouted, indicating that we could leave the dorm for dinner. Our dorm was relatively close to the cafeteria. Meals were a big thing in prison. As we exited the big dorm, we saw several guys standing by the door waiting for the CO to open it. For many of the guys, the food in the cafeteria was their only access to a meal, which meant that, if they missed dinner, they would not eat again for about another twelve hours when breakfast was called at five in the morning.

Some of the guys would skip going to the cafeteria and prepare a break: a meal of noodles, canned meat (usually tuna, bar-b-que beef, or roast beef), mayonnaise, cheese, and pickles. Though to prepare a break entailed having money in one's account, which many inmates did not.

Booger and I followed the other guys to the cafeteria. We stood in the long line waiting to pick up our trays, silverware, and cups. A chalkboard on the wall detailed the meal for the day: Hungarian Goulash. I placed my tray on the serving line, as an inmate who worked as a server dropped a lump of the Goulash on my tray. It hit my tray with a loud, "thump." I moved on down the line. I was given Jell-O and three slices of bread. *Wow! What a meal!*

We sat down to eat our food. I ate what I could stomach and threw the rest in the trash can. After Booger had finished eating, we got up to leave.

"I'ma go to the gym," Booger announced.

"Okay. I'll go with you. Can you go to the library with me, first? I want to get me some books to read."

"Yeah, I'ma see if I can find me something, too," Booger said. "A, you know where the library is?" Booger asked a guy who walked by us.

"It's around the corner and up those stairs," the guy stated, pointing in the direction of a doorwell.

"All right. Thanks," Booger replied.

We walked up the winding staircase to the library. There were not too many people in the library yet, since dinner had just been called. I looked for the books of fiction. I found a bunch of V.C. Andrews' books. I checked them out at the counter and waited for Booger. Seconds later, he arrived with several Iceberg Slim novels.

I really did not have an interest in going to the gym. I had much rather go to my bed and read, but I wanted to look-out for Booger. He was far more sociable than I was, so he tended to invite the wrong guys into his circle. Just as I was not going to let anyone mistreat me, I was not going to let anyone treat Booger unfairly.

A guy told Booger how to get to the gym, so I let Booger lead the way. We walked down the long hallway and then down a ramp that led into the gym. It, too, like the library, was a bit deserted. A basketball court with six baskets was to our left. As we passed the basketball court, we could see that there were six pool tables in another area of the gym. Walking farther into the gym and down a flight of stairs was a full-sized weight room. Weight benches, squat racks, and dumbbells were placed neatly throughout the area.

"This weight room is nice. I want to start working out, again. I couldn't get a rhythm going in C.R.C," I said.

"Yeah, me, too. I wanna play some ball!" Booger said, as we walked back pass the basketball courts and out of the gym.

Chapter Ten

Two weeks had gone by since Booger and I arrived at Lima. The first two weeks of an inmate's incarceration is known as his orientation to the institution. During that period, we were made aware of the prison's rules and given work assignments. Generally an inmate is assigned one of three work duties: the cafeteria, Safety and Sanitation (S&S), or as a dorm porter.

Cafeteria detail was the least desirable job assignment. The inmates who worked in the kitchen typically began as a dish washer or table wiper. While there was an opportunity to be promoted as a cook, one usually had to work for several months to be granted such a privilege. Inmates assigned to the cafeteria also had to spend long hours in the kitchen completing their work.

S&S was a more preferred job assignment. S&S entailed cleaning the institution. The work was oftentimes quick and easy, such as dust-mopping sections of the institution's main hallway. The assignment typically took about fifteen minutes. Though, there were times when the work was more detailed and laborious, like waxing the floors, scrubbing baseboards, or cleaning the many windows throughout the institution.

As a dorm porter, an inmate could be assigned any number of jobs: cleaning the dayroom, the bathrooms, the showers, or sweeping and mopping the floors. Work as a dorm porter was also highly sought, especially if an easy assignment, such as sweeping the dorm hallways, became available. Dorm porter positions were assigned by first-shift dorm COs. Therefore, in order for an inmate to get a job as a dorm porter, he had to request that the first-shift dorm CO hire him. If the CO did not like him or was unfamiliar with the inmate's work ethics, he would not be hired.

Booger was assigned to S&S. His job was to sweep a portion of the institution's hallway each night. I was assigned to the kitchen as a pot and pan washer. The work was grueling, not only because I was responsible for washing the large pots, but also because of the heat. It was extremely hot in the kitchen, though, specifically, in the pot and pan area. The dish water was hot in order to thoroughly clean the pans, and the floor was slippery-wet, which made walking across it a tight-rope act.

Luckily for me, however, I only worked in the pot and pan area for a couple of days, and then I was transferred to the serving line. Technically, I was not supposed to be given the position. There was a work hierarchy in the kitchen. Those who had worked in the kitchen the longest had first choice of work duty. However, someone showed me favor, for when I reported to work the following morning, the CO told me that my work description had been changed.

I was happy to be out of the pot and pan room, though with every job there were advantages and disadvantages. Although the work in the pot and pan area was awful, I did not have to deal with anyone bothering me, namely COs and other inmates. In the pots and pans area, I was basically unsupervised by COs, and I only dealt with the half dozen or so inmates that worked in the pots and pans area with me. For me, not having to work under the scrutiny of a CO or having to deal with the varied personalities of inmates were perks. However, as a line server,

I was constantly bombarded with requests for more food by the inmates and, more often than not, the meanest COs supervised the serving line.

"A, man, let me get another piece of chicken?" An inmate asked one of the line servers.

"I can't, man. You know the CO gone say something," a guy working on the serving line responded.

"You bitch ass, mutha fucka! Yo' punk ass come to prison and wanna get scared and shit!" The inmate yelled.

"Man, fuck you. I ain't going to the hole for yo' stupid ass!" The line worker shouted back.

"Hey, hey!" The CO pointed at the inmate who requested more chicken. "Move out, inmate, or you'll find yourself in the hole eating your chicken!"

The guy continued moving down the line getting the other foods being served, "bitch ass, mutha fucka! I'ma see if yo' ass talk all that shit when you get off!" The guy hissed before exiting the serving area.

I was serving bread, something rarely sought as an article of controversy. I shook my head at the guy. It was unbelievable how riled some of the guys were because of food. Although, I had to admit, the portions served were miniscule. I had a healthy appetite, though a healthy appetite in a 5'7," 138 lbs., frame. I could not imagine being bigger and hungrier and served such small portions.

"What's up, man?"

Oh, God! Where had he come from? I only had my head lowered for a moment and there he was. He was like a magician--appearing from nowhere. I raised my head.

"What's up?" I replied coolly. For the last couple of days since I had been working on the serving line this guy had been speaking to me. He seemed cool, but I was not looking for any friends. I was cool having my cousin as a friend.

"A, what dorm you on?" He asked.

"6A," I said, flatly.

"Oh, yeah! I'm in Delta Unit, too! I'm supposed to be moving to 6A!" He said, excitedly.

"Okay."

I did not know how to respond to his news.

"You go to any of the softball games?" He asked.

"Naw. I usually go to my dorm to read when I leave here, unless I go jogging," I said.

Sports were huge in prison. The other inmates, and some COs, revered the players as though they played for the NBA, NFL, or the Major Leagues. I was not trying to be mean to the guy, but I really was not interested in being his friend. My focus was on doing my time and going home.

"Inmate, is there anything I can do to help you down there?" The CO yelled, sarcastically.

"Naw, you can't help me," the guy said menacingly to the CO. I smiled a little to myself. Unlike most of the other guys, this dude was not afraid of the COs.

"I'ma holla at you," he said before he slowly walked from the serving area, as though for effect. Though who was he trying to affect, me or the CO?

~~~~

As the days passed, I had settled into something of a routine. As a line server, I was awakened every morning at four-thirty, so that I was prepared to leave for work at five o'clock. We, line servers, worked all three meals: breakfast, lunch, and dinner. I did my work, returned to my dorm, and either read or went for a jog.

Booger and I had begun to drift apart. He seemed to like doing things by himself. On several occasions I tried to partake in the things that he enjoyed, like playing basketball, pool, or card games; though, he would always decline my request. Eventually, I stopped asking him. I did not know what had changed in our relationship. I started to feel that maybe Booger had begun to absorb the full understanding of our being incarcerated, and that perhaps he blamed me for his being in prison. If that were the case, there was nothing I could do about it. I had done the very best I could during our trial by telling the truth and letting everyone know that it was me who had handled the gun as it discharged. I could not do anymore, so I gave him the space that he seemed to need.

I still worried about Booger, though. I did not want him to deal with whatever he was going through alone. I also did not want him to give up hope that we would be released soon and to succumb to the vices of prison life.

Despite my understanding and respect of Booger's need to be alone, I was hurt. He was all I had in there. I felt that God had blessed us to be together, not just in the same institution, but on the same dorm. I thought that we should honor that blessing by doing our time together. Though, perhaps the desire to spend our time together was a need of mine and not Booger's. So, I settled into the quiet life that I had created for myself, vowing to be available to him should he need me for anything.

~~~

It had been a couple of days since I had last seen the guy who never failed to speak to me. I was surprised that I had not seen him, because he never missed a meal. Then, as though I had conjured him, he suddenly appeared.

"What's up, man?" He said.

"Not too much. I haven't seen you for a few days. You been all right?" It was the most I had ever said to him. Generally, I just responded to his statements and questions with a nod of yes or no.

"Awww, you missed me?" He asked, smiling like a Cheshire cat.

"Huh? Naw! I was just saying that I hadn't seen you in awhile!" I said a little too defensively.

"Yeah, whatever, nigga! You missed me!" He said smiling as he walked out of the serving area. I looked around me to see if anyone had overheard our exchange, though I could not imagine anyone not hearing. He made no attempt to be discreet. His outburst was the first time that he had openly suggested anything other than a simple friendship between us. I forced him from my mind and went back to doing my work.

Dinner was served rather quickly. Before I knew it, we were breaking down the serving line: throwing away the leftover food and putting the pots and pans in the back area to be cleaned. The meal of stuffed cabbage was not one of the most desirable to many of the inmates; though, surprisingly to me, they were actually good.

I quickly ate my meal and rushed from the cafeteria. I wanted to shower and get back to my novel. The library had recently acquired a new shipment of books, and Terry McMillan's latest novel, "Waiting to Exhale," was a must-read.

I hurriedly walked down the hallway to my dorm; as I did so, I heard someone shouting down the hall.

"A, man!" I continued walking without looking back. I assumed that the person could not be someone yelling for me, since I did not really know anyone there.

"A, man!" The guy continued to yell. I looked around. There was no one in the hall, but the guy and me. Most everyone was outside enjoying the beautiful sunny day and preparing to watch the softball game.

"Yeah?" I shouted back. The guy ran until he reached me.

"Man, you heard me calling you!" He said, smiling. He had an affable manner about himself. He reminded me of the actor Chris Tucker. Although, I remained guarded, I liked him, immediately.

"I didn't know who you were yelling to," I said in a calm manner.

"Man, ain't nobody in this damn hallway, but us! Who else I'm gone be hollerin' for?!" He said, laughing.

"Well, I ain't used to people yelling down hallways at me." I said, sarcastically.

"I like yo' ass! You got a smart-ass mouth and you fine as fuck!" He said, still laughing. I did not know whether to take his comment about being fine as a compliment or what, so I disregarded the comment, as if he had not said it.

"You know my nigga after you?" He said, looking half-serious and half-joking.

"What?" I asked.

I knew what he was talking about, but I did not know about whom he was talking.

"Man, you know damn well what I'm talking about!" He shouted in a joking manner.

It should have dawned on me who his 'nigga' was, but I really had no idea to whom he was referring.

The practice of homosexuality was commonplace in prison. Some of the guys who knew me from home had told other guys that I was friends with Leslie and Erin, and before I could bat an eye, the news of my sexuality had spread around the prison like wildfire.

I continued to look stupefied. "Man, Moe-Moe!" He said, impatiently.

Moe-Moe? I did not know anyone named Moe-Moe. I searched my memory trying to remember where I had heard the name. Moe-Moe! I remembered! While at work I had heard someone in the line shouting to the guy who spoke to me every day. His name was Moe-Moe. We had never exchanged names, which was the reason the mentioning of his name did not jar my memory.

"Oh, yeah, I remember him," I said, nonchalantly.

"Yeah, whatever," he said, not believing that I did not initially remember him. "Anyway, he after you," he said, as though he had just shared some classified information with me.

"All right," I replied, unenthusiastically.

I really had no interest in the guy, or any of the guys there. I had seen how they scampered after the gay dudes; oftentimes paying the homosexuals with cartons of cigarettes for sexual favors. I would not be one of the many gay guys that the "heterosexual" population used for their selfish needs.

"Yeah, you say that shit now! He movin' up on 6A! We gone see if you still actin' like you don't give a damn, then!" He laughed, playfully.

"I don't care what dorm he moves on. I'm not interested in him," I said, evenly, as I walked up the stairs to 6A, leaving the guy downstairs with an astonished look on his face.

I had become slightly irritated by the guy's rallies for his friend. I thought of the stories I had heard about the gay guys being penetrated in secluded areas, or cubby holes as they were referred to throughout the prison. I did not judge my gay comrades for what they did. I understood that, for some of them, they had to do what they felt they must to survive in there. Though, I refused to allow myself to become a sexual doormat for the prison population.

~~~~

I absolutely loved to read. I would much rather had picked up a good book to read over watching a television show any day of week.
Maya Angelou was my favorite author, though I appreciated the works of many other African American authors as well: Zora Neale Hurston, J. California Cooper, Alice Walker, Richard Wright, and a host of the contemporary authors; like, Yolanda Joe, BeBe Moore Campbell, and Rosalyn McMillan (sister of Terry McMillan).

I had gained a love for books, particularly those written by African Americans, as a teenager when I lived in Washington, D.C. The discovery of books was paramount to my becoming the person I was. Through the beauty of story-telling, I was able to see my story, as an African American, told by others like me. Maya Angelou's, "I Know Why the Caged Bird Sings" was my first literary conquest. Ever since I first peeled back the pages of her monumental autobiography, I acquired a ferocious love of books of all kinds and by varying authors.

My genre of choice during the early years of my incarceration was romance novels. V.C. Andrews' novels particularly appealed to me. I loved that the central character was always a person of integrity who was eventually blessed beyond measure in the end.

I was engrossed in reading, "The Casteel Series" of V.C. Andrews' books when he walked into the dorm.

"What's up, man?" He asked with a huge smile on his face. My mind was quickly transported back to the prison.

"Hey. What's up?" I said, moving the book from my face for a moment to look at him. I went back to reading, though I was disrupted, again.

"What you reading?" He asked.

"A book by V.C. Andrews," I responded.

I did not want to be rude, but I did not like being interrupted while I was reading. I raised the book again to continue reading.

"What's it about?" He asked.

I smiled, despite myself. He was persistent.

"Do you really want to know, or are you just asking to make conversation?" I asked, smiling.

"Kinda both," he said, smiling.

I laughed. He was not a bad looking guy. He had a thuggish-appeal about himself. He was six feet tall and extremely muscular. His well-developed muscles were clearly visible through his immaculately ironed state shirt. His hair was neatly French-braided. He resembled Allen Iverson, the basketball player.

Oh, god! What was I doing? I had no business thinking of him in that manner, I chided myself.

"Uhn huh! I told you my nigga was gone get you!" His friend yelled, as he entered the big dorm and dropped Moe-Moe's locker box beside his bed. My smile quickly faded from my face.

"Come on, Foster! Man, don't start that shit!" The guy said.

Foster? He did not look like his name would be Foster, even though it was his last name and not his first.

"I'm just saying, man! I told this pretty ass mutha fucka that you was gone get him, and look at y'all! Lookin' at each other with stars all in y'all damn eyes, and yo' ass just got up here!" Foster said.

"Don't call him out of his name, Foster, man," the guy said before I could.

"Damn, you taking up for him already!" Foster said, laughing.

"What's your real name?" I asked, trying to change subjects.

"Don't be trying to change subjects now!" He replied.

"I want to know for real. You don't look like a Foster," I said.

"What I look like, then?" He asked.

"I don't know, but you don't look like your name would be Foster."

"His name is Cameron," the guy interjected. Cameron? I liked that name. It was a pretty name. It matched Cameron's beautifully-colored eyes.

"Do you know my name?" The guy asked, directing my attention back to him.

"You never told me your name," I responded.

"Moe-Moe," he said, smiling, as though he had been presented a million dollars.

"Okay. I'm Chris," I said.

"Man, he know your name! Everybody know yo' name! You the talk of the camp!" Cameron exclaimed.

"Okay, Foster, man, thanks for bringing my locker box up. I'ma catch back up with you." Moe-Moe said, dismissing Cameron.

Cameron was getting on Moe-Moe's nerves. I think he felt that Cameron was vying for my attention. Though, he was not. Cameron was cool, but in a friend-kind-of-cool-way, not the kind of guy that I would be attracted to romantically.

"Alright, man, I can catch a hint! I'll holler at you, pretty boy!" Cameron said.

"See you," I responded to Cameron as he ran from the dorm.

Technically, Cameron was not supposed to be on the dorm. We were not allowed to go on dorms on which we did not reside. It was considered out-of-place. Many inmates had gone to the Hole for being on dorms that was not their own.

Moe-Moe looked down at the book that I still held in my hand. "You know, I used to read a lot, too. I used to tutor, too, but now I ain't got time with baseball practice and shit," he expressed.

"Did you? I love it. It takes my mind off of being in here," I said.

"Yeah, for real though," he said, understandingly, "All right, I'ma let you get back to yo' readin.' I just wanted to say what's up to you." He said, patting my bed as walked off.

"All right...thanks for speaking," I replied.

I watched him as he walked away. He was sleu-footed, like a penguin. He had a nice muscled butt, too. I had every intention of continuing my reading, but I could not stop thinking of Moe-Moe. Despite his rough exterior, there was something very pure and gentle about him.

~~~

Over time Moe-Moe and I had become good friends. We talked about everything with one another. As I had suspected, his outward demeanor was quite different from the person he truly was: intelligent, kind, sensitive, and very thoughtful. Moe's childhood was particularly harsh. His mother was incarcerated and had worked the streets as a prostitute. Moe and his sisters were orphaned and sent to live with different people; he was adopted and his sisters moved in with relatives. Moe's adopted parents were a senior couple who truly loved him, yet they were unable to meet the emotional needs of a child with a troubled history.

Despite the limitations of their age and resources, they supported Moe-Moe with what they had—an unconditional love and dedication to him. Moe's adopted father sent him ten or fifteen dollars every other month. Fifteen dollars seemed like little, though to a person whose only source of income was social security, fifteen dollars was a huge sacrifice.

I shared with Moe-Moe the details of my case and my hope of being granted super-shock probation. He, like most Black people who knew of the circumstances of my incarceration, was outraged. Yet, he felt that I was fortunate to receive a sentence of nine to twenty-five years, considering the time I could have been given. Moe encouraged me to apply for a position in the education department tutoring inmates who were trying to achieve their G.E.D. He also felt that I should enroll in as many institutional programs as I could, such as anger management and positive attitudes, regardless of whether I needed them for my personal well-being. He insisted that the parole board or judge would look favorably upon my having taken them.

I was promoted to the position of a breakfast cook. I only worked two or three days a week, so I had more time to read, exercise, and to spend with Moe-Moe. After much thought, I decided to enter a romantic relationship with Moe. He was delighted by my decision. I was not in love with Moe, but I did love him. He was a great person. My separation from my family and friends was starting to wear on me. Moe offered me the companionship for which I had come to long. Booger, who was still a bit distant, seemed to like Moe as well. Sometimes the three of us would accompany one another to lunch or dinner.

In time, I settled into a comfortable relationship with Moe. We gave each other names of endearment: he called me Brown Sugar; and I called him Moses, after the prophet in the Bible. I attended his softball games in the blazing July heat, despite my disdain for the hot summer weather. I would watch him as he searched the rows of bleachers from the softball field until he spotted me. Once he saw me, he would smile like a child on Christmas.

I still spent most of my days reading on the dorm. Moe was a social butterfly who loved being outdoors. Throughout the day, he would come in to check on me. My mind would be fixed on what I was reading.

"What's up, Brown," Moe greeted.

"Hey. What's up?" I responded.

"Nothing. I was thinking about you," he said, as he searched under the linen for my foot.

No matter what the temperature was, I always covered my body with at least a sheet. After he found my foot, he began to rub it tenderly. My feet were always sore from jogging. His sweet gesture was always welcome, albeit risqué. We inmates were not allowed to touch one another, especially in an intimate manner. I did not say anything to stop him, though. He understood the ramifications of his actions, without me having to remind him.

I smiled at his act of kindness. "Well, thank you for thinking of me," I said, still smiling.

"You know I gotta see if you all right," he flashed me one of his signature smiles. "What do you want to eat tonight?"

Moe made it his responsibility to ensure that we ate every

night, whether we had gone to the cafeteria for dinner or not. Sometimes he would prepare a break, which was always tasty, or he would buy something from the guys who worked in the kitchen. Some of the cafeteria employees smuggled food from the kitchen. It was their hustle or way of supporting themselves.

The kitchen smugglers would sell cheeseburgers, steaks, fried egg sandwiches, or anything on which they could get their hands. The food was typically prepared in the officers' dining room, so it was always scrumptious. A pack of cigarettes could buy at least one sandwich, or sometimes two, depending on the relationship the buyer had with the seller.

Moe would always prepare or buy enough for us to eat and Booger as well. It really touched my heart that he would think of my cousin, without being asked or prompted.

While our relationship had it beautiful aspects, it was not without its issues. Moe was incredibly jealous-hearted. He did not want anyone around me. If he saw anyone talking to me, he automatically went into a jealous rage. Although, he believed in his heart that I was faithful and honest, there was always an underlying element of distrust in him.

"A, Chris, can you get this ingrown hair out for me?" Carlos asked, pointing to a bump on his face.

"I don't know. I've never gotten one out before, but I can try," I said, putting down my book and getting up from my bed.

"Thanks, man. Here you go," Carlos said, as he handed me a safety pin for extracting the hair from under the skin, and a pair of tweezers for removing it from the follicle.

"What the fuck y'all doing?" Moe asked the moment he entered the big dorm. I heard him, but I was so focused on removing the hair from Carlos' face that I did not notice his tone or his foul language.

"Hey," I said without looking up from Carlos' face.

"I said, what the fuck y'all doing?!" Moe repeated. I looked up this time. The anger in his voice was more obvious to me.

"I'm getting an ingrown hair out of his face," I said nonchalantly, unaware of how my actions could be misconstrued.

"Nigga, why he gotta get it out of yo' face?! How come you didn't ask one of these mutha fuckas around here to do it?!" Moe asked Carlos angrily.

"Man, gone with that shit." Carlos calmly said, keeping his eyes on Moe. Moe was known throughout the prison for his fiery temper and ability to fight well.

"Naw, nigga, y'all slick ass niggas talk all that shit about not fuckin' around and the first gay dude that moves on the dorm, y'all all in they face!" Moe yelled.

Everyone in the big dorm turned their attention to what was going on. Most anyone else would have been concerned that the CO would overhear the commotion and that he would be placed in the hole, but not Moe. He did not care who heard him.

"Man, I don't know what you talkin' about," Carlos said calmly.

"Nigga, you know what the fuck I'm talkin about! Now all of sudden yo' punk ass want to act all innocent!" Moe fumed.

"I ain't go be too many of yo 'punk ass niggas.'" Carlos said, still in a calm manner as he looked directly in Moe's eyes. Carlos, unlike most of the other guys in the prison, was not afraid of Moe.

"Well, what the fuck you gone do, punk ass nigga!?" Moe asked, instigating a fight with Carlos.

Moe was not a bully, which was one of the things that I

liked about him. Though, he knew he was good fighter, he usually did not use his ability to fight well to take advantage of people, unless he was dealing with White guys. He took every opportunity he could to misuse a White guy.

I turned completely in Moe's direction. "Moe go on...don't start that shit."

I did not like being the cause or center of nonsense.

"Brown, I keep telling you how these niggas is!" Moe said trying to control his anger. I looked deeply into his eyes. The anger that was so prevalent a moment ago was being replaced by hurt. I turned to Carlos.

"I can't do this, Carlos."

I gave him back the safety pin and tweezers.

"It's cool, Chris," he replied, understandingly.

I walked over to where Moe stood, "Come on," I said calmly to him.

I walked pass him and into the ten-man annex, where he slept. He followed behind me. When we were both in the ten-man, I turned to him.

"What's up with you?" I was somewhat used to Moe's jealous ways, but this was the first time
I had seen him in a rage because of them. I did not like it at all. In times past, he had always maintained a certain degree of control. This time, however, he not only acted like a damn fool, but he acted like one in front of the entire big dorm. Ordinarily, I did not care what people thought of me; though, in prison, things were different. Everything I did was scrutinized by other inmates, including my relationships.

"I don't know, Brown...I just got mad when I walked in the dorm and saw you in that nigga's face," he said quietly, with tears in his eyes.

It was remarkable to me how he could be a big, bad grizzly

bear with these guys, but was a gentle cub with me.

"Well, what did you think I was doing, Moe?! I mean, I was in the big dorm, where everybody can see me! I won't cheat on you, Moe," I said, emphatically.

"I know, Brown," he replied, softly.

"I'm not him or them, Moe. You can't judge me according to how they were," I said, referring to whoever had hurt him in the past.

"I know…I know, Brown. I'm trying. I love you," he said looking into my eyes with the tenderness of a child, but the love of a grown man. I understood at that moment how great a responsibility I had to protect his heart. I knew that I would not do anything as selfish as to cheat, but my responsibility went beyond being merely faithful. This man had placed his heart in my hands. It was my responsibility as his lover to protect and nurture his heart much like a parent protects and nurtures a child's.

~~~~

Moe's insecurities were the least of our problems. Although Moe, like so many other men in prison, considered himself to be a heterosexual, he had other relationships with men (casual and significant) prior to me. I knew of two gay relationships he had previously: Nee-Nee and Blake. His relationship with Blake was his most recent and would ultimately become the biggest threat to our relationship.

Moe and Blake had been in a stormy, romantic relationship for about a year. As I understood it, Moe was madly in love with Blake and, while, Blake may have loved Moe, his love did not equal Moe's love for him. According to Moe, they fought and argued a great deal. Moe had also caught Blake having sex with another guy. After much heartache, they finally severed their relationship about two months before I arrived to the institution.

Per Cameron, my arrival to the prison had stirred some previously checked feelings Blake had for Moe.

"Man, Blake mad as hell you came here!" Cameron said to me one evening as I walked around the East yard.

"Why is upset with me?" I asked. I liked Cameron. He had a fun personality, though sometimes he concerned himself with things that were not of interest to me, and they should not have been of interest to him.

"Cause, man, you took Moe-Moe away from him!" He said.

"I didn't take Moe away from him. They had already broken up by the time I got here," I said.

"Well, that nigga want him back. His punk ass jealous 'cause you here, and Moe-Moe don't want him no mo'!" Cameron surmised.

"That's something he needs to take up with Moe. I don't have anything to do with how Moe feels about him, and he definitely doesn't have any reason to be jealous of me."

"Well that nigga don't see it like that. He feel like you took Moe from him. His stupid ass been buying Moe all kinda shit from commissary, tryin' to get Moe back and shit!" Cameron said.

I did not like Cameron telling me about Moe's dealings with Blake. He did not know whether Moe had shared with me the details of his relationship with Blake, specifically that Blake had bought him some things from the commissary. Cameron violated his friendship with Moe by telling me all that he had. His actions also seemed messy, like he was trying to get something started between Blake and me. Cameron and I were cool, but we were not close friends.

"All right. Well, I'm headed back to the dorm."

I was finished with the conversation. I really did not want to be a part of such petty stuff. I had far more on my mind with which to contend, and I did not have the desire to concern myself with prison drama.

"Cool, man. I'ma holler at you," Cameron said as I walked off.

~~~

I sat at the foot of my bed washing my clothes out of a five-quart, gray bucket. I had moved to a bottom bunk against the wall. It was nice to no longer sleep on the top bunk in the middle row.

I scrubbed my socks and underwear until they were bright white. We were allowed to send our clothes to the laundry once a week, though, every time I sent them, my white clothes always came back a shade or two darker. I now understood why so many of the inmates refused to send their clothes to the laundry, choosing to wash their clothes by hand. The problem was one of two things: either the persons who worked in the laundry did not use enough washing powder and bleach, or there were simply too many clothes being washed at one time for them to be cleaned adequately.

Moe walked into the big dorm just as I was finishing my last pair of socks. The East and Center Yards had closed; meaning it was close to evening count time. He walked over to my bed and sat on the bunk opposite of mine, so that we were facing one another.

"Look at you! Damn you got those socks white as hell! Hold on, let me go get mine!" He said smiling.

Although Moe was joking, I would have washed his clothes for him. I could not count the number of times he had just grabbed my soiled laundry and washed them alongside his.

"They were starting to build-up. I didn't want to be sitting here all night washing, so I decided to knock them out now. You want me to do yours?"

"Naw, I was just fucking with you. I did mine this morning when you went to work," he said.

"Aww! So that's what you do when I'm gone! That's a shame! When the cat is away, the mouse will surely play!" I said teasing him.

"Aww, nigga, you can gone with that! You know I don't do shit that I don't tell you about!" He said, smiling.

"I know. I was just playing with you," he said, as we looked into each other's eyes for a long moment.

Loving someone felt wonderful, but it felt better when you loved and trusted the person with whom you were in a relationship, as we did.

"How was your day?" Moe asked.

"It was cool; same ole, same ole," I replied.

"Yeah?" He said with a troubled look on his face.

"What's wrong?" I asked.

He smiled, "You can always tell when something is on my mind, can't you?"

"Well, most times, but it's kind of obvious by the look on your face," I said.

"Listen, Brown, if Blake comes over here, don't go to see what he wants. Okay?" He asked.

"Yeah, but, why not?" I asked him.

"Nothing. He just been talking crazy, saying he go pick a fight with you, so that we ain't on the dorm no more. His ass just mad and jealous 'cause we together. I wouldn't fuck with him at all, if he wasn't paying me," Moe explained.

"Moe, you don't need him to 'pay' you. That just keeps all of this stuff going. If you don't want to be with him, then you'd just cut it off," I stated.

"Brown, you don't understand. See, you got your family looking out for you. You don't know what it's like to be hungry. You know that all you have to do is pick up the phone and some money is on the way. I ain't got it like that…ain't nobody sending me nothing, but my pops, and that's only every other month. If this stupid nigga is willing to buy me anything I want from the store, then I'ma get that shit and share it with you," he said, empathically.

"But we don't need what he has to offer, Moe. We are cool. We break every night; we don't go to bed hungry. What more can we ask for? Are you using this as a reason to be around him?" I asked, earnestly.

"Hell, naw! Brown, I'm telling you, I can't stand that nigga. I listen to the shit he talk about and I'm like, 'you stupid as hell!' I deal with his dumb ass, 'cause I'ma make him pay for doing me like he did," he said, angrily.

"Is that what this is about? You're trying to get revenge for him hurting you? You need to let that go, Moe. I'm telling you, it's not worth it," I reasoned.

"That ain't it…well, kinda that's what it is, but, at the same time, I could use that shit he gone get me. Man, you don't understand…what if I get shook down and the COs took all of that shit in my locker box? You don't know how it is. You just like Tyler Matthews. Y'all got family, so y'all don't know what it's like to be in need," he said, appearing simultaneously hurt and irritated.

Moe operated what was known as a store. He would loan someone, say, a bag of chips, the borrower would have to pay

Moe back two bags of chips for the one bag that the guy borrowed. Anything could be sold as two for ones: cigarettes, canned meat, mayo, soap, etc.

Operating a store was illegal. If a CO shook-down (searched) an inmate's locker and the inmate did not have a receipt showing that he purchased the items, the items were confiscated from the inmate. The inmate could not offer a rebuttal in the matter, because he did not have a receipt to verify that the items were his. The COs, therefore, assumed that the merchandise was either stolen or acquired by way of operating a store.

"Okay, Moe. Do whatever you feel like you need to do."

We had had the same conversation before and it always ended the same. I did not believe in using anyone for anything. I understood what it was like to be without, but, perhaps I did not in the manner that Moe did. Still, even without our situations being the exact same, I refused to 'use' someone to get what I wanted or needed. What goes around has a way of coming around; what one does to others will inevitable happen to him.

Ironically, in actuality, it was Moe that was being used, not Blake. Moe allowed Blake's gifts to buy him: his time, his conversation, and his energies. In the end, it was Moe who was being duped, not Blake. Blake had the money to spend frivolously. It was nothing for him to spend his money on Moe, especially when he was getting what he wanted.

Chapter Eleven

I thoroughly enjoyed cooking. I was very passionate about making certain that everything I cooked was prepared well. A few mornings each week, I was awakened at three o'clock in the morning to begin my shift as a breakfast grill-cook. As a grill-cook, it was my responsibility, along with three other inmates, to prepare pancakes, scrambled eggs, waffles, or anything else that was cooked on the grill for the nearly two thousand inmates. The task was daunting at times, because we had a little less than two hours to prepare the food.

Generally, I was finished with my work by seven-thirty in the morning. However, one morning, in particular, was different. After we cooked breakfast, we had to thoroughly clean the kitchen in preparation for the institution's inspection. I was still cleaning at nine o'clock when I received word that the CO wanted me.

"Hey, Chris, the CO wants you up front," Mohammad, an inmate supervisor, told me. Mohammad was a Muslim. He was responsible for me getting the job as a grill-cook. Usually guys would pay persons in Mohammad's position for such a job as a grill-cook. However in my case, he merely walked up to me and asked me if I wanted the job. After careful consideration, I told him, yes. Although Mohammad was a member of the Islamic faith, which, according to his faith, meant that he was not supposed to engage in homosexual relations, he let it be known that he was attracted to me sexually. I did not like accepting things from anyone, especially someone who expressed an interest in me; for, more times than not, there was an expectation attached with accepting favors.

At the time that I was offered the position Moe and I were still friends and not yet lovers. I mentioned to him that Mohammad had offered me the position and asked what he thought about me accepting it. Moe encouraged me to accept the job.

"Man, that's a cool job. These niggas around here wish they could get a job working the grill," Moe said.

"Yeah, but, what about his attraction to me? I don't want him thinking that, just because he got me the job, something is going to go on between us."

"Man, forget what that nigga think. Shit, tell his ass that you ain't interested in him like that."

"I don't know. It doesn't seem right to me," I expressed.

"Man, you can eat as much as you want, you don't have to deal with these knuckle-head ass dudes on the serving line, and you only have to work two or three days a week," he persisted.

I did not care about having access to as much food as I would have liked, though the thought of having more time to myself was appealing. Not to mention, as Moe said, I would not have to deal with as many people as I did while I worked on the serving line. I decided to accept the position. I told Mohammad where I stood. He respected my stance and me.

"He wants me?" I said incredulously. I could not believe that any CO would want me for any reason. I tried as best I could to follow the institution's rules, ensuring that our paths seldom crossed.

"Yeah, that's what he said," Mohammad responded.

"Okay."

I walked from the back area of the kitchen to the dining area where the CO sat.

"My name is Price, 307-720," I said, identifying myself by my last name and institutional number to the CO.

"Yeah, you need to head back to your dorm. You have a visit," he said.

"All right. Thanks," I replied.

As I walked back to my dorm a guy who lived on the dorm with me passed me en route.

"Hey, Chris! You got a visit!" He said, enthusiastically. Although we lived on the same dorm, I did not know him.

"Okay, thanks," I said, smiling.

Visits were humongous in prison. They were a time for the inmate to connect with his family and to get away from the monotony of prison life; though, far more than anything else, visits communicated to the inmate, and those around him, that he was loved by someone. Many of the guys formed real, sustaining friendships with one another while in prison, though being loved and appreciated by someone outside of the prison meant far more than the love expressed by prison friends. Because many of the guys led a less than exemplary life prior to their incarceration, few of them had visits from family members and friends.

As I walked up the stairs leading into the dorm, Carlos passed me.

"What's up, Chris! I hear you got a 'V'!" He said, gleefully.

"Yeah, that's what they tell me!" I responded.

"Alright, man. Have a good one!" Carlos said.

"Okay. Thank you!" I said, smiling.

I entered the dorm, walking down the long hallway until I reached the CO's desk.

"Hey, I was told that I have a visit." I said to the CO.

"What's your name? Price?" The CO asked.

"Yeah, that's me," I answered.

"Yeah, you've got one. You have to get down there before they close the halls, or else you'll have to wait until after count," the CO informed me.

"Okay," I said.

I started to undress as I walked into the big dorm.

"Brown, where you been?!" Moe asked.

"I was at work," I responded matter-of-factly.

"I mean, they called for you over a hour ago for yo' visit!"

"Oh. They didn't tell me until a few minutes ago. I came up here right after the CO in the kitchen told me," I replied.

"What you doing?!" He asked, watching me undress.

"I'm about to take a shower."

"Man, you can't take no shower! You got to get out there for your visit!" Moe exclaimed.

"Yeah, but I've been working," I explained.

"Man, you done had your people waiting all this time! You better gone like that! You can't have them waiting!" He responded, passionately.

I looked down at my clothes and boots. I looked a mess. My pants were slightly soiled and my shoes had bits of dried eggs on them.

"Okay," I said, shrugging my shoulders.

I grabbed my picture ID and hall pass. I walked over to Booger's bed where he laid.

"Booger, I'm going to a visit," I said.

"Okay. You know who coming?" He asked.

"I think it's my daddy. He said he was coming down," I replied.

"All right. Tell him 'what's up' for me," he stated.

"Okay. I will," I said before walking off.

As I walked up the aisle leading out of the big dorm, Moe appeared.

"Man, you got to hurry up!" Moe said persistently.

"Moe, I'm on my way, now," I said with a little irritation in my voice. He must have heard it. He shook his head.

"Man, y'all spoiled ass niggas don't appreciate nothing!" He said in disgust.

I opened my mouth to say something sarcastic, but I decided against it. I did not feel like arguing with him. Instead, I ignored his comment and walked to the visiting room.

In a way, he was right. I had not been at the institution long enough to truly appreciate the significance of a visit. I had come from the county jail where visitors arrived frequently. Someone was always requesting to visit me in the County. I had not endured the loneliness and pain of being separated from my family, without seeing them for long periods of time yet, though all of that was soon to change.

~~~

I stood outside of the visiting room waiting for the CO to unlock the gate that separated the visiting room from general population. After several minutes of waiting, he finally opened the gate, allowing three of the six of us into a room to be patted-down and searched.

"Okay. You two come on!" The CO barked. A couple of guys sat in chairs in front of us putting on their clothes. Two of us stepped before the CO.

"Take your clothes off, squat, spread your cheeks, cough, raise your palms face up, and open your mouth!" He bellowed.

Although the strip-search procedure was a duplicate of the one performed in the county jail, the process still annoyed me. Inmates sometimes smuggled in drugs through visits. The drugs were hid in their mouths, between their butt cheeks, in their rectum, or between their fingers. As demeaning as the strip-search process was, I fully understood its importance. Yet, still, I deplored being searched.

I did as the CO commanded, put my clothes back on my body, and then exited the changing room. I entered the visiting room, looking around to see a familiar face. I walked to the CO station to make her aware of my presence. As I did so, I spotted my daddy sitting at a table. It was an amazing feeling seeing him sitting there. I was overwhelmed with joy at the sight of him.

Moe oftentimes would tell me to forget about my life on the street. In doing so, he believed I would make my bit (or time in prison) go by more quickly and smoothly. He encouraged me to acclimate myself to my new environment.

I refused to do so. I did not want to become acclimated to prison. I wanted to keep my memories of my family and my life before my imprisonment fresh in my mind. I intended to allow those memories to guide and govern my actions while I was confined, so that I would not become consumed by prison life. I felt that the reason why so many of the inmates fell prey to the depravities of prison were because they had forgotten that a whole other world existed beyond their present circumstances.

Yet, as I looked at my daddy, I wondered if I had subconsciously disconnected a small part of me, so that I would be able to adequately focus on getting through the time I was given to serve.

I smiled broadly as I made my way to the table where my

daddy sat. He looked up as I approached.

"Hey," I said beaming.

He stood up as I neared the table.

"Hey, junior. You're looking bad, aren't you?" He said smiling, as he looked at my clothes. We hugged firmly before sitting down.

"Yeah," I laughed. "I just got off from work. I didn't have time to shower and change before coming out here."

"Not a problem, it's just not how I'm used to you looking," he laughed. "You've been alright?" He asked.

"Yeah, I'm doing okay. Oh, Booger, told me to tell you 'what's up.'" I said.

"Did he?!" He laughed. "Tell Boo I said, 'what's up.' How is he?"

"He's cool. I think he likes it down here."

"Why do you say that, son?" My daddy asked, laughing at my statement.

"Uhm hmm…I don't know. He just seems happier than he did when we were home. He was so depressed sometimes. I guess mainly because of his relationship with Raymond, but now he doesn't seem so sad anymore." I explained.

"Oh, he and his father didn't have a good relationship?" He asked in a more serious tone.

"Well, not really. I think Raymond wanted Booger to be someone he was not. Plus, you know, Booger didn't graduate from high school and he wasn't working. All of that affected their relationship," I said.

"Oh, okay. I see," he said.

"But, like I said, he seems cool, now. He has a few friends, he works-out, and plays basketball and card games a lot. It just doesn't seem like he minds being here. I thought that he was angry with me for him being here, but I realized that he's just an independent person who likes to do things on his own." I said.

"Well, that's good. It seems like he's adjusting well. Maybe he just needed to come into his own; you know, just to grow and mature into his own person," he assessed.

We spent the next four hours playing two-handed spades and talking about all that was going on at home. Afterwards, we had the inmate-photographer take two pictures of us. I kept one of the pictures, and my daddy took the other one with him. I laughed as I looked at the picture. My clothes really did look bad!

I ate quite a bit of the food that my daddy bought from the vending machine. One of the bonuses of having a visit was that we inmates were allowed to eat something other than the food that was served in the cafeteria. If we were not incarcerated, the food from the vending machine would not be anything spectacular, but, because of our circumstances, it was a real treat.

"Well, junior, I'm going to be heading home." My daddy said after being there for nearly five hours.

"Okay," I said. I thoroughly enjoyed the visit, but I was sleepy.

I had awake since three o'clock that morning for work, so I badly needed a nap.

"I'll send you some money when I leave here, and don't forget to send me the clothes and food box forms," he reminded me.

Every six months we were allowed to get clothes and food boxes. They were highly treasured commodities. As was the case with visits, clothes and food boxes communicated that the inmate was loved, appreciated, and needed.

"Okay. Thank you for coming down here to see me…I love

you," I said, as we stood to hug one another.

"I love you more, son. Take care of yourself," my daddy said, kissing me on the cheek before we parted.

"I will. Bye-bye."

I walked to the room where we were patted-down and searched. I looked to the visitor's exit. My daddy raised his arm and waved good-bye to me. I waved back, mouthing the words good-bye.

"Who was that, your brother?" A guy waiting in line in front of me asked.

"Naw, that was my daddy."

"Damn, y'all could pass for brothers!"

"Yeah, that's what a lot of people tell me. Who came to visit you?" I asked the guy.

"Aww, my girl came down. A nigga needed that visit. It get rough down here without yo' family and shit coming to see you," he said.

"Yeah, I know what you mean," I replied, sincerely.

~~~

Count had just cleared as I entered the dorm. Our dorm had not yet been called for dinner. Moe was the first person I saw as I entered the big dorm. I gave him one of two sodas we were allowed to bring with us from the visiting room. It was an honor to be given a soda from someone after his visit. It meant that the two of you shared a special relationship.

"Thanks," Moe said, as he accepted the can of Hawaiian Punch.

"You're welcome."

"How was your visit? Who came to see you?" Moe asked.

"It was nice...my daddy came," I said, handing him the

picture we took.

"Damn, you look just like your dad. This dude stays G'd up, huh?" He said, complimenting my daddy on how nicely he was dressed.

"Yeah, I guess so. He doesn't wear anything, but suits and dress slacks. He doesn't even own a pair of jeans."

"Yeah, that dude is sharp," he expressed.

"Thank you. Where is Booger? Have you seen him?" I asked.

"Yeah, he's in the dayroom playing bid whist."

"Okay. Give me a second. I'll be right back. I want to give him this pop before it gets warm," I said.

"All right. I'll be in the ten-man."

I walked to the big dorm. Several of the men were sitting around watching television until dinner was called. In the far end of the room, I saw Booger sitting at a table with three other guys.

"Here, cousin," I said, giving Booger the soda I brought back for him.

"Aw, thanks. Who came to see you?" He asked, concentrating on the card game.

"My daddy. He told me to tell you, hi. I told him how much you like it down here," I said.

"Yeah?" He said laughing. "What did he say?" He asked.

"Nothing. He just asked me why I thought you like it and I gave him my reasons."

I did not want to delve too deeply in the conversation with everyone sitting around the table, possibly listening to our conversation.

"Yeah, it's cool down here," he said, looking at his cards and what was being played by the other persons at the table.

"Okay, I'm going to go back to the big dorm. I don't think

I'm going to dinner. I ate a lot on the visit," I said.

"Okay. I don't think I'm going either," he said.

Booger had a healthy appetite, but he could go all day without eating, especially when he was engrossed in a card game, as he was then.

Just as I was leaving the dayroom, the CO announced that it was dinner time. Moe was exiting the big dorm and headed in my direction.

"You going to chow, Brown?" Moe asked.

"Naw, I ate too much when I was out there on my visit. If you want me to go with you, I will, though," I offered.

"That's okay. You can stay here. I know you tired. You been up since early this morning."

"Yeah, I am," I said, truthfully.

"Well, go ahead and take your daily nap, and I'll wake you up in a couple hours with a foot massage," he said, smiling mischievously. "Oh, don't forget you have to tell me how your visit was!" He said, smiling.

"Okay. I'll see you."

I laughed at his remark about my nap. He always teased me about having to take a nap everyday, like a pre-schooler. I could not help taking them. I had been taking naps for years. They always made me feel refreshed and vibrant afterwards. My mind was clearer, and I had more energy to deal with other things during the remainder of the day.

~~~

Just as my daddy had said, he sent me a food and clothes box. The CO called me to his desk right after eleven o'clock count.

"Price, you've got a couple packages in the mailroom. You

can go on up there and get it. Give me a second, I'll unlock the doors," he said.

The doors of the dorm stayed locked until lunch was called. Ordinarily, inmates were not allowed in the halls during that time, though because I had a pass to go to the mailroom, I was exempt.

"Okay," I said.

I made my way to the mailroom. There were only a few people walking the halls. Lunch had not been called for many of the dorms, so most of the inmates were still locked in their dorms. A small crowd had already gathered in the mailroom. I waited impatiently in the line, shifting from one foot to the other until my turn had come. Forty-five minutes later, I stood before the CO.

"Do you have a pass?" He asked.

I gave him the passes the dorm CO had given me. He took the passes and searched amongst the other boxes until he found the one with my name on it, and then located the second box.

"You've got two, huh?" He said smiling.

He was one of the nicer COs. I had heard about him. The other inmates called him "P".

"Yeah," I said, smiling sheepishly.

"Well, somebody must love you," he said, genuinely.

The CO opened the food box. He pulled out the institution's formal food box list, which stated what an inmate could receive. He checked off the items, making certain that everything in the box was marked off on the list. After everything had checked-out, he placed the items in paper bags and handed them to me.

"Here you go," P said, handing me the final bag.

"Thank you," I replied, as I grabbed the bag.

"Okay, I'm going to go through the clothes box now."

He turned around, picked up the box from off of the floor, and placed it on his work station. After locating his box cutter, he sliced through the packaging tape, revealing the contents inside. My dad had neatly packed two sweat suits, a pair of black running shoes, house slippers, several pair of underwear, socks, and T-shirts.

Just as I was placing the clothes in paper bags, I heard an all-too familiar voice.

"What's up, man? What you got in there for me?" Cameron said in his high-pitched Chris Tucker-like voice.

I turned around, smiling at him. He was always in a chipper mood.

"What's going on, Cameron?"

I could not help laughing at him. Even when he was not doing anything particularly funny, he was still amusing. The humor lied in his mannerisms: the way he spoke; the way he walked; his energy.

"Nothing, man. I came up here to see if you needed some help carrying your stuff back to the dorm."

"How did you know I was up here? And, won't you get in trouble for being up here?" I asked quietly.

We were not allowed to be in the mailroom, unless we had a pass to be up there. P would not place Cameron in the hole, but if another CO caught him there, there was a possibility that he would have him placed in the hole.

"Man, fuck these mutha-fuckas! They know I run this Joint! Ain't that right, P!" Cameron yelled toward the direction where P stood.

"Yeah, that's right, Foster," P said, laughing at Cameron and his antics, which was all the fuel Cameron needed to hear to continue his behavior.

"See, I told you, man. This is my Joint!"

He began to pimp-walk over to where my bags were. He looked more like George Jefferson from the sit-com, "The Jeffersons" than he did a pimp, though. He grabbed as many bags as he could, and I grabbed the remaining ones.

"Man, what's all this shit you got. I ain't never seen nobody with this many damn bags!" He complained.

"It's two boxes: a food box and a clothes box," I said.

"Shit, I was about to say! Damn...now that I think about it, I ain't never known nobody to get no food and clothes box in one day either! P's ass like you! That nigga ain't foolin' me! I know he fuck around!" Cameron was suggesting that P was attracted to me. It was not uncommon for COs and inmates to have relationships with one another, though, generally, the relationships were amongst the female COs and inmates—although I had heard of instances where the male COs copulated with the gay inmates as well.

"Well, it ain't gone happen with me!" I laughed.

Besides the fact that I was in a relationship with Moe, P was far from my type. He appeared to be a very nice man, but some boundaries I did not believe in crossing—and the CO-inmate boundary was one of them.

We finally reached my dorm after walking seemingly forever. It was amazing to me how it appeared to take longer to reach a destination when something heavy was being carried.

"I ain't carrying this shit upstairs!" Cameron announced.

"Oh, no! Not you! I know you're not scared to go on the dorm!" I said, teasingly.

"Man, I ain't thinking about these fools. Out-of-place don't mean nothing to me. I was just fucking with you!" He said, defiantly.

We walked up the stairs leading to 6A. Just as Cameron said, he walked in the dorm without a care in the world. The

CO merely looked at him.

"Where yo' bed?" Cameron asked.

"It's over there against the wall," I said.

"All shit! You got a wall-bed!" Cameron shouted.

I smiled at him. I was not nearly as enthused about having a bed against the wall as Cameron and Moe were. Although I thoroughly enjoyed not being in the middle-row, I came to understand that a bed was bed, no matter where I was in the dorm. I was, after all, still in prison.

Cameron and I placed the bags in front of my bed. I sat down on the bed to unlock my combination lock. I instinctively knew by looking at the things I had been sent that all of it would not fit in my locker box.

"I'm 'bout to go to chow. I ain't eat, yet." Cameron exclaimed after sitting my bags down.

"Okay. Thank you. Do you want anything from my food box?" I asked. It was customary to share things from our food boxes with our close friends. Although Cameron and I did not have the relationship to warrant a close relationship, I was appreciative of his help.

"Save me something!" He yelled as he ran from the dorm. Cameron's energy was boundless; he was always running somewhere.

I started to rearrange my locker box to make room for the recently acquired things. Just as I was taking the last of things out of the locker box, Moe and Booger rounded the corner, entering the dorm.

"What's up, Brown?" Moe asked.

"Nothing: trying to organize this stuff, so that it'll fit in my locker box," I said.

"Damn, yo daddy sent you all this!" Moe said, enthusiastically.

"Yeah. Where y'all coming from? Lunch?" I asked,

directing my question to Booger.

"Uhn huh," Booger responded.

"What did they have? Was it good?" I asked.

"Chicken and noodles. It was cool," Booger replied.

"Brown, you gone have to put some of your clothes under your mattress and me and Boo can put some of the food in our locker boxes, 'cause it ain't all gone fit in yours," Moe suggested.

Technically, we were not allowed to put things in other person's locker box. As with things bought from commissary, if a food box list did not show that the items belonged to the inmate, they were considered contraband and confiscated. Again, the mentality of the prison officials was that the inmate could be operating a store; or, worse yet, the inmate could have acquired the things by way of extortion (bullied them from their owner).

Moe was right, though. There was no way that all of the stuff would fit in my locker box. One of the perks to having a bed against the wall was that I was given an upright locker box, as opposed to a foot-locker box. The foot-locker box slid under the bed and was smaller than a wall-locker box. Though, despite the presumed extra space, it was still too small to fit all of my things into it.

"Okay. We'll separate the things as you see fit. Booger, my daddy put a couple extra bags of chips in the food box for you," I said.

Booger loved potato chips. I asked my daddy to include something that Booger would enjoy in the food box. Booger could eat a whole bag of chips by himself and think nothing of it. Luckily for him, his metabolism was fast enough to burn off the added calories.

"Good looking out," he replied, appreciatively.

Chapter Twelve

Moe and I had been in our relationship for nearly two months. While we shared many moments of intimacy, we had yet to consummate our relationship. Sex was commonly practiced in prison. Yet, despite the frequency of its occurrence, it was still against the rules of the institution. An inmate found engaging in a sexual act was punished with a sentence of forty-five days in the hole for his first offense; though, the amount of time an inmate spent in the hole increased by thirty days, depending upon the number of times he had committed an infraction, such as a sex act.

The hole was nothing more than a small 6X9 cell, much like the cells in the county jail. However, there was a difference between being confined in the county jail and being confined in the Hole. In the county jail an inmate was allowed to leave his cell whenever he pleased, whereas in the Hole he was almost wholly confined to his cell for forty-five days.

The only exception to this rule was that those confined in the Hole were given an hour, three days a week, for showers and recreation; that is, if the inmate behaved himself. Recreation was a privilege, not a right; at any time such a privilege could be revoked, leaving the inmate to do most of his time in absolute confinement.

My concern did not lie in being confined in the Hole, as it was for other inmates, but in how negatively it affected my chances of receiving probation. Judges did not look favorably upon inmates who were reprimanded to the Hole. Such infractions communicated to judges that the inmate had not been rehabilitated, and, therefore, he was not ready to be released into society.

Although my body and mind longed to be sexually intimate with Moe, I was fearful of doing anything that would jeopardize going home early. I wanted to return home to my family and friends. I simply could not risk doing anything to lessen my chances of an early release. Yet, despite my obvious concerns, Moe and I still planned where and when we could make love.

"Brown, I spoke with my dude on F-Block about renting his room." Moe said one evening, as we sat on my bed talking.

"F-Block?" I queried.

"Yeah, he got a two-man cell, with a door we can close for some privacy. I can have my dude look out for us, so we 'on get caught. What you think?" He asked.

The inmates who resided on F-Block were either students or teacher's aides. The administrators of Lima felt that the inmates should have a dorm that was more conducive to learning. As a resident of F-Block the student-inmates did not have to contend with the noise that was common on traditional dorms. As an added bonus, the inmates on F-Block slept in two-man cells, as opposed to sleeping in big dorms with fifty to seventy inmates in one room.

"I don't know...I guess, it sounds cool," I said, thoughtfully.

I tried as best I could to weigh the pros and cons of my decision. There really were not any real pros and cons. There was simply a pro and a con: the pro being, consummating my relationship through love-making; the con was getting caught. Against my better judgment, I went with my carnal proclivities.

"Let's do it," I said, firmly.

"You sure, Brown? You know you ain't got to do this. I'll be all right with our relationship as it is," Moe said.

I looked into Moe's brown eyes and saw a tenderness and concern in them. His regard for me was touching. I knew full well that he was just as drawn to me sexually as I was to him, yet he cared enough for me to consider my needs above his own. His selfless attitude was endearing to me.

"Yeah, I'm sure," I said, resolutely.

Having made our decision, Moe went about securing the room for us to copulate. We tentatively set the date for July 25th, the day of my twenty-second birthday. The date was not etched in stone, however. Our primary obstacle resided in which COs were working on F-Block and the halls leading to F-Block. Both COs had to be "cool" by inmate standards. Being cool meant that the COs did not walk around searching for possible illicit activities. If either of the COs were the type to patrol their areas, Moe's well-laid plans would be ruined.

"Brown, you ready?" Moe asked, as I sat reading on my bed early one morning.

"Ready for what?" I said, looking up from my book at him.

"I got a room," he said.

"Already? My birthday is still two days away. I thought you were supposed to get the room on my birthday?" I asked.

"Dre said Ms. Taylor working on F-Block and Jones working the halls. Ain't neither one of them gone move around," Moe replied.

"Dre?" I asked.

"Yeah, that's the dude on F-Block whose room I'm renting," he said.

"Oh," I said.

I suddenly realized the totality of our decision to have sex.

The mere thought of us going out-of-place sent nervous shivers throughout my body, not to mention the consequences of getting caught in a sexual act. If we were caught, it would destroy any chance of my receiving probation. Without the hope of probation, I would have to remain in prison for at least six years until my parole hearing. And, even after going before the parole board, my freedom was not guaranteed. I was sentenced to nine to twenty-five years, which meant that the parole board could make me serve the entire twenty-five years; a frightening thought, to express the least.

"Okay. What time should I be ready?" I asked, ignoring my better judgment.

"We gone have to leave when they call us for chow. We got an hour to use his room," Moe informed.

"Alright," I said.

Although I felt a strong sense of apprehension, I illogically pushed it aside. Instead, I foolishly forced myself to focus on the resulting ecstasy our love-making would bring. I looked at Moe walking ahead of me. I envisioned his beautiful, well-muscled, naked body lying against my own. I longed to kiss him deeply and passionately without reservation. I desired to connect with him emotionally and mentally in a way that could only be achieved through love-making.

"You ready?" He asked as we neared F-Block.

"Yeah," I replied through the lump in my throat.

I walked close behind Moe as he entered F-Block. A guy stood on the stairwell, who I presumed was Dre. He waved his hand, indicating that we should follow him up the stairs. We did so, quickly and quietly. Dre peeked around the corner of the stairwell to see where the CO was. After determining that the CO sat at his desk, he walked up the second flight of stairs. Moe and I followed closely behind him.

As we were walking up the last staircase, an inmate turned the corner startling us. The guy looked at Moe and me for a long moment, before he continued down the stairs. My heart nearly leapt from my chest. The encounter with the guy made me that much more nervous. The guy could make our presence known to the CO. Such tattling was not uncommon amongst jealous-hearted inmates who resented inmates like Moe, who had prison companions.

We continued up the stairs, entering a hallway lined with steel doors on both sides. The old steel doors were humongous. Although the doors were no longer operational (they did not lock), I cringed at the thought of a time when mentally disordered patients were locked behind them.

Dre led us to the third room on the left. We entered the small room. The cement walls were painted white; a stainless steel sink and toilet sat on one side of the room; a bunk bed sat on the other.

"I'ma let y'all have some privacy. If anybody come, I'ma tap on the door three times to let y'all know to get out of here," Dre said in a deep, husky voice.

His words of caution should have offered me some security, but instead I felt more nervous.

"Alright, man. Good lookin'," Moe replied.

Moe did not seem nervous at all. Though, when I thought about it, this scene had occurred many times for him with Blake. It was only a novelty for me.

"You alright, Brown?" Moe said to me, after Dre closed the door of the cell.

"I'm a little nervous, but I'm okay," I said.

Moe walked over to where I stood. He placed his hands on my neck and began to gently massage it. He covered my head within his big strong hands, rubbing away the tension. I began to relax under his firm grip.

"You want to leave?" He asked as he cupped my face between his hands. He softly kissed my lips, allowing his tongue to slowly enter my mouth, searching for my tongue. Our tongues intertwined, sensually moving around the other.

"No," I said in a deep, passion-filled voice.

He led me to the bed, where he slowly began to undress me. I stood still as he unbuttoned my shirt, sliding it off my shoulders, and placing it on the top bunk-bed. I suddenly remembered that I had not worn any underwear, just in case we had to make a hasty retreat. Fearing that my penis would get caught in the zipper of my pants, I quickly removed the pants myself before Moe had an opportunity.

I stood stark naked before Moe. He embraced me firmly.

"I love you, Brown," Moe breathed deeply, whispering in my ear.

"I love you, too, Moe," I responded, passionately.

Unlike the care and sensuality Moe took in taking off my clothes, he shed his own in one deft movement. Moe's body was purely exquisite. His six-foot tall frame was heavily muscled: his chest, arms, and shoulders were thick and rock-hard. I relished in the beauty of his body.

I gently placed my index finger under his chin, slowly moving my finger down the front of his neck to his chest, making small circles around his areola. I moved my hand to the back of his head, running my fingers through his neatly lined corn-rows, as I guided his face down to mine. We kissed sweetly at first, then ferociously as with the passion of two estranged lovers.

I directed our bodies down to the bed, allowing him to lie on top of me while we continued our kissing frenzy. For a fleeting moment, I thought of the risks we were taking.

Though, the transient thought moved from mind just as suddenly as it had appeared.

We lay motionlessly in bed for a moment, both of us breathing laboriously. After a short while, he leaned towards me, kissing my forehead tenderly. Tilting my chin upward, he looked into my eyes warmly.

"I love you, Brown," he said, softly.

"I love you, too, Moe," I smiled, kissing him gently on his lips."

An hour had gone by quickly. Before Moe and I knew it, a soft tap was heard at the door; our indication from Dre that it was time for us to leave and return to our prison environment. We reluctantly, albeit speedily, put on our clothes. We had no time to bask in the afterglow of our love-making: no time to look into one another's eyes; no time to hold each other until we fell into a deep sleep; no time to exchange soft words of love. We were still incarcerated, after all.

Although everything had gone smoothly so far, we were still in harm's way. The CO could still catch us on the dorm and arrest of us for being out-of-place. After we put on our clothes, Moe peeked out of the room to look for Dre. Outside the cell, Dre stood at attention like a bodyguard. He was prepared to safely escort us from the dorm.

Once again, Dre used his hand to indicate that we should follow him. We obediently did so. With Dre in the lead, we walked down the stairs. Dre looked around the corners, surveying the stairwell and hallways. Finding nothing, he motioned for us to continue behind him. We had one more flight of stairs to descend and we would be home free. Dre stealthily walked down the stairs. Moe and I remained on the stairwell, as Dre looked up and down the hall that led to the dorm, ensuring that there was not any COs in the hall. Finding none, he signaled for us to exit the dorm. Surreptitiously, we walked out of the dorm unseen by anyone.

~~~

My twenty-second birthday had come and gone uneventfully. The hallmark of my week lied in my love-making session with Moe a few days prior. The succeeding days were blissful. Our love-making united us in a way that we were not in days past. We developed an intimacy that made being incarcerated a little more tolerable. Although, I still longed for the love and companionship of my family, my relationship with Moe buffered the pain I felt from being separated from them.

I spent the majority of my days much like I had before: working, reading, and jogging. I still regularly attended Moe's softball games. He was looking forward to the start of the football season. Already, he was being asked by various team captains to join their squad. He was highly favored amongst the players, because of his speed and strength. Although, I was not a sport enthusiast, I shared in his joy and excitement.

Occasionally, Moe and I worked-out together. Many of the other inmates were openly taken aback by my desire to work-out. Although none of them expressed their disapproval directly to Moe or me, their discontent circulated throughout the institution. Homosexuals in prison were pigeon-holed, much like women were in free-society. Working-out was considered a man's activity. Because male homosexuals were seen in the same manner as women, it was considered unbecoming for a gay guy to work-out.

I refused to allow a bunch of chauvinistic men to determine what I could and could not do. I adamantly bucked their narrow-minded beliefs. Fortunately, Moe was not one who cared about the opinions of others. He took pride in being a rebel and feeding off the murmurs of naysayers. I was lucky to have him; though, quite honestly, I would have worked-out, whether he supported my decision or not.

Despite having to contend with the opposing views of some of the men, I had adjusted well to my life in prison. I had settled into a smooth rhythm of sorts. Nothing seemed able to disrupt the easy flow that I had established, until one beautiful, late summer day.

The sun shone brilliantly, revealing an exquisite cloudless, blue sky. Although, it was mid-August, the hottest month of summer, the midday temperature was surprisingly pleasant. I had just returned from lunch. Our dorm was one of the first to be called. With the exception of the inmates who resided on privilege housing dorms, many of the inmates were still in their dorms waiting to be released.

I sat on the ledge of 6A's huge dorm windows looking out at the Center Yard. Several inmates walked the perimeter of the Center Yard on the cemented sidewalks. I drank a cup of cold water, as I watched them walk and talk amongst themselves.

"A Chris, can I holler at you?" I heard a guy bellow.

I had no idea who the person could be. The voice did not at all sound familiar to me. I looked down from my position on the second floor through the barred windows in the direction in which I heard the voice. As I peered down, I was completely surprised by who I saw. Blake.

"What did you say?" I asked, looking down at him.

He was a really nice looking guy. I had, of course, seen him many times before, though I had never really looked at him. Light complexioned guys were not my color of choice, but beauty was beauty, no matter the skin color, and he was undeniably attractive. His dark, wavy hair glistened under the rays of the sunlight, framing his narrow face wonderfully.

"Can I talk wit you?" He repeated in the same heavy, unassuming voice. A thin, dark-skinned guy stood beside him looking around. He appeared agitated, nervous.

"Yeah, give me a second," I said.

I jumped down from the short window ledge, taking my cup into the big dorm, and placing it on the floor next to my bed. I retraced my steps, walking out of the big dorm, to the landing, down the stairwell, and entered the main hallway of the prison. I crossed the hallway, and exited the door leading to the Center Yard.

Wow! The sun is extremely bright!

I shielded my eyes with my hand. Blake stood below the stairs.

"What's up?" I said, after spotting him.

"Can you come down here, so I can talk to you?" He asked in a soft-spoken manner.

"Yeah," I said, descending the stairs. I had forgotten all about Moe's admonishments a few weeks ago.

A sixth sense should have gone off in my head, but it did not. At the very least, I should have been on guard. Instead, I walked down the stairs, approaching Blake as though I was meeting an old acquaintance, rather than an ex-lover of my partner's. As I neared him, I felt him sizing-up me. Perhaps he was really seeing me for the first time as I had him, or he could have been assessing my physical prowess.

"Um, you know Moe and I are getting back together, don't you?" Blake asked me matter-of-factly.

I laughed at his statement.

Why did I do that?

I did not mean to openly laugh, but the way he stated that they were getting together amused me. He said it as though he were talking about going on a long-awaited trip around the world. He was proud to the point of being cocky. He had a lot to learn about men.

"Are y'all?" I asked innocently.

Moe and I had discussed his conversations with Blake. He also told me in great detail the things he expressed to Blake, including that he led Blake to believe that there was a possibility of them rekindling their relationship. I did not agree with what Moe was doing, specifically that he was playing with Blake's emotions. I told Moe on countless occasions that trying to get back at Blake would not resolve or change anything that had occurred during their relationship. He needed to get over the abuse that he suffered during their relationship. Though, he would not listen. He was intent on making Blake suffer as he had.

"Yeah, we are and you're in the way!" He said, vehemently.

I really had nothing against Blake. In fact, I felt sorry for him. As a child, my mother had unknowingly prepared me for life as a gay man. I do not mean to suggest that she wanted me to be gay, because she did not. Though, because of the many conversations that she and I had about her dealings with men, I gained a wisdom and understanding of how to deal with men romantically.

The first lesson I learned is the importance of self-love. There is absolutely nothing wrong with loving a man fully and wholly, though, in doing so, one has to understand the value of loving himself first. If a person has not achieved a healthy love for himself, chances are he will not love another person healthily.

"I am? How am I in the way?" I retorted, as we walked along the sidewalk of the Center Yard.

"Cause Moe-Moe told me that you won't leave him alone…that you keep asking him to be with you!" He responded, hotly.

I tried to maintain my cool, though it was incredibly difficult. I could not believe what I heard. I did not know if what Blake said was true, but I did know men. I knew that many men would say whatever they needed to say to get what they wanted.

"And, you believe everything that Moe tells you, huh?" I asked coolly with a hint of sarcasm.

My sarcasm rubbed Blake the wrong way; he was livid. His light-colored face flushed a bright crimson.

"You got a smart-ass mouth!" Blake fumed.

"Yeah, that's what I've been hearing my whole life. Join the crowd," I said, bitingly.

I should not have antagonized him. I could not help myself, though. I felt that it was stupid of Blake to approach me about a man. I would never do anything so degrading as to take issue with someone because of a man. It always sickened me to hear of scorned lovers arguing or fighting with the person with whom their partner had cheated. Their issue should not have been with the third party, but with their partner. After all, it was in their partner with whom they had placed their hearts and trust, not the other person.

"You just a young, stupid ass, bitch, who run around chasing men who don't want you!" Blake hissed.

Aside from my smart remarks, I had remained somewhat cool, however, I could not hold back the flood gate any longer.

"Stupid?! Stupid?! Yo' dumb ass is the stupid one! You running around believing every damn word that a nigga say to you! You stupid as hell! Moe is using your dumb ass to get back at you! He don't want you, dummy! He wants what you can do for him! Stupid ass idiot!" I yelled.

People had begun to enter the Center Yard. I had a naturally loud voice, though, when I was upset, it reverberated like a blow horn. After hearing my tirade, all eyes were on us. Inmates began to look out the windows. Several of them laughed and applauded after hearing the mean things I said to Blake. Senselessly, I had created a public spectacle for the entire institution to see. Nothing was more amusing to a crowd of chauvinistic men than to see two gay guys fighting…except, perhaps, two women.

I could not believe what I had just said to him. I should have had better control of my emotions. I behaved as foolishly as Blake. I prided myself on being mature and above senseless behavior. Yet, I had conducted myself like an immature teenager.

"Bitch!" Blake hissed vehemently. He looked like the devil incarnate as he charged toward me.

I quickly gained my footing. I grabbed his outstretched arms, pushing him away from me.

Blake stumbled a bit, before he charged, again, like an enraged bull. His face was contorted in anger. I grabbed him by the waist as I attempted to throw him to the ground. I resolved in my mind that I was not going to fight him, though I was not going to allow him to hurt me, either.

I lost my footing as I tried to toss him. We both crashed to the ground. He landed on top of me. Blake was taller and weighed slightly more than me, though he was not stronger than me. I wiggled and squirmed until I wrestled myself on top of him. My intention was to simply hold down him until he came to his senses, but I soon realized why his wiry, little friend had accompanied him. Just as I had gained an advantage over Blake, his friend pushed me from behind, sending me toppling over. I tried to jump up to regain my position, but my tight, unyielding state pants and slippery state boots prevented me from moving as quickly as I had liked.

I succeeded only in looking like a total klutz. I was able to rise to my knees, but it was not for long as Blake pulled me back down to the ground. I crashed down atop of him. The entire farce looked more like a mud wrestling event than a fight. I could only imagine what our spectators must have thought.

When I thought I had finally succeeded in holding down him, I was knocked down again. This time, however, I was not pushed by Blake's friend.

"Come on, guys! Break it up!" A male voice boomed above us. When I was able to focus my eyes beyond the glare of the sun, I saw two COs standing above us. The CO turned me onto my stomach to handcuff me; though, in doing so, the other CO failed to restrain Blake. While I was being handcuffed, my head had landed near his feet. Taking the opportunity before him, Blake thrashed about trying to kick me in the head. Fortunately for me, he did not succeed.

After the COs pulled us up to our feet, I looked around the Yard. Hundreds of inmates had gathered around to watch us as we made fools of ourselves. I felt humiliated. I could not believe that I had unwittingly behaved like a buffoon for the inmate population.

We were escorted to S/C (Security Control)-D/C (Discipline Control), also known as the Hole, where we waited to be seen by the RIB (Rules Infraction Board).

The Hole was not a dark hole in the ground where inmates were served only bread and water, as was commonly believed by many. In truth, the Hole was nothing more than a dorm set aside for the housing of inmates who had violated the prison's rules. At Lima, the Hole was structured much like F-Block. Each cell was equipped with sinks, toilets, and a bunk bed. Like the cells on F-Block, each of the cells had big, heavy steel doors. The doors in the Hole were constantly locked, however; unlike the doors on F-Block.

Blake and I stood outside one of two locked doors waiting to enter the Hole. After the door was unlocked electronically by a CO working in the control booth, the two COs escorted us into a waiting area where we stood before a locked gate. One of the COs reached for a ring of keys that he held fastened to his belt. Locating the correct key, he unlocked the gate, ushering Blake and me into an area where we were instructed to take off our clothes and to put on a white jumpsuit. After following the COs directions, we were taken to two separate cells.

The CO locked the cell door and instructed me to place my hands through an opening in the door, so that he could remove the handcuffs. Once the CO had un-cuffed me, I looked around the cell. The dingy walls were a yellowish color. The room was filthy: dried feces clung to the stainless steel toilet; old toothpaste and crusty, mucus-filled saliva was in the sink; the green, plastic mattress was cracked, revealing the heavily-soiled inner material of the mattress. I felt as though I was in the bull-pen, again.

I sat in the Hole for three days before my case was reviewed by the RIB. During that time, I was entirely confined to my cell. Our meals were served to us three times a day through a hole in our cell door, though I ate very little while I was in there. Although I had been given cleaning supplies, which I used liberally to clean the toilet, sink, and to wipe down the mattress, the room still had an unclean feel to it.

There was no television, and I was not allowed to shower. I also did not have a cell-mate, which, for me, was just fine; I had no desire to do much conversing. Instead, I read two of the several books that were left behind by an inmate who had previously occupied the room. Finally, on the third day, I received word from the CO that I was scheduled to go before the RIB.

I had no idea what to expect, but I was prepared to meet with the panel. Shortly after noon, a CO spoke through the hole in my cell door, instructing me to place my hands through the hole for cuffing. After being cuffed, the CO unlocked the door, and escorted me down the hall to several chairs outside of the room where the RIB conducted their meetings. I sat in one of the chairs until my name was called.

"Price, 307-720, come on in," a female voice boomed from the other side.

I stood up and walked into the room. Two COs wearing white shirts, which indicated that they were lieutenants, and a guy dressed in civilian clothes sat behind a long table.

"Inmate Price, state your name and institutional number for the record," the female lieutenant demanded.

"Christopher Price, 307-720."

"You can sit down in one of the chairs behind you," she commanded.

"My name is Lt. Hassleford, this is Lt. Michaels, and this is Case Manager Richards. We'll be reviewing your case. You are charged with fighting and instigating an institutional riot. How do you plead?" Lt. Hassleford asked.

I frowned at the mention of instigating an institutional riot. I knew that I was being charged with fighting, but how did I instigate a riot, I wondered?

"Not guilty to both charges," I responded.

Lt. Hassleford looked up from her paper work. She had not expected me to plead not guilty.

"Would you like to tell your version of the events that occurred, Inmate Price?" She asked in an annoyed tone.

"Yes," I related the events, beginning with Blake coming to my cell and ending with the COs breaking-up us.

"Sounds like you were fighting. Why, then, are you pleading not guilty to fighting?" Lt. Hassleford asked, pointedly.

"Because, I wasn't fighting. I was engaged in a fight, but I was not fighting. I was preventing him from hurting me, but I never hit him. What was I expected to do, let him beat me?" I said, resolutely.

Lt. Hassleford looked at me incredulously.

"Step out of the room, while we make our decision, Price," she directed.

Blake had already related his version of the events. I could only imagine what untruths he told. He did not strike me as a person of integrity. I believed in telling the truth no matter what the consequences were, good or bad.

Within five minutes Lt. Hassleford called me back into the room. I entered the room.

"Price, take a seat." I sat down. "The panel finds you guilty in the charge of fighting. We relied on outside resources to make our decision. In the charge of instigating an institutional riot, we find you not guilty. You will be released after serving three days. You will receive time served in S/C-D/C for three days, which means you will be released today. Do you have anything to say?" She asked.

I actually had quite a bit to say. I wanted to contest the conviction of fighting. I still maintained my position that I had not fought. I recognized how my actions could have been construed, though I insisted that I was not fighting. If I had fought Blake, he would have known it, I reasoned cockily. While I thought all of these things, I did not express any of them. I did not want to remain in the hole for another minute, so I accepted my conviction with a closed mouth.

"No, I don't have anything else to say," I replied, begrudgingly.

"Wait outside for your release," Lt. Hassleford instructed.

I walked out of the room and took a seat in one of the chairs. I was irritated by the entire ordeal. I wondered how being found guilty of fighting would look to the judge when I filed for probation. Again, I had gotten myself involved in a situation that was not my own. I could not help to think of the circumstances of my incarceration: if I had told Tookie that I would not go with her, I would not have been entangled in the events that transpired; had I not gone downstairs to see what Blake wanted, I would not have been involved in Moe and Blake's mess. I was disgusted with myself for foolishly making the wrong decision yet again.

~~~~

I looked awful: I had not showered in three days; my hair had not been brushed; and, although I had brushed my teeth with the flimsy toothbrush I had been given by the CO, I still had a foul taste in my mouth. I changed out of the white jumpsuit back into the state uniform I wore when I was taken to the hole. The light blue shirt was soiled in places from rolling in the dirt with Blake. Apparently, I had also ripped my pants in the tussle, so that a gaping split was evident in the crouch of my pants.

A CO unlocked the doors of the hole, releasing me back into general population. As soon as I stepped out of the Hole, I felt somewhat better. A soft, warm breeze entered through the open windows in the hallway. The air moved around and through me, erasing the filth of the Hole from my mind and spirit. I felt as though I was being bathed in the grace of God; a feeling of being comforted enveloped me. I instinctively knew that all would be well.

I began to walk toward the mailroom, where my possessions were being held. Because the prison was vastly overcrowded, when an inmate was placed in the Hole his bed was quickly given to another inmate. My personal belongings were taken to a room adjacent to the mailroom, where I was instructed to go to re-claim them.

As I turned the corner of the hallway, I saw Moe pacing back and forth awaiting my release. News in prison traveled fast; he had already been informed of the time of my release. He looked distraught.

"What's up, Brown?" He said, solemnly.

"Not much. What's wrong? What happened? Why are you looking like that?" I asked each question in rapid succession of the others, not really giving him time to answer any one question.

"I'm sorry for getting you caught up in this bullshit," Moe said, forlornly.

I had not considered that he looked as he did because of my ordeal. I thought that something had happened to Booger in my absence.

"It's alright. I shouldn't have gone down there in the first place," I said.

"Yeah, but you wouldn't have been in this shit if it hadn't been for me. You just got to the camp and you already going to the Hole and shit. You ain't even that kinda dude. You just keep to yo' self, not fuckin wit' nobody and I got you in my shit wit' Blake," Moe stated.

Moe was correct, as I had previously deduced. I was unwittingly enmeshed in his and Blake's relationship, though I did not express that to him. He seemed to be having a hard enough time dealing with things as they were, without me verbalizing my thoughts.

"It's cool. You told me to avoid him should he try anything."

"Yeah, but you shouldn't have to avoid nobody about some shit that ain't got nothing to do with you," he offered.

He was right, again. This time, however, rather than to justify his part in all of it, I just kept quiet. Instead, I allowed him to share in his responsibility in the matter.

"That's all these niggas been talking about around here. Sayin' I'm a bad ass man to have two fine broads fighting over me."

I looked at Moe as he spoke. I did not like being referred to as a 'broad.' Many of the gay guys took pride in being associated with names that were traditionally reserved for women, including derogatory names. Though, I did not delight in such misnomers at all.

Yet, this time it was not the mention of being referred to as a broad that piqued my interest. I wondered just how detached Moe was to the stir that had ensued. Many guys would feel a certain amount of esteem to have two guys fighting because of him. Moe was different in many ways than most guys, yet I still wondered if he delighted in having his friends and others guys in the prison refer to him as "the man," because of the altercation between Blake and me.

"I aint on that shit, though. I feel fucked up that you had to go through that shit, for real!" He said, as though reading my mind.

I continued listening to him. I wanted to hear his take on all that had occurred. As we walked toward the mailroom several guys spoke to us, many of whom I did not know. Just as we were about to walk up the stairs leading to the mailroom, Cameron whistled to get our attention. We stopped to wait for him to get to where we stood.

"What's up, Bonnie and Clyde?!" Cameron said.

"Come on, Foster, man," Moe said, nearly pleading with him not to start his antics.

"I thought Moe-Moe was the fighter in this duo, both of y'all some bad mutha-fuckas in the ring!" Cameron said, loudly.

I smiled at him, despite myself.

"Not me. I was not fighting!" I said, adamantly.

"Shiiiit! I heard about what you did to him!" Cameron countered.

"That ain't nothing but hear-say. These niggas ain't doing nothing, but pumping up the story. I didn't even hit him, if anything it was more like a version of the WWF (World Wrestling Federation)," I said.

"Yeah, whatever, nigga! If you kicked his ass…you kicked his ass! That crazy bitch needed his ass kicked anyway!" Cameron continued.

"I didn't kick his ass. I…." I abruptly stopped trying to explain myself. Cameron and the others were going to have their opinions, regardless of what I said.

"Come on, Foster. Let it go, man. You see he ain't on that shit," Moe interjected.

"All right, man…y'all going to get yo' shit?" Cameron asked me.

"Yeah," I said.

"Good! Cause yo' ass lookin rough as hell!" He said, laughing.

As usual, I could not do anything, but laugh. Cameron was a constant jokester.

"Yeah, nigga, you can help us get this shit!" Moe said, smiling at his friend.

Chapter Thirteen

Being placed in the Hole had cost me a lot: I was in jeopardy of losing my chance of receiving probation; I lost my bed against the wall, which meant that I had to move back to a bed in the middle row; and, I lost my job as a grill cook and my seniority in the kitchen. I would be assigned to the pots and pans area, again. I had thoroughly screwed things up for myself.

On top of everything else that was going on, a rift had begun to develop between Moe and me. While I did not wholly blame Moe for the altercation between Blake and me, I had the wherewithal to know that Blake would not have had a foot-hole in our relationship, if Moe had not given him room in it. Moe perpetuated the situation by playing both sides from the middle. Truthfully, I did not know whether he was being completely open with me. He could have been telling me what he wanted me to know about his supposed animosity for Blake and the reasons for his involvement with him.

After Blake and I were released from the Hole, Moe absolutely refused to have any dealings with him. He even went as far as to threaten Blake that he would fight him, if he came anywhere near either one of us. Blake was seemingly unmoved by Moe's threats. He did not approach Moe directly, though he would send messages to Moe through mutual friends of theirs. Moe initially dismissed the messages asking the persons not to mention Blake's name to him. Yet, as the days and weeks wore on, Moe weakened more and more in his resolve.

Rather than consume myself with the jail-house soap opera that my life had become, I began to focus more on my life outside of prison and less on my relationship with Moe.

"Hello? Mymomme?" I said into the phone receiver.

"Hey, bae," Mymomme said, after the automated operator connected our call.

"What's going on with you?" I asked.

I had long since moved passed our ordeal in the county jail. Our argument was a thing of the past. In order to survive in life, one has to constantly rid himself of negative feelings. Failure to do so allows the ill-feelings to set up residence in his temple, which poisons the body like a cancer.

"Nothing much, just getting home from work," Mymomme responded.

"You start cooking, yet?"

"Yeah," she laughed. "I'm in the kitchen now."

"Mmm! What are you cooking?" I asked. "I can't tell you how much I miss your cooking!"

She laughed, "I put a roast in the slow cooker last night, so it's about ready now. I'ma cook some mashed potatoes and green beans with it. It's too hot to be in this kitchen. I been bar-b-queing all week to keep the house cooler, you know what I mean?"

"That's sounds so good! I'm so tired of this food in here, I don't know what to do! Where is Miah-Miah and Sam?" I asked, referring to my little brother and my mother's boyfriend.

"Sam in there in the living room, and Jeremiah is somewhere outside running around. You know that boy ain't gone stay in the house no time!"

I laughed. My brother and I were truly like night and day.

I was more of a homebody. I loved to be indoors reading or watching television; Miah-Miah grew agitated if he was in the house for too long.

"When did you get out of the Hole?"

Booger had informed our family about my being placed in the Hole.

"A few days ago."

"Boy! And, you just now calling...I was worried about you!" Mymomme yelled.

"I'm sorry. I was getting settled back into my environment...I lost my bed and job."

"Yeah? Well, why did you go to the Hole? Booger said something about you getting into a fight."

"Nothing really; just some crazy prison stuff. This guy got jealous, because I'm in a relationship with this dude he used to be in a relationship with, and he didn't like it. It's really not a big thing. I can tell you more in detail when you come to visit me," I said, hinting at a possible visit from her.

I had not seen her since I was transferred from the county jail nearly six months ago. My parents and I had always had a very open relationship, so it was nothing for me to talk to them about the personal details of my life.

"Okay. I'll see you next Tuesday on my day off from work."

"You have one minute left of your phone call," an automated recording announced on the phone. No matter how long I had been incarcerated, I still did not like those recordings!

"Okay, Mymomme. The phone is about to hang up. I love you and I'll see you next week!" I said enthusiastically into the phone receiver.

"Okay, bae. I love you, too!" She said in her usual deep voice.

I woke up bright and early for work on Tuesday morning. I had been reassigned to the serving line, which was kind of nice. It was not as enjoyable as working as a grill cook, but it was better than being assigned to clean the pots and pans.

I finished working and eating breakfast at six-thirty. I went back to my dorm and took a short nap before the dorm doors were unlocked at eight o'clock in the morning, allowing us to leave the dorm as we pleased. After napping, I ran a brisk three miles around the East Yard.

The day promised to be a great one. I ironed my nicest state pants and shirt in preparation of my visit with Mymomme. I would not look as I did when my daddy visited. I could still see in my mind's eye the faded, soiled pants and shirt that I wore to our visit. I looked horrible.

I went to the barbershop the day before. Although haircuts were free, I paid a barber a pack of cigarettes to cut my hair. Such a payment was illegal, though its practice went on anyway. Paying for a haircut was an inmate's way of ensuring that he received a quality haircut.

I washed my hair and showered after my run. After putting some lotion on my body, I laid down to read until the CO announced that my visit had arrived. I could not wait to see her. I missed seeing her beautiful, radiant smile.

I read for an hour before my eyes began to get tired. I put down my book for what I thought would be a moment; however, I awakened to the CO's whistle, indicating that it was time for eleven o'clock count. *Wow, I slept an entire two hours!*

After the CO cleared his count of the dorm, Booger came to my bed.

"Lawanda still coming, Chris?"

"Yeah, I guess so. I'll call her house after the institution's count clears."

"All right. Let me know when you call."

"Okay. I will."

The institution's count cleared an entire half of an hour later than it normally did. I rushed from the big dorm hoping to get to the phone before anyone else did. I was lucky; no one was using the phone. I stepped into the phone room and closed the door. I dialed Mymomme's number. The phone rang several times, though no one picked up. I was getting a little worried. I picked up the receiver, again. I dialed her number and waited for someone to answer. Again, there was no answer.

I hung up the phone. I was apprehensive that something had happened to her. I left the phone room, deciding to call her back should she not arrive soon. I was just about to get in my bed as Moe came out of the ten-man annex.

"What's up, Brown? Your visit ain't came, yet?" He asked with a smirk on his face.

"No," I said worriedly. "I hope she's okay.

"You sure she comin'?" He asked, amusedly.

I looked up at him, "What?" I asked in a tone of irritation.

"Man, I'm just saying," he said chuckling, "She might not come. Y'all dudes go have to learn the hard way. Just 'cause somebody say they comin' don't mean they go come!" He laughed.

I could not believe that he was getting a kick out of my mother not being there, yet. Anything could have happened to her, and the only thing he could think to do was to vent his bitter thoughts about being imprisoned and the lack of support he received from his family and friends.

"Well, I don't know about your people, but if mine say that

they are going to come, they are!" I said, angrily.

"Yeah, whatever. We'll see!" He said, laughing as he walked away.

I was incensed. He did not know the first thing about being a friend, let alone a lover. *That's alright. I'll show him that not everyone disappoints you, as his family had him. Just wait.*

~~~

Another hour passed by. I got up from my bed to call Mymomme, again. I walked to the phone and peeked in the window to see if anyone was using the phone. No one was in the phone room. I opened the door and dialed my mother's number. The phone rang several times, as it had last time; yet, still no answer. She did not have an answering machine, so I could not leave a message. I disconnected the call to Mymomme, and then dialed my grandmother's phone number.

The phone rang two times. "Hello?" Mama said in her familiar southern drawl.

"Hi, Mama," I said into the receiver.

"How you doin', baby?" My grandmother asked.

"I'm doing okay, Mama."

"I heard you got in a little trouble down there," she said in a tired voice.

"Yeah, I did…are you okay, Mama? You sound tired."

"I am tired, baby. I just got home from work and yo' grandmother is wearing me out… oh, she's yo great-grandmother, isn't she?" Mama asked, referring to her mother.

Mama had moved her mother in to live with her a little over a year ago. Mother Frazier had Alzheimer's and was no longer able to care for herself.

"Yes, she's my great-grandmother, but I guess it's all the

same," I said, laughing.

Mama laughed, too. "Yes, I guess, you right, baby. You probably think yo' old granny losing it, too, huh? I can't even remember if you my own child or not," she said, joking.

"No, I don't think you're losing it. Just because you slip up every now and then doesn't mean that you have Alzheimer's."

"That's what the doctor tell me, too. He gave me some kind of test and he said I don't have it. I make sure I go to the doctor regularly. That old grandpappy of yours! I can't get him to go to the doctor for nothing! I keep tellin' him, 'Allen, you need to go to the doctor and get yo'self checked out!' But you think he'll listen to me? No sir-a-ree! That man just does whatever he wants! He been like that ever since I married him and it don't seem like he gone change, either!" Mama rambled.

I listened to her go on and on from one subject to the next, until I remembered that our phone calls were timed. I needed to know if she had seen Mymomme.

"Mama," I said, when she paused to take a break, "have you seen or talked to Mymomme?"

"Naw, baby. Why, what's wrong? Oh, she was supposed to come visit you today, wasn't she?!"

"Yes," I replied.

"Aww, baby…I'm sorry. That girl! Boy, I'm tellin' you the truth! These kids of mine! I don't think they ever gone grow up! You know, I think her and Sam messin' with that stuff, again, but don't say I said nothing," she confided in whispered tones.

"That stuff" was a reference to crack-cocaine.

"Yeah, I know, Mama," I said, disappointedly.

"Oh, who told you, baby? I try not to tell you all that stuff, 'cause I don't want you worryin' no more than you have to in there," Mama explained.

"I know, Mama. I suspected that she was using when I was in the county jail. I can handle it. I'd rather know what's going on at home just in case something bad happens to any of you all. It won't come as a surprise to me. Can you promise that you'll continue to confide in me like you always have?" I asked.

Mama and I had always shared a very close relationship. She and I talked about everything. She would always remark, "I can't believe I'm sittin' up here talkin' to my grandson about this

kind of stuff!" Yet, she would continue to tell me whatever the topic of the moment was. I missed those times we shared.

"I'll try, baby, but you know how I am. I just worry so much about you in there, and I don't want to put too much on you, baby."

"Okay," I said, although I knew in my heart that she would not tell me everything as she once had. She worried about my well-being too much to burden me with our family's issues.

The automated operator could be heard again informing us that the call would be ending soon.

"Okay, baby. I heard that lady. I don't know where that mother of yours is, but if she shows up here, I'll let her know that you called. I love you, baby. Always remember that C.P." She said, referring to me by the initials in my name as she sometimes did.

"Okay, Mama. I love you, too. I'll call…" The call was disconnected before I could finish what I was saying.

I went back to lie down on my bed to try to do some reading. However, just as fast as I picked up the book, I put it back down. I could not concentrate on what I was reading. It was three o'clock. Visiting hours ended at five. I seriously doubted that Mymomme would arrive that late in the day.

I was sad that Mymomme was not coming, but to compound my sorrow was the fact that she was using drugs, again. As I expressed to Mama, I suspected that she was using drugs while I was in the county. Though, if Mama was aware of her habit that meant Mymomme's addiction had gotten worse. The fact that she continued to work meant very little as well. She was a functioning addict, as I called her; like a functioning alcoholic, she was able to maintain a somewhat functional lifestyle: she worked, paid the bills, and continued to run her home as if things were normal. Though, her substance use was a clear indication that things were not normal.

"What's up, Brown? Your visit ain't came, yet?" Moe laughed teasingly from one end of the big dorm.

I could not understand why he insisted on picking with me. Whatever his reasons, my patience and tolerance had worn thin.

"Did yours come, yet? Oh, I forgot. You have not had a visit in how long?" I asked, facetiously.

I know I should not have teased him, but I could not help myself. I got tired of being the mature, understanding person. I wanted to be left alone, but he insisted on bothering me.

"Fuck you, nigga! You spoiled ass bitch!" Moe yelled, hotly.

Fuck me?! Spoiled bitch?! I could not believe he had gotten upset over what I said when he had been taking jabs at me all day. His response was a clear indication that some people can dish things out, though they could seldom take them in return.

Without thinking I quickly sat up, yelling, "Yo' mama, nigga!"

As soon as the words escaped my mouth, I quickly

regretted them. I would not have expressed them had I been more sober-minded. I did not believe in talking about a person's parents, especially Moe's mother. Over the past couple of months, he had shared quite a bit to me about her, including her struggle with chemical dependency, prostitution, and imprisonment.

Upon hearing Moe's mother's story, I instinctively joined in her hardships. Although I had never had the pleasure of meeting her, I felt a kinship with her. I understood her struggles as an African American woman. Having had such intimate relationships with Mymomme and her sisters, I was aware of the difficulties women endured because of their gender. I knew firsthand the perseverance it took to remain grounded as a woman amid racism, sexism, poverty, and, in many cases, physical and sexual abuse.

Moe rushed between the beds toward me before I could fully grasp what was happening. He raised his outstretched hand well above his head and sent it slamming into my face. I did not have time to think. The only thing that registered was that this man had slapped me. I jumped up from my bed with lightning speed, grabbing him by the legs as I did so. I raised his six feet tall, two hundred pound frame high from the floor, shaking him as though he was a rag doll. I desperately tried to slam him to the floor, but, using the strength and length of his gorilla-long arms, he held on to the sides of two bunk beds. The beds shook violently, threatening to collapse inward as I pulled and tugged at his body.

I was incensed. *How dare he put his hands on me!* I tried with every muscle in my body to pull him down, but he continued to hang onto the beds. Several of the guys in the big dorm stood staring at us. Booger heard the commotion and ran to where I stood with Moe high in the air.

"Chris, come on, man! You gotta let go! The CO is going to hear y'all!" Seeing that I had no intention of letting him go without a fight, Booger urged, "You gotta let him go, man!"

Booger's words began to permeate my mind. I slowly began to loosen my grip on Moe's legs. Booger grabbed his legs as I let go to prevent Moe from falling and hurting himself. I stood back fuming, as I watched Booger lower him to the floor. I could not believe that he had put his hands on me! I wanted to charge him. I knew full well that what I said was mean, but he had no right to touch me, especially considering that he started it all. I could not get pass him smacking me!

"Nigga, you got me fucked up! I ain't one of these punk ass niggas or White boys that's scared of yo ass! You put yo hands on me again and I bet yo ass regret it!" I yelled.

He looked at me as if I was crazy. He walked backwards to the ten-man annex where he slept, mindful of not turning his back to me.

"Chris!" Booger whispered, "You gotta calm down! The CO go hear you and put you in the hole!"

I was still livid, though I heeded Booger's warning. I had not been in the institution for three months and I was already involved in two fights. At that rate, I could only guess what the rest of my time in prison held for me.

~~~

Later that evening, Moe came to my bed as I was reading.

"A, Brown, can I talk to you?" He asked.

I looked up at him. I was still upset with him for smacking me. I kept re-playing the scene in my mind. He had a lot of nerve putting his hand on me in any inappropriate manner. As

I had expressed before: I was not going to allow any of those guys to mistreat me. I felt that Moe thought he could treat me any way he wanted because of his size and my presumed status; meaning that, as a gay male, I was presumed to be weak and cowardice.

"What you got to say?" I asked angrily.

"Can we go in the ten-man, these niggas go be all in our mouths out here?" He asked.

I did not want to make things convenient for him at all. He should have thought about what other people would think before he smacked me.

"Come on," I said, stubbornly. I was not going to let him think that he had gotten what he wanted, so I led the way into the annex as though it was my idea that we talk in there, rather the other way around. Things would truly be changing in how we dealt with one another; gone was the nice, obsequious Chris.

"What's up?" I asked as soon as we crossed the threshold of the ten-man annex.

I did not want to waste any time. He needed to say what he had to say, and he had to say it quickly.

He stammered a bit. "I just wanted to say I'm sorry." He said, humbly.

"Sorry for what?" I asked.

I wanted him to take full responsibility for his actions. Simply offering a general apology to me was not enough; he needed to be very specific.

"I'm sorry for slapping you, and I'm sorry for the way I acted earlier today," he said softly in his baritone voice.

I looked at him for a long moment. I was unable to say that I wholly accepted his apology. I believed that he was sincere, but every time I thought about him striking me, I became angry all over again.

"Okay," I said, obstinately.

Fighting in a romantic relationship was a major no-no to me; something that should never be done amongst people who loved one another. My relationship with Kevon was filled with fighting and arguing. I refused to be in another volatile relationship.

"Blake's ass made me mad this morning and you was so caught up in your visit and not showing no interest in me that I took it out on you," he explained.

"So, you are openly admitting that you took out the crap that you and Blake went through on me?" I asked, not believing that he was foolish enough to say something so damning.

"Yeah," he said, sheepishly.

"Okay," I replied, nonchalantly.

At that very moment, I resolved in my mind that I would soon end the relationship. It made no sense for me to continue to be in a relationship that had caused so much destruction and turmoil in my life, and we had only been together for a few short months. The relationship was a done deal, as far as I was concerned.

Chapter Fourteen

Summer had ended. To my delight, autumn was quickly ushered in. Spring and fall were my two favorite seasons. The temperatures were typically very mild; not too hot and not too cold. Both seasons offered something different and exciting: spring signaled new beginnings; fall represented an ending of some things and the promise of better things to come.

Although Moe and I were still technically together, our relationship had changed drastically. In some ways, we were still the same with one another: he still prepared breaks; we continued to talk at night once the doors to the dorm were closed; and, from time to time we copulated. However, those were the superficial qualities of the relationship.

Beneath the surface of our relationship, where my feelings laid, was a different matter. I had emotionally disconnected myself from Moe: I did not care how long he stayed away from the dorm; I did not care how much time he and Blake spent together; I did not care what he did or did not do. My one concern was in catching a sexually transmitted disease. I felt that, as long as Moe protected me in that sense, I was content; or, so I believed.

Moe gradually became more open in his relationship with Blake. Although he still maintained that he was using Blake, he went to greater lengths to please him. They ate together in the cafeteria, which in itself was significant. Dining together in prison was comparable to having a candlelight dinner in free society. Under normal circumstances, sharing a meal with someone may not have been important, though when the persons involved were romantically linked at one time and one of the parties was in a committed relationship, having a simple meal took a different twist. Blake also began to regularly attend Moe's basketball games, which, again, was noteworthy.

Yet, despite all that Moe did to sabotage our relationship, I remained loyal to him. My greatest issue lied in my environment. I did not want to begin a relationship with someone else while I was in prison. The prison community was far too small. Nearly everyone knew one another. I felt that, if I ended my relationship with Moe, after a few short months, I would eventually be in a relationship with someone else. I did not want to go from one relationship to the next.

I had to be mindful of whom I shared myself with romantically. My dilemma was not unlike that of women. My sexual and romantic choices were viewed differently than Moe's were. If he was to have sex with multiple partners while confined, he was looked upon as being 'the man'; whereas, if I committed the same sexual choices, I would be deemed a whore. Besides the inequities that existed, I simply did not want to invest the necessary energies in learning the idiosyncrasies of another inmate's personality.

Yet, I understood my sexual appetite. Abstinence was not an option for me. I did not believe that I could remain abstinent indefinitely. I knew that as time passed I would want to have sexual relations, which was one of the reasons I chose Moe as a partner. I needed to be with someone whom I could trust and whom loved me wholly. Moe appeared to possess the qualities I wanted in a mate, though, most importantly, he valued monogamy—or so I thought.

It was a beautiful mid-autumn day. I had gone for a nice, brisk jog earlier during the day. I always felt invigorated after a good run. My lungs seemed able to take in more oxygen, my muscles felt exhilaratingly exhausted, and my mind was clearer. The leaves had mutated into vibrant, red, yellow, and orange colors; signaling their descent-to-come. Moe and I had dinner together; talking and enjoying each other's company as we did when we first met. As we sat at the dining table, we intimately bumped into one another, relishing the feel of the other's touch.

It had been quite some time since we had had sex. We were both burning in our desire for one another. Perhaps a good love-making session would ease some of the tension in our troubled relationship. We haphazardly planned our meeting.

"Where you wanna go?" Moe asked.

"I don't know, not to the back bathroom, though," I said.

There were three bathrooms on the dorm; one bathroom in the dayroom, and two general bathrooms. We had sex in one of the two general bathrooms on occasion. Although, F-Block was a more ideal location, because of the level of comfort it provided, it was riskier to go on F-Block. More people were able to see us going and coming from F-Block, making us more susceptible to being caught.

Only one of the two general bathrooms was fit for using. Fewer people used it, and the dorm porters took greater care in cleaning it. In times past, we had taken bath towels with us and made love on the floor with the bath towels beneath us. It was not the best place to copulate, though we were in prison and had to make do with what we had available.

"How about the bathroom in the dayroom?" Moe offered.

"Umm mmm. I don't know. It's still relatively early in the evening. There will be a lot of people in there," I said.

A half-bathroom was located in the dayroom. It was always clean; perhaps the most clean of the three bathrooms. Though, the problem was its location. It was located in the dayroom where everyone congregated. None of the areas were particularly private, but the bathroom in the dayroom seemed to offer the least amount of privacy. Plus, it was the closest of the three bathrooms to the COs desk, offering little cover should he decide to roam the dorm.

"Well, it's up to you," Moe said.

I was as horny as I could be. I reminded myself that none of the areas were safe, considering at any time a CO could walk in and catch us. Before we had used a look-out person, maybe we could do the same thing this time.

"Do you think Pig would look-out for us if we used the bathroom in the dayroom?" I asked.

Pig was an acquaintance of Moe's. He had looked-out for us previously.

"Hell naw! I ain't asking that nigga to do shit for me! I think his ass is the police!" Moe said.

Pig was a suspicious person. He liked me a lot as a person, but that did not mean that he was not a snitch. In prison, most persons were capable of doing anything to anyone, whether the individual was liked or not. Being in prison was truly an act of survival of the fittest.

"Well, what do you propose? It's too risky to go in there without a look-out," I queried.

"We've done it before in there without a look-out. We just gotta do it fast."

"Yeah, but the time we did it before, we knew more about the CO. This dude is new; he might be a walker," I said, referring to the likelihood that the CO could walk around the dorm checking to ensure that it was being run smoothly.

"It's up to you, Brown."

He had a lot of nerve leaving the decision up to me. I did not know what to do. My carnal-self was under the influence of my hormones and only wanted to satisfy them; while logic dictated that I should wait for a more opportune moment. Yet, being young and horny, I allowed my less than rational side to govern my actions.

"Okay. Let's go to the bathroom in the dayroom," I decided.

Doing anything at all was incredibly risky; though going to the bathroom in the dayroom was simply foolish. Yet, cleanliness and foolishness prevailed, perhaps costing me my freedom and dignity.

~~~

Moe entered the dayroom clad in a maroon bathrobe. He held a bath towel under his arm on which we were to lie. I walked in the dayroom minutes after him in similar apparel. Ordinarily, two guys in bathrobes would look strange, but it was Friday evening, which meant that we inmates were allowed to stay awake until two a.m., pass our usual eleven-thirty curfew. Many of the inmates in the dayroom donned nightwear, allowing us to blend into our environment.

I entered the bathroom first with Moe close behind me. We laid our bath towels on the floor. Moe stepped around our pallet, careful not to step on it with his soiled slippers. He reached for my arm, and gently pulled me toward him. The light in the bathroom was off, though the glow from the moon spilled into the room, creating a soft amber-colored ambience.

We found each others' mouths. We kissed with the fervor of estranged lovers. Moe reached down, untying my robe with one hand, while massaging my neck and back with the other hand. My knees buckled under the feel of his touch. I needed to lie down, or else I would fall. All of my pent up frustrations and passions culminated to that moment.

I reached for Moe, savagely disrobing him. I did not want him, not after all that had taken place with Blake because of him…not after he had slapped me...yet, I needed him. I needed the reprieve that he could give me. If I was a marijuana smoker, I would have asked for a joint. If I drank alcohol, I would have asked for hooch. I was neither, so I resorted to what I was familiar…what I knew he could give me.

The desire to escape my environment was overwhelming…my mind longed to be free of thoughts of prison. I needed to forget the rude, red-faced COs and the advantageous, conniving inmates. I needed to lose touch with the reality of my circumstance…if only for a moment. I needed to make love, despite the obvious consequences.

I gripped his full, muscled chest with two hands, kissing the well-placed tattoos on his pectorals. We descended onto the towels. Moe lied on his back as I mounted him like an experienced jockey. I bent over, allowing my lips to find his lips in the near darkness of the room. While kissing him, I located the neatly wrapped petroleum jelly in the pocket of his robe. I unveiled its contents, slowly caressing it onto his hardened penis. He moaned in ecstasy. I massaged his penis, while kissing him passionately. Pre-cum began to escape from his firmed member. I released his penis, wiping the petroleum jelly from my hand.

I kissed his neck…his ear, sucking sensually on his lobes. He wiggled under the power of my tongue. I smiled…I had located one of his spots. My tongue looped in and around his ear a moment longer, until I felt that he would wiggle himself off of the towel. I reached for the petroleum jelly, placing the remainder of it on my anus. I put the head of his penis on my opening. I relaxed my anal muscles in preparation for his entrance….the bathroom door creaked open. Light flooded into the room, temporarily blinding me. I covered my eyes against the harsh, bright light.

"Come on out, fellas," The CO said.

He stood above us for just a moment before he closed the door behind himself, giving Moe and me an opportunity to dress in private. I remained atop of Moe, straddling him. I was unable to move from my position. I hung my head low, allowing it to rest on his chest. *We had been caught!* I thought in disbelief. Slowly, I dismounted him.

"You okay, Brown?" Moe asked softly in concern.

I could not speak. I did not know what to say. *Was I okay? Could I handle the ramifications of yet another one of my stupid decisions? What would my family think? Did I ruin my chance of going home on probation?*

"Yeah, I'm okay."

I stood up to begin putting on my bathrobe. Moe looked at me as I did so. I had decided that there was no time for me to wallow in pity. I had made my bed; I now had to lie on it, so to express. Moe dressed in silence.

"You ready?"

"Yes."

Moe opened the door of the bathroom. I looked in the dayroom to see how many inmates were present. It was empty, save the CO. He had waited patiently for us to emerge from the bathroom. After handcuffing us, we walked down the hallway to the doors exiting the dorm. Along the way, inmates stood in the doorwell of the big dorm looking as we passed by them. Although most, if not all, of the inmates on the dorm knew of my relationship with Moe, it was humiliating to walk pass them in handcuffs.

"I'ma call Mama and them, Chris," Booger yelled.

I looked up at the sound of his voice. It was customary for friends, or family in our case, to call loved ones of the person being placed in the Hole to let them know that their relative was being placed in the Hole. Even if the situation was the fault of the inmate's, it was always wisest for his family to be made aware of his circumstances. Anything could happen to the inmate while he was in the Hole. I believe the courtesy began as a precaution against CO brutality and mistreatment. It was not uncommon for an inmate to be placed in the Hole unfairly, nor was it particularly uncommon for a healthy inmate to mysteriously die while in the Hole.

"Okay," I said, as I looked into his eyes.

I tried to manage a smile, though I was unable to do so. Although Booger seemed unfazed by the trouble I had gotten myself into, I still felt ashamed. I had promised myself that I would protect him, yet there I was being carted off to the Hole, leaving him alone amongst wolves.

~~~~

Moe and I were taken to S/C-D/C (Security & Discipline Control). Once there, Moe quickly made arrangements for us to be placed in the same room. At that time, inmates who were assigned to work in the Hole were able to place inmates in whatever cell they chose. However, as a consequence of our being in a sex-act, a separation was placed on us, making the arrangement too difficult. Instead, the

inmate-worker placed us in cells across the hall from one another. The arrangement worked out well. We
were able to open the chutes that were used for passing our meals to us as a channel through which to communicate. Several times throughout the day, Moe called my name through the chute.

Again, as Moe was when I was last holed, he was incredible remorseful. I tried to convince him that the fault was not his, but he still blamed himself. He felt that he should have known better than to try to have sex while a new CO worked. I did not blame him. I knew the possible consequences of our actions, and yet I still decided to go along with our plans.

As if things could get no worse for us, we were faced with another assault to our relationship; one that ultimately threatened its cohesiveness.

I sat on my bed reading one of the books that had been left behind by a previous occupant of the cell. Moe called my name through the chute in his door.

"Brown," Moe called in an urgent whisper. I placed down my book as I got up from the bed.

"Yeah," I said, after I had opened my chute.

"I got some bad news," he said in a distraught voice.

Oh, boy! What now?!

"What happened?" I asked in concern.

"Blake did some stupid shit to get in the Hole, so that he can be in the cell with me," he expressed.

"Oh, yeah? What did he do?" I asked, unconcerned.

"Shit, man. I don't know. Aint no tellin' wit his stupid ass! He probably cussed out one of the COs; some little ass shit just to make them put in him the Hole for a couple of days. He paid the trustee a box of cigarettes to put him in the cell with me," Moe expressed.

"He is crazy. There is no way I would go through all of that for a man," I said, senselessly. I was, after all, in the Hole for attempting to engage in sex with a man that I professed not to want romantically. "Does he have any dignity for himself?" I asked, rhetorically.

I usually did not say anything, good nor bad, about Blake's actions, though his behavior was both frustrating and confusing to me. I could not understand his mentality. He was a good-looking, well-educated guy who, according to Moe, came from a wealthy family; yet, he behaved as though he had nothing and came from nothing.

"Man, I told you that nigga is spoiled ass hell. He don't care about going to the Hole 'cause he got flat-time. He stole some shit from his daddy's business and his daddy pressed charges on him."

Moe had explained once before to me the circumstances of Blake's incarceration, and that he was given two years flat-time, which meant that, when his two years of incarceration expired, he would go home. He had a definite sentence, as opposed to an indefinite sentence like many of us who were incarcerated. Being sentenced to flat-time also entailed that Blake did not have to go before the parole board, so being placed in the Hole did not concern him in the least. However, in spite of the knowledge of Blake's criminal offense, his subsequent sentence, and his family's socio-economic status, his behavior still baffled me.

As a poor person myself, I understood the mentality that sometimes accompanied a life of poverty. Poverty was powerful and pervasive; it penetrated to the soul and mind of the individual. Living amongst dilapidated homes, being educated in schools by teachers who did not care about one's success as a student, or wearing soiled, ill-fitting clothes all communicated to the poor person that he was not worthy of a general standard of living. Such living conditions oftentimes rendered the poor person short-sighted; in that, he could not see beyond his circumstances. As such, many of us poor persons fell as prey to self-destructive behaviors, such as drug abuse and criminal activity. A life of poverty had prevented many of us from seeing pass the misery of our situations.

Was there a possibility that Blake's position of privilege had eroded his sensibilities in the same manner that poverty sometimes adversely affects the mentality of the poor?

"I can refuse him as a celly, but they gone give me more time in here for refusing a celly," Moe said, looking through the opening in the door at me.

"Well, it sounds like there's nothing that you can do, but let him come in the cell," I said.

"You not worried about him being in here with me?"

"No…should I be worried?"

"Naw, you ain't got shit to worry about. I ain't even gone talk to that nigga!" Moe proclaimed.

"Okay," I responded nonchalantly.

In truth, I was not at all concerned. My indifference had little to nothing to do with any security I had in myself or my relationship with
Moe, and more do with my feelings about Moe and our relationship. I was weary of dealing with Moe and Blake. I did not care what he did sexually or otherwise. I had always upheld a strong belief in monogamy. The fact that I was apathetic regarding Moe's dealings with Blake was a clear indication that my heart was not in the relationship.

Several hours later, just as Moe had said, Blake moved into his cell. I was lying on the bed reading when he arrived. Minutes after his arrival, Moe came to the chute.

"Brown?" He called.

I got up from the bed and opened the chute. "Yeah," I responded.

"What you doing?" He asked, uneasily. He was trying to gage my feelings.

"Nothing; just reading."

We stood there for a few moments in silence, until I finally said that I was going back to my bed to continue reading.

"Okay...I love you," Moe said.

"I love you, too."

I walked away from the door to return to my book.

~~~

I opened my eyes. It was dark in the cell. The only visible light came from the chute in the door. I laid there in the bed for a moment trying to gather my thoughts. I had been reading. I had planned to close my tired eyes for a brief moment; instead, a moment had turned into several hours. I got up from the bed to stretch my aching back. The thin mattress was horrendous on my back and neck. I felt like I had slept on a slab of concrete.

Instinctively, I walked to the door, looking out the chute. The chute to Moe's cell was closed. For the past few days since we had been in the hole, Moe's chute had remained open. I shook my head in disbelief. I had not really expected Moe and Blake to have sex so soon, especially with me across the hall from them. I thought that Moe had more respect for me than do something so insensitive. I shook my head once more before I walked back to the bed to lie down. Perhaps, Moe sensed my presence or possibly he and Blake were finished copulating, whatever the case the chute to his door opened.

"Brown!" Moe whispered, urgently.

I continued to lie on the bed. I listened to him call my name, though I was not motivated to answer his call.

"Brown!" Moe called again.

I continued to ignore his call. Eventually, he stopped calling. Within minutes, I fell into a deep sleep. A couple of hours later, I heard the chute of Moe's door close; a half an hour or so later, it re-opened. The process continued several times throughout the night until breakfast arrived at 6:30.

The CO rapped on my door.

"Price, you want your breakfast?" He bellowed from the other side of the door. The past few days, I had declined breakfast, but the night's events had given me a different perspective on my relationship with Moe.

"Yeah," I said as I stood up to get my breakfast from the chute. I retrieved the tray, removing the lid. The food was unappealing:

scrambled eggs, two slices of white bread, an apple, and a small carton of milk; much of the same, as always. I placed the tray on the top bunk while I brushed my teeth. I did not like using the facilities in the cell, though I resolved that I had to get used to them, since I would be in the Hole for a while.

Hearing my exchange with the CO, Moe took the opportunity to communicate with me.

"Brown?" He called.

I walked to the door with my toothbrush in my mouth.

"Hold on," I said after reaching the door.

I walked back to the sink to finish brushing my teeth. After I finished, I walked to the chute. I looked across the hall. Moe stood at the door to his cell looking like he had lost his best friend.

"Yeah," I said flatly.

"You want another apple," he asked.

Wow! This was his attempt at an apology?

"No, I'm cool."

We looked through our chutes for a long moment at one another. Although, he looked forlorn, I was unmoved. I was tired of his pity-parties after his mishaps. I had thought that I would be unaffected by Moe's actions of infidelity, yet I was. As I began to think more deeply about what he did, I was pained. In truth, I cared deeply about him. I had given myself mentally, emotionally, and physically to him and only him. I could have easily been with someone else romantically. Moe was not the finest, the most intelligent nor the kindest person in the prison, though, because of the commitment I had made, I remained true to him. I trusted and believed in him; I listened and consoled him when he shared stories of his childhood abuse and neglect; I had encouraged him during the times when he felt devalued.

I was not in-love with Moe. I did not have the Earth-moving, soul-shaking feelings for Moe that I had for Kevon or the other lovers that I would have after him, but I did love Moe. As such, I was saddened that he could betray me as coldly and callously as he had. Though, beyond sadness or any other emotion that I could have attributed toward my feelings for Moe's action, there was disappointment. I expected him to care enough about me not to behave so carelessly.

"Foster gone send me some stuff; I'ma give you whatever he send," Moe said.

By stuff, Moe meant candy or whatever he requested. Although, it was illegal to send things to those in the Hole, it was a common practice for friends of those in the Hole to send them whatever could be smuggled in there. The actions of the friends communicated empathy; the gifts allowed the person in the Hole to feel the care of his friends.

"Naw, I'm okay," I said, before I walked away from the door to eat my breakfast.

~~~~

Blake was released from the Hole later that morning. He had only committed a minor offense, which required just a couple days of being in the Hole; long enough for him to accomplish his objective with Moe. Moe called to me as Blake was being released.

"Brown?"

I was tempted not to answer his call, yet I got up from the bed and walked to the door.

"Yeah."

"I'm sorry, Brown."

I looked at him through the chute. My mother had raised me to accept an apology when one was offered, though I did not want to accept Moe's. I felt mistreated and unappreciated by him. So, instead of accepting his apology, I simply looked at him.

"I told Blake everything…that I love you and only you, Brown…that I'm not giving you up for him or nobody else!"

Just as Moe spoke, Blake appeared at the door, he called to the CO, informing him that his things were packed, and that he was ready to be released. After the CO opened the door, Blake stepped into the hallway. We met one another's eyes. He looked drained and defeated, as if he had been in a war and lost. The CO closed and locked Moe's cell door. Moe's face reappeared in the chute.

"Moe, you should have thought of me and your feelings for me before you slept with Blake. No, actually you should have thought about them before you started this crusade to supposedly hurt him. I'm done with you," I said, calmly through the chute before I walked back to the bed.

"Brown, please, Brown, I'm sorry. I ain't never loved nobody like I love you!" Moe yelled through the chute.

"I'm going to sleep," I yelled from the bed, not giving him the courtesy of going to the door. He called me a few more times before he eventually stopped calling. I know that it was mean of me to ignore him, but I was wounded. I had given him all that I could give; I had been all that he wanted me to be, and, yet he still did as he did. I had enough.

~~~

A few days later, our case was reviewed by the RIB. Although, Moe and I had not been actually caught having sex, we were in the commission of engaging in sex. Therefore, we were convicted of a sexual act and sentenced to L/C (local control). I was imposed a sentence of forty-five days; fifteen days in S/C-D/C and thirty days in L/C. Moe had received a sentence of seventy-five days. Our offense was his second L/C violation. Whenever a person had previously been placed in L/C, they were given thirty additional days to serve.

After serving our time in S/C-D/C, we were transferred to L/C. Local Control was no different than S/C-D/C, in that we were still confined to a cell for a great part of the day. Two or three days of the week we were allowed to shower. We were typically given an hour to shower. After showering, most of the inmates would spend the remainder of their hour in the recreation room; however, I did not.

I always opted to return to my cell. I saw the recreation room as another way in which the COs exercised control over us inmates. If we were "good," we were allowed to go to the recreation room; if we were not, the privilege was taken away from us. Although I did not do anything that was against the rules, I did not want to give the COs the power to further control me with something as miniscule as being allowed to leave my cell to enter another cell for a few short minutes.

~~~

Prison life in itself was monotonous, however being in the Hole was even more so. I busied myself by reading. I also wrote letters to my family. I received a heart-warming letter from Mama. She admonished me to 'straighten up and fly right!' I could see her in my mind's eye, wagging her index finger at me as she spoke the words with a big, bright smile on her face. Mama's letter inspired me to better look at the choices I made and the consequences of my choices.

I eventually forgave Moe. I could not hold ill-emotions in my spirit for long. Moe and I used letter-writing as our conduit of communication. We wrote letters to one another frequently. Through our letters, I gained a better understanding of him and the reasons for his behaviors, or perhaps he just said the words my heart and mind longed to hear. A part of me wanted, and possibly needed, to know that he was remorseful; that he regretted the choices he made, and that he valued me. Such admissions of his made me feel as though the energies and the love that I put into our relationship were not in vain. He apologized profusely, beseeching me to allow us to continue as romantic partners. Yet, I was hesitant.

I realized that I had chosen to be in a relationship with Moe for the wrong reasons. When I had initially decided to be with him, I was impressed by his strength. He handled his responsibilities well, and he seemed very capable of ensuring that my needs were met. All that I had experienced the previous year in the county jail had begun to wear on me. After a year of battling the judicial system; of writing letters to countless people in an attempt to make them aware of my case; of being strong for my family; and, of ensuring that Bradley and my cousins' attorneys represented us well had finally taken its toll on me. I was mentally and emotionally drained. I needed to take an emotional and mental break.

Moe offered me that reprieve. I was able to lie on my bed, and not have to worry about anything other than whichever novel I was engrossed in at the moment. However, I soon learned that I could not abdicate my personal responsibilities onto someone else, even if the person was willing to accept those responsibilities. My responsibilities to myself were mine and mine alone. It would have been nice to have a partner through which I could weather the storms of prison life, though to give Moe control of my life was a mistake. I had to be in control of myself and what affected me. No human being should be given the right to govern another person's life.

Having gained that insight, I came to understand that the best thing I could offer Moe was my friendship.

~~~

The days in L/C passed without incident. I developed an uneventful routine of reading and writing letters. I immersed myself in my books, allowing them to carry me away from the confines of prison. I dreamed and hoped for a better day. I welcomed each day with a recital of Maya Angelou's poem, "Still I Rise." Every day, I allowed the words to reverberate through my spirit, comforting and encouraging me to rise above my circumstances. Until, finally, on a cool day in December, I received a loud bang on the cell door.

"Price! Bunk and jump!" A CO shouted from the other side of the door.

I had hoped to hear those words while in the county jail, though, nevertheless, they were welcomed. I hurriedly gathered my few belongings, walked out of the cell, down the hall, and through the doors of L/C to freedom—of sorts.

I was finally released from the Hole. I served a total of forty-five days of being confined to a 6X9 feet room. I felt invigorated as I walked down the halls to retrieve my belongings from the mailroom. I imagined the feeling that I felt must have been akin to what one feels upon his release from prison. As much as I wanted to fight the euphoria that had come over me, I had to admit that it felt good to be out of the small, dingy room. My footsteps were lighter...my disposition was happier...my spirit was free!

After getting my possessions from the mailroom, I made my way to the dorm where I would reside. I was no longer on 6A with Booger, which was a major disappointment to me. The beds on 6A were all filled, so I was placed on a dorm where a bed was available. I felt that Booger and I were blessed to be on the same dorm with one another, and I had gone and disrupted things.

The yellow piece of paper I had been given upon my release from the Hole stated that I would be housed on 7A. I had heard quite a bit about 7A. It was said to be one of the rougher dorms; the "ghetto" of Delta Unit. The guys on 7A were younger and more prone to being involved in illegal activities; 6A was the opposite, the guys were older and laid-back.

"Hey, Chris! You need help wit' that locker box?" An

unfamiliar person asked.

"No, I got it. Thanks," I responded, smiling in appreciation of the offer.

I continued to make my way to 7A, though before I could walk another two steps, "you made it out! Good to have you back amongst the living!" Another unfamiliar person yelped.

I smiled shyly, "Thank you."

I was not used to people speaking to me so freely.

I was well-known throughout the institution, simply because I was gay. Every gay person was known, whether he wanted to be or not. Yet, it seemed that people whom I did not know, and those who ordinarily were afraid to speak to me, because of Moe's possessive ways, were more inclined to be friendly. Moe, speaking through his insecurities, had warned me of this kind of reception.

"Brown," he had professed through the small opening in my cell door, "those niggas gone really be at you, since I'm locked up in this mutha fucka. They thinkin' I aint gettin' out of here. My fake-ass friends and all them niggas that was too scared to holla at you 'cause of me, gone be in yo' face. Just watch and see!" He had prophesied.

Moe had been given the position of trustee, which allowed him to leave his cell in the Hole to walk to other cells without being supervised. Although he and I had a separation on us for being caught in a sex act, he was unafraid; choosing to live by his own rules as usual.

I searched his face, reading his eyes. His words, spoken in his deep, raspy voice, sounded sure, yet his eyes communicated something altogether different. He was afraid; worried that I would choose to be with someone else.

I met his eyes with my own, in a gentle, yet firm voice, "I'm not thinking about these dudes; none of them."

He half-smiled in a manner that only he could, his eyes brightened for a moment, our hearts connected for a brief instant in a place that knows no time, no boundaries, no limitations…and then, as suddenly as it appeared, it was gone…

"Yeah, that's what you say now," he retorted before walking away.

As I walked down the corridor to retrieve my possessions, I was in awe of how accurately Moe had predicted the other inmate's reception of me. I had finally made it to 7A. I walked up the long staircase and down the hall to the CO's desk. I gave her my yellow slip, indicating that I was moving to the dorm. After making my presence known to her, I went into the big dorm in search of my bed.

As was the case before, I was in the middle-row. I did not fret over where I slept, however. I vowed to myself that this would be the last time that I went to the Hole. Mama's words resounded in my mind, 'straighten up and fly right, my grandson!' I would make her proud.

I went about the task of getting my possessions in order. I made my bed, and then took a nice hot shower. I quickly put on my state uniform. I exited the dorm in search of my cousin. I went to 6A. I was not allowed to go on the dorm anymore, since I no longer lived there. I paced up and down the hall, until I saw someone who lived on the dorm.

"Hey. Can you get Booger for me?" I asked the stranger.

"Yeah, how you doing, Chris?" The guy asked.

I had no idea who he was, but I responded anyway.

"I'm doing okay."

"I know you're happy to be out of the hole!"

"Yeah, I am." I said smiling.

"Hold on. I'll run up there to get him."

"Thank you." I yelled as he ran up the stairs.

After a couple of minutes, Booger came down the stairs. I missed my cousin! I realized just how much so when I saw his face.

"Hey there!" I said as I walked to him.

"What's up, cousin!" He exclaimed.

I gave him a big hug once we were close enough, despite the rule against such intimate behavior. I did not care about the rule. He was my cousin, and I missed him terribly.

"When you get out?" Booger asked.

"Just a little while ago; long enough for me to take a shower and to put my stuff away. I'm about to go to the barbershop now. My hair looks a mess. What are you doing...letting yours grow out?" I asked, touching his thick mound of hair.

"Yeah, I'ma get it braided."

"You know, they say we can't let it grow longer than three inches."

"Yeah, I know. I'ma just keep it braided, so if it gets longer than that, they won't know."

"Moe said sometimes they make you take the braids out just to mess with you and see how long it is."

"Uhn huh. I ain't worried. If they say something, I'ma just get it cut. It'll grow back." He reasoned.

We had walked a full lap around the interior of the institution.

"Alright," Booger said once we had reached his dorm. "I'ma finish my game. I was playing bridge wit the fellas.

"Okay. I'm going to get my haircut. I'll see you tomorrow. I love you." I said as we hugged, parting ways.

"I love you, too."

I walked around to the barbershop to get my haircut. Kevin, my barber, was working.

"A, Kevin, can you get me in?" I asked, leaning over the half-door into the barbershop.

"Fa sho, Chris. Give me about five minutes. Cool?"

"Yeah, that's cool. I'm going to the library to get a couple books. I'll be right back."

"Aight."

I was glad that he was able to get me in. I did not like getting my hair cut by other barbers. There was too great of chance that they would give me a bad haircut. Though as bad as I needed a haircut I would have taken the chance, if Kevin had said that he could not cut it. Kevin was one of the best barbers in the institution. It had been an entire two months since I last had a haircut. My hair resembled Kunte Kente's from the movie, "Roots"!

~~~

I was lying down on my bed reading when he approached my bunk. I was so enthralled in the book that I did not hear him speak to me. He hit my foot to get my attention. He startled me. I moved the book from in front of my face. I gazed down towards him.

"What's up, man?"

"Aww, what's up?" I responded. I knew him or, rather, I knew of him.

"Ain't you Booger's cousin?"

"Yeah"

"I'm Tyler. I know yo whole family!" He said smiling.

"Yeah, I remember you. Austin introduced us when Booger and I first got here."

Austin is my oldest maternal cousin. He was actually responsible for Booger and me being on the same dorm. Our family had informed him that we would be arriving at the institution soon, so he made arrangements with one of the inmates who worked in the Unit to place us on the same dorm. He was transferred to another part of the institution the day after our arrival. Booger and I did not really have an opportunity to bond with him; since he was gone so soon after we arrived.

"Aww, yeah! That's right! Man, my memory is fucked up. I be forgettin all kinds of shit!" Tyler said laughing.

I laughed with him, not really knowing how to respond to his statement. I had not paid close attention to him before, but seeing him so close I saw how attractive he was. He was about my height, but he had a thicker, more muscular frame than my own. His face was round, with chubby, baby-like cheeks. His face was the color of rich, milk chocolate with innocently set doe-like, dark brown eyes.

"You just got out of the hole, huh?" He asked.

"Yeah, I thought they were going to put me back on 6A, but I guess there weren't any beds available." I said.

"Nigga, where you come from talkin' like that?! All proper and shit! Don't know nigga talk like that!" He laughed.

I laughed along with him. Not so much because of what he said, but because he was so amused with what he said. He laughed as though he had just heard the funniest joke ever.

"Man, you in the dungeon now! You go have to talk like one of us 'round here!" He said through fits of laughter.

He did not know me. Although I spoke with Standard English, I had a real potty mouth; I cursed like a sailor, so to express. His laughter was contagious. He really seemed to enjoy himself. His face lit up every time he laughed. His round cheeks rose high on his face, forcing his eyes shut, tears slowly escaping from them. I began to laugh at the sight of him. I could barely breathe; I had laughed so fully. I did not know exactly why I was laughing, but I knew that it felt good. I had not laughed so wholly since before I was incarcerated. It felt wonderful to reconnect with my own laughter.

After about two minutes of hearty laughter, we were able to continue talking.

"Yeah, man, me and Austin came down here together on the same van: me, him, Donald, James, and a few other niggas." He said enthusiastically.

"Did y'all?" I asked.

"Yeah, I grew up with Tookie, Booger, Jaden, and Raylin! We all went to Keyser together. I use to like Tookie's chocolate ass! She still sexy?!"

"Tookie or Raylin?!" I asked in surprise.

It was not that I thought Tookie was unattractive; she was a very pretty girl. Though, I had always heard people refer to her older sister, Raylin, as being pretty. Perhaps, I was more accustomed to people referring to Raylin as being pretty, because she and I were so close to one another as young children. Everyone always seemed to either remark on her long hair, how well she danced, or how intelligent she was. I quite naturally assumed that Tyler was referring to her.

"Naw, Tookie, man! Raylin was cool, but Tookie is sexy ass hell to me! And, she got long ass legs, too!" Tyler said excitedly.

He was definitely referring to Tookie. Raylin stood at about 5'3; Tookie was 5'6, though her lengthy legs made her appear taller.

"Yeah, she looks good. She has a daughter, now. In fact, her daughter just turned three years old on the seventh of November."

"Yeah?" Tyler laughed amusingly. "You got any pictures

of yo' family? I ain't seen none of them in years."

"Yeah, let me get my photo album from my locker box."

"Cool, man! I'ma grab mine, too!"

Sharing photos was a sign of friendship. Typically inmates only allowed others who they liked to view pictures of their loved ones. I retrieved my photo album from my locker box and followed Tyler into the ten-man annex where he slept. His bed was on the top bunk, closest to the entrance of the annex. As I entered the annex, I saw that he had already jumped on his bunk.

"Come on in," he said as he saw me approaching. "A, y'all this my dude, Chris." He said, introducing me to the other guys who slept in the annex.

"All hell! Not another pretty boy! We got our hands full with this one!" One of the White guys said laughing.

"Well, get used to another one, mutha fucka!" Tyler said as he laughed.

"No, I'm just teasing," the White guy said sincerely. "It's nice to meet you. I'm Frank." He said extending his hand.

"Nice to meet you, too." I said, shaking his extended hand.

"Hey, Chris!" The other guys yelled and waved.

The institution was racially divided, so that there was an even amount of Whites and Blacks throughout the prison. The ten-man annex, for example, consisted of five Black inmates and five White inmates. Latinos were classified as either White or Black, depending upon the number of the other two races in the institution. There were no other races present at Lima, though if there were, they, too, would have been designated as either White or Black, according to the racial composition of the prison. The administrators felt that the best way to prevent race riots and to encourage the inmates to get along with one another was to force the different races to live together; as opposed to allowing them to choose their bunk/cell mates according to their race or familiarity with one another.

It was refreshing to see how well Tyler and the other guys got along. Such was not the case in other areas of the dorm, or on other dorms in the institution. Generally expressing, Black inmates had power over White inmates at Lima. There were some White guys that were respected;
though such respect was uncommon. Most of the White guys were exploited for either money or sex. Some of the Black guys would force or intimidate the White guys into having sex with them. Those Whites who were not sexually desirable to the Black guys were extorted financially; they would be made to surrender their commissary, or things they acquired in food/clothes boxes.

Tyler, however, was a genuine friend with the White guys whom shared the annex with him. He did not partake in such behavior as the other Black guys in the institution.

"Man, I know all yo' people!" Tyler said again as he looked at the photos of my family.

I laughed at his enthusiasm over seeing familiar faces.

"Who is that?" He asked.

"That's my ex-girlfriend, Karen." I said.

"You got a girlfriend. You ain't always been a..." He stammered trying to find the right word.

"Gay. Say, 'gay'. It's not polite to call someone a fag," I said, "And, yeah, I've had a few girlfriends, but she's my ex. We broke up in the county." I said.

"Damn, y'all did? I know that hurt. Me and my girl broke up, too. This place a mutha-fucka...she a good girl, though; she just couldn't handle having her dude being locked up and not knowing when he comin' home. I gotta understand that, you know? She got needs, too. We got a son together, though!

That little nigga look just like me! You got any kids?"

I felt sorry for him. Judging by the look on his face and the sadness in his voice, he seemed to really love his ex-girlfriend. I did not know what
he had done to be in prison, but I prayed that he would be released soon, so that he could be a father to his son and perhaps a partner to his girlfriend. It was evident to me that he was not yet over their separation.

"Naw, I don't have any kids, at least none that I know of," I said smiling. "Karen got pregnant when we were in college, but she aborted the baby." I shared.

"Damn, nigga, you was in school?! I knew you was a smart ass dude! I'm going to school here. Why she have a abortion?"

"I went to Central State and UT," I said, answering his first question.

"I heard Central is off the hook…parties and shit all the time!" Tyler said.

"Yeah, it was a lot of partying going on, but I think that's any college. I only stayed there one quarter, though. I was coming home every weekend…I missed my family too much, so I transferred to UT," I said.

"Man, I wouldna never came home! All them women and liquor! You ain't never say why yo' girl had a abortion." Tyler reminded me.

"Oh, yeah, that's right…It's kind of hard to say. I guess, we were too young and her father wanted her to have an abortion. She asked me what I wanted to do, but I took too long to respond. I was indecisive, so she had the abortion on Christmas Eve; my daddy's birthday."

"Damn, I know that had to be hard. Me and my girl…I mean ex-girl had my son when we was young, too; but, man,

I'm glad she had him."

"Yeah, I kind of wished Karen had kept ours, too. Maybe I wouldn't be in here. I probably would've been somewhere taking care of him or

her hopefully." I surmised.

Tyler and I continued to talk for hours. I felt like he and I had been friends all of our lives. I told him about my desire to continue pursuing my college education. He encouraged me to enroll in the University of Findlay. According to Tyler, instructors from the University taught at Lima five days a week during the evenings. Students were able to achieve Associate's and Bachelor's degrees in business and social services.

I was very interested in the social services program. While attending Central State and the University of Toledo, I had majored in Social Work, like my daddy. I did not know exactly how soon I was going to go home, but while I was there I wanted to do all that I could to be better myself. I made a mental note to go to the unit on Monday to enroll in school. I concluded that the best thing that could come from my time there would the completion of my education, or at the very least accumulating some educational credits until I was awarded super-shock probation.

Chapter Fifteen

The holiday season had come and gone, bringing an end to yet another year. Holidays were largely uneventful in prison. Thanksgivings fell short of the traditional gratitude accompanied by the day; Christmas and New Years were void of the festive exuberance of the season of giving and new beginnings.

For me, however, the New Year looked bright and promising. I had been at the institution for a little over six months, which allowed for enough time for me to file super-shock probation. One of the criteria for filing was that the inmate must be incarcerated for at least six months. I was going to wait another few months, since I had been in the hole twice already during that six month period.

I started school at the University of Findlay during the first week of January. It felt great to be in school, again. I had not realized how much I missed the joy of learning new things. I started the first semester off by taking four classes, primarily prerequisites to my actual degree. Although, I had taken a few classes prior to being incarcerated, not all of the credits transferred from the other institutions. I really did not care about receiving credit for the classes I took at Central and UT. The only thing that mattered was that I was able to do something positive. I was disappointed with myself for having gone to the hole. I needed to do something that was more in tuned with who I really was as a person.

Tyler and I had become great friends. My friendship with him proved to be a real blessing from God. I had not fully realized how desperately I needed someone like him in my life. In many ways, Tyler was like my family I had left at home. He was trustworthy, kind, understanding, and, most importantly, he cared about my well-being in much the same manner as my family had.

Moe was still in the hole, though he was due to be released soon. While I still cared for Moe, I felt that our relationship had run its course. It was time for us to move on. Moe, on the other hand, felt that he still had a fighting chance with me. He vowed to get me back and to be a better partner. I tried to dissuade him in his pursuit, but he was unrelenting.

Although it was illegal to communicate with persons in the hole, many of us still did. The windows of L/C faced the Center Yard. At any given time, I, along with a number of other inmates, would walk outside and inconspicuously attempt to talk with those who were confined in L/C.

"Moe!" I yelled with my back turned away from the windows in an attempt to camouflage the fact that I was talking to an inmate confined in the hole.

"What's up, Brown?" Moe yelled back.

"Not much. How you feelin?" I asked.

"I'm cool. Who is that you got with you? Is that little Tyler?" Moe asked in pseudo-ignorance. He and Tyler were good friends.

"What's up Moe-Moe, man?" Tyler yelled towards the window, smiling from ear to ear.

"Nothing, man; in here trying to survive. How come yo ass ain't been out here to see about me, nigga? I thought we was better than that!" Moe yelled, his attitude had changed abruptly.

"Nigga, I told yo' ass the last time you got in some shit that I wasn't go be coming out and getting' hemmed up. Stay out of trouble and yo ass ain't got to worry about nobody coming out here to see you!" Tyler said angrily, unyielding to Moe's attitude.

I had not expected Moe to respond to Tyler in the manner that he had. After all, they were friends, but it was always difficult to judge Moe's moods.

"Yeah, whatever, nigga!" Moe said, dismissing what Tyler said. "I heard about y'all love birds! What, y'all came out here to rub in my face how much y'all in love or something?!" Moe yelled sinisterly.

"What?!" I said in irritation.

I was already bothered by the way Moe treated Tyler; someone who had placed his freedom in jeopardy to see about him, so it took very little for me to explode. In my anger, I turned to face his window, forgetting about possibly being seen by a CO. "You see, nigga! That's why I don't like fucking with yo'ass! Every time I try to help yo ass and deal with yo' shit, you do or say some stupid ass shit."

"A, man, a CO gone hear you!" Tyler urged.

I ignored Tyler's whispered pleas, even though they were for my benefit. I continued my rampage.

"I don't have to come out here to see how you are, but I do! Ain't none of yo other so-called friends out here checkin' on you and the ones that come out here, yo silly ass treat like shit! I ain't coming out here no more!" I said, walking away.

"Brown! Brown! I was just joking…I'm sorry!" Moe yelled through his window.

"I know damn well you are!" I said as I walked into the institution, ignoring his last minute apologies.

Once inside the institution, my anger had begun to subside

some, but I was still incensed by Moe's words. Rumors had begun to circulate around the institution that Tyler and I were together romantically. I understood that people were going to talk, but it angered me that I could not even have a friendship with a guy without them talking. My entire life I had heard men say how women gossiped, but I did not know true gossip until I entered the walls of Lima--and those doing the talking were not women.

"Man, you crazy as hell!" Tyler laughed as he ran to catch up with me.

"What?! He gets on my nerves with that shit!" I said, fuming.

"Man, you crazy! All this time, I thought you was quiet and nice!" Tyler said in between fits of laughter. Tyler had never seen me upset before.

I laughed. "I am nice, but I'm not going to let him walk all over me! He is always trying to play the victim, like everybody has done something to him and owes him something!" I vented.

"Man, why do you fuck with these niggas?" Tyler asked in a serious tone.

"Huh?" I asked. I knew what he had asked. I just did not know why he had asked the question. Tyler and Moe were very good friends, yet Tyler, like so many other persons, knew about the issues in my relationship with Moe.

"You just don't seem like you would be caught up in no bullshit like that." Tyler said.

"What do you mean by 'bullshit', being gay or being in a relationship with Moe?"

"All of it! Moe my dude, but you don't seem like the kind of dude that would be caught up in all that shit that you and him went through, and you don't seem like you would be gay, either." Tyler expressed.

"You think being gay is bullshit?" I asked him.

"I'm just saying, you could have any woman you want...a woman would love to have you, and you fuck around with these dudes." Tyler said.

I understood Tyler's perspective, though I was not foolish enough to think that if I was heterosexual, I would have less, or any, romantic problems. Straight people went through the same things that gay people went through in their romantic relationships: fights, arguments, infidelities, break-ups, and make-ups. As much as I would have liked not to think it, I may have encountered the same partner in a woman as I did in Moe. It simply was not guaranteed that I would find emotional bliss as a heterosexual.

"I cared a great deal for Moe. There was a tender side of him that was beautiful to me. I shouldn't have stayed in the relationship as long as I did, but at the time I felt like I could handle the other stuff—at least until he and Blake slept together in the hole. Regarding being gay: I don't know that a person chooses to be gay. I mean, who would intentionally choose to live a life of homosexuality amid prejudice and discrimination? My sexual and romantic choices are just a part of who I am. In homosexual relationships, there can be beautiful moments
filled with love, understanding, compassion, and a true meeting of spirits, just as there can be in heterosexual relationships. I think that many of you straight people sometimes fail to see the other side of gay relationships. Instead, y'all tend to focus on the negative aspects and what the Bible says about homosexuality."

"You just seem too good of a dude to be gay." Tyler said.

"Huh, too good?" I asked rhetorically. "None of us are too good for anything. Society has determined that gay people are the scum of the earth; and, consequently, it has brought about this thinking of better than and worse than amongst heterosexuals and some misguided gay people. In truth, no one person is better than another person; and no people are better than another people, including gay and straight people. Who are we, as flawed human beings, to say who is good and who is bad? That responsibility should be left to someone or something perfect, and God is the only being whom I know to be perfect."

"Yeah, I get what you sayin'…I just would rather you be with a woman." Tyler said obstinately.

Our conversation was the first of many that we would have about homosexuality, specifically, my sexual orientation. In many ways, Tyler's position reminded me of the way some of my cousins felt about my sexuality. Because of my cousins' and Tyler's love of me and society's negative portrayal of homosexuality, they could not understand my relationships with men.

~~~

"A, Chris!" Someone yelled as Tyler and I left the cafeteria after lunch.

I turned in the direction of the person's voice, "Huh?"

As Moe had correctly surmised, ever since I had been released from the hole, quite a few guys had been approaching me. I was considered "free game", as some of them had the audacity to express to me. Other persons in my position may have been flattered by all the attention that I received. Prisons, after all, held some of the finest Black men in the nation. Whatever one's flavor, whether he was dark-hued, light-complexioned, or somewhere in between, he could have been found in prison. The best of Black America's male minds, its most athletic, and its most artistic were caged within America's penal institutions, yet I was unmoved by the presumed praise.

It was not an honor to be sought after by a bunch of men who wanted to be with me simply to fulfill their sexually deprived needs. I valued myself far too much to be regarded as a sex tool. If I was going to be in a relationship, I wanted it to be with someone with whom I could build something substantial; a relationship that would exist beyond the walls of prison.

"Can I talk to you?" the guy asked.

His name was Michael. We met when I first arrived at Lima.

"Hold on, Tyler. Let me see what Michael wants." I stood in front of Delta Unit as I waited on Michael.

"What's up?" He asked smiling. His bright smile looked radiant against the backdrop of his smooth dark skin.

"Not much. What's up with you?"

I liked Michael. He was different from many of the other guys in the institution. He was polite, and he never treated me as though I were an object. I respected him for that.

"You got any plans later this evening?"

"I need to do some reading for this class I'm taking, but nothing other than that. Why?"

"You wanna watch a game with me in the gym? They got two A-league teams playing."

I laughed to myself. *He was asking me out on a date.* The thought amused me. Since I had been in prison I had been placed in the role of a woman. Although I had had date-like experiences with guys before my incarceration, they did not seem like dates in the sense that they did while I was in prison.

"I don't know...can I let you know after I leave dinner? I

need to see how much reading I get done." As much as I liked Michael, I did not know if I wanted to start any kind of a relationship with anyone. My ordeal with Moe had left me leery of beginning something new. Suddenly, I remembered that I left Tyler waiting! I quickly turned away from Michael, scanning the area in search of Tyler. I did not see him.

"Did you see where Tyler went?"

"He took off that way when I started walking toward you. What's up with yo dude?"

I instinctively turned around again looking for Tyler, though I knew he would not be there.

"I don't know." I said, perplexed by his departure. "Okay. I'll let you know what's up after dinner." I said absentmindedly. I had to check on Tyler. I was concerned about him.

"Okay. I'll see you." Michael said smiling.

I half-smiled back, though my mind was far from Michael or our so-called date. I needed to check on my friend. I immediately walked back to the dorm. I went into the ten-man. As I turned the corner leading into the annex, I saw Tyler lying on his bed. I sighed in relief. I did not know what to think. I had become a worry-wart ever since I had learned that I delivered the fatal shot leading to Adam's death. The least little thing sent me into a panic.

"Tyler!" I said in a slightly contained voice. "What happened? Why did you leave?"

Whatever his reason, I could tell that it was not too severe for he was reading from his school textbook.

"Nothing. I had some reading to do." He said, continuing to read.

"Boy, you must be crazy if you think I'm going to believe that you just up and left without a single word, because you had to study!" I said incredulously.

I stood there for a moment waiting on him to respond. After a few moments without a response, I cleared my throat. "Uh, hello? I'm still here."

"Look, man, I told you how I feel about you and these niggas. I don't think you should be fuckin wit 'em."

I spoke without thinking. "Aww! Ain't that cute? You're concerned about my well-being?" I said teasingly.

I should not have teased him. He was genuinely concerned about me.

"I'm just saying," he said irritated. "If you want to keep going through shit like you did with Moe-Moe and end up messing up yo chance of going on home on shock, that's on you." Tyler replied defensively.

I understood his concern. If the situation was reversed, I would feel the same way that he did. I absolutely would not want him to be involved in something or with someone that I knew would interfere with his being released. Yet, I was obstinate. While I knew that Tyler's concern was legitimate, I felt that he was attempting to control my actions or my choice of friends in the same way that some of my family members had.

Although my dad had embraced my sexuality to a certain extent, he did not like that I chose the friends I had, specifically Erin. He felt that Erin's flamboyance would ruin my positive reputation in the community.

My cousin, Andre, thought much like my dad, except that he did not embrace my sexuality. While Andre and I are first cousins, we were raised as though we were brothers. After our other aunts and cousins had moved out of our grandparent's home, Andre and I stayed there with our mothers. For several years, Andre was like the younger brother that I did not have, until my brother Jeremiah was born. I saw Andre's stand concerning my sexuality as the action of an over-protective younger brother.

While I appreciated the love my dad, Andre, and Tyler had for me, I would not allow them to dictate my actions.

"Tyler, I'm cool. I'll be alright. Besides, Michael isn't like Moe, anyway." I reasoned.

"Yeah, okay." Tyler said unconvincingly.

~~~~

Moe was finally released from the hole after serving nearly three months. However, his freedom was short-lived. Two days after his release, he was placed back in the hole.

"Chris, Moe-Moe back in the hole!" Cameron said to me as I left the gym. I had begun working out regularly since my release from the hole. Working out had become my way of regulating the stressfulness of being incarcerated.

"What! What did he do?"

"They got him in there for extortion."

"Extortion?"

"Yeah. Him and a White guy was in the shower, and Moe started beating up the dude, so he could get the dude's commissary." Cameron explained.

"That's a shame. Moe ain't gone ever learn."

"I told Moe-Moe to quit fucking wit that dude!" Cameron slipped.

"What? Moe had been bothering him for some time?"

"Yeah," Cameron said hesitantly. "Every since he got out of the hole." Cameron looked suspicious, like he wasn't telling the full story.

"There something you ain't saying. What? Was Moe

trying to have sex with him or something?"

"Man, I ain't getting in it!"

"Listen, I ain't the least bit concerned about what Moe did or does! That part of our relationship is long over! Hell, I know how his ass is now!" I said hotly.

While Moe was in the hole the time before, a number of people had come to me with stories of Moe's conquests. Apparently, Blake was not the only person in their relationship that was unfaithful.

"Yeah, well, he want to know if you can send him something? They talking about riding him out to another camp."

I sighed deeply. It was always something with Moe.

"Yeah, come by my dorm this evening. I got some granola bars and Little Debbie's you can send him."

Although Moe and I were not together anymore, I still felt a sense of loyalty to him. I did not risk going to the hole by going outside to speak to him every day as I had before, but I did what I could to make his time a little more bearable while he was in the hole.

~~~

Rumors began to circulate more and more regarding the sincerity of my friendship with Tyler. Most of the inmates refused to believe that he and I could have a genuine friendship. The rumors upset me. Had something been said about me, I would not have cared, though, because Tyler was involved, the rumors affected me. Tyler was unfazed by them, however. His mentality was incredibly mature, especially considering that the rumors were about homosexuality. I expected him to be perturbed, but he felt that the only thing that mattered was that we knew the untruthfulness of the rumors.

It irritated me that everything I did centered on my sexuality. I could not be friends with someone without something being made of my association with the person: if I smiled as I spoke to someone, it was rumored that I wanted the person sexually; if I sat at a table in the cafeteria with someone other than a gay person, it was rumored that we were romantically linked; if my line of vision happened to cross someone's path while I worked out, a rumor began that I was attracted to the person. It was even rumored that Booger and I were sexual partners!

As such, Tyler was not the only person it was rumored that I was involved with; though, because I spent the bulk of my time with him, our friendship became the focus of most of the scrutiny. The unwanted attention was what I assumed the life of a celebrity to be, though without the money or fame that accompanied such a status.

~~~

Each unit within the institution had a privilege housing dorm. Delta Unit's privilege housing dorm was D3. In order to be placed on the waiting list for privilege housing, an inmate could not have any hole-bound infractions for six months. The benefit of being on privilege housing was that the entire dorm consisted of cells or small cubicles, which offered far more privacy than traditional big dorms. The other advantage was that the inmates were allowed to have their own personal television in their cells.

Booger and Tyler had long since been residents of D3. After being released from the hole, I had to wait several months before I was allowed to request that my name be added to the waiting list.

The waiting period had come and gone. Then, finally, I received a yellow slip from the CO late one afternoon, informing me that I was to move to D3. I was ecstatic about the move. I missed being around Tyler and Booger; eating breaks and talking late at night until the CO hollered, "lights out!"

Michael had also placed his name on the waiting list. Ironically, he and I, along with two other guys, moved to D3 at the same time. Rarely were so many beds available on D3 at one time. Usually a bed became available once every couple of months, but we were lucky.

Over the course of the past few months, Michael and I had grown closer. He proved to be the man that I thought him to be. He was kind, loving, respectful, and incredibly understanding. When I was not spending time with Tyler and Booger or studying, I was with Michael.

We thoroughly enjoyed one another's company. We took long walks on the East Yard, where less people congregated and where we had more quality time to ourselves. We shared our fears and joys, and our hopes for the future. In addition to our romantic attraction to one another, we had become very good friends.

I shared a fantasy-game with Michael that Tyler had introduced to me. The game was called, "daydreaming". Tyler and I loved the game. We introduced Booger and a few of our friends to the game, but they did not seem to be interested in it. The game entailed daydreaming about what our lives would be like upon our release. Tyler and I thought and talked about home constantly, so for us "daydreaming" was just an extension of the conversations we shared with one another every day.

For many inmates, as I suspected was the case with Booger and the others, "daydreaming" was a difficult game to engage in, because it forced the persons to think and imagine a life outside of prison; which was the last thing many of them wanted to do. One of the keys to surviving being incarcerated was by forgetting one's life prior to prison. Though for Tyler and I, the reverse was true: remembering the lives we had and the family we left behind was a means of inspiration for us. Our memories fueled our positive decisions and acted as an emblem of hope for us during the difficult times.

"Okay," I said to Michael as we walked the perimeter of the East Yard. *"Imagine you are at home... on the streets."*

"Cool." Michael responded in his smooth, baritone voice.

"It's a beautiful sunny day in late spring. The sun is shining brightly; a soft breeze is blowing; the temperature is a pleasant 74 degrees. You were released from prison six months ago, so you've had time to establish yourself: you landed a job in your field as an electrician; you have a nicely decorated apartment; and, you have a new, black Cadillac Escalade.

You are feeling good and looking good. You just got your hair cut: it's faded close, but not so close that your brush waves aren't able to be seen. You are casually dressed: you have on a pair of white jersey sweatpants, with a sky blue stripe down the center of them. Your gym shoes are the exact same sky blue, as is your white/blue gym shirt. You are wearing a few pieces of choice jewelry, nothing too gaudy: a stylish, white-gold, Movado watch on your left wrist and a bracelet on right wrist; a white-gold chain; diamond earrings in both ears; and a diamond ring on your right hand. Your broad shoulders and thick muscled arms look sexy as hell under your shirt.

You drive your Escalade to Pearson Park. You scan the park. Finally, in the distance, you spot them. You step out of your truck, walking towards the crowd of people. The lush, green grass feels good under your feet. The pink and white buds of trees in full bloom create a wonderful aroma in the air. As you get closer to the crowd, the smell of the season is replaced by the scent of meat being bar-b-qued. Everyone is enjoying themselves; children are running and jumping around; the melodious sound of laughter fills your ears; the soft sounds of the O'Jays gently flow to the symphony of birds.

'There go Big Mike right there!' A cousin yells.

'What's up, man!' You reply exuberantly, as the two of you shake hands.

'Come here, Mikey baby!' Your mother calls, placing serving dishes of strawberry shortcake and banana pudding on a picnic table. 'This is your cousin, Patricia. We used to spend the summers together in Alabama at Big Mama's! Patricia, this is my baby, Mikey!'

You feel the love from your family...you look good...you feel good..."

"SssssSsssSssss," a whistle was blown by a CO.

"Clear the yard!" Another CO shouted.

"Dang, they're clearing the yard already? It's only six o'clock. The yard is not supposed to close for another hour and a half," I said, quizzically.

"Move out!" A third CO shouted.

"I wonder what's up. They ain't never got this many COs out here to clear the yard," Michael said, as we walked toward the institution.

As we entered the prison, "get to your dorm, now!" A CO yelled.

The halls were packed with inmates returning to their dorms. Chaos was amuck. Michael and I walked in the direction of D3, though the throngs of inmates in the halls made the journey painstakingly slow.

"I wonder where Booger and Tyler are. I need to check to see if they're in the gym...they said something about going to play basketball," I said, turning in the direction of the gym.

"Baby, we need to head back to the dorm," Michael said, gently grabbing my arm. "Something's up. Look at all of these COs they got out here. I ain't never seen this many COs and some of them don't even work here. We better get to the dorm. Boo and Tyler are probably there already."

I did not want to go to the dorm without making certain that Booger and Tyler were not in the gym, yet I heeded Michael's advice, "okay," I said, turning back in the direction of D3.

As soon as we walked onto the dorm, we were met by several COs and many other black-clothed officers with guns.

"Get the fuck to your cells and on your fucking beds, now!" One of the black-clothed officers yelled.

Although the institution's COs were not the picture of cordiality, they were not as rude as the black-clothed officers. Those of us inmates that were in the halls turned to look at the black-clothed officer, as if to say, "who in the hell are you talking to?"

Our dorm CO saw the potential problem and de-escalated it before a bigger one began.

"Come on, guys. Can you go to your rooms, please?!" Our CO yelled, raising his hands as though in submission.

We lingered in the hall a moment longer before we began to walk to our individual cells.

"I'll talk to you in a minute," Michael said.

"Okay," I responded.

Booger and I shared a cell together with two other guys. When I entered the room, Booger was sitting on his bunk bed.

"Man, these mutha-fuckas crazy!" Booger said as soon as he saw my face.

"I know. What happened? Why did they make us come back to our dorm?" I asked.

"Shiit, I'on know! Me and Tyler was at the gym playin' some ball and a bunch of damn COs came in talkin' crazy and shit, tellin' us we had to get back to the dorm!" Booger said.

Gonzalez, our Latino cell-mate, leaned in to whisper, "I heard something happened to one of the counselors in Gamma Unit."

"What do you mean 'something happened'?" I asked.

"See, what I hear is that that short, stout counselor was killed, but that's all I'm saying?" Gonzalez shared.

"What the fuck!" Booger exclaimed. "You talkin about the Black one?"

"What!" I said shockingly, as I looked from Gonzalez to Booger. "Who told you that?"

"I don't know…I ain't sayin," Gonzalez stammered.

Gonzalez was something of a prison-know-it-all; he knew all of the gossip that went on in the prison. No matter what it was, if there was something to be known, one could trust that Gonzalez knew about it.

"Well, who killed her, since you can't say anything else?" I asked, exasperatedly.

Gonzalez liked to have information teased from him. It was all a part of a game he played. In truth, he could not wait to share whatever he learned. One simply had to be very patient and play his game with him.

"I hear some of the guys on Sigma Unit had something to do with it," Gonzalez whispered.

"What did they do?" I asked.

"I hear a bunch of 'em raped her and then killed her," Gonzalez answered.

"Oh, my God! Are you serious?!" I asked, not wanting to believe him.

"I'm tellin' ya, man," Gonzalez said, as though his word could not be debated.

Our dorm CO blew his whistle and yelled, "Count time!"

Seconds later, he walked pass, counting the number of us in the cell before he moved on to the next cell. After the CO counted us, another CO yelled for us to stand outside of our cells. After exiting our rooms, we all stood single-file outside of our cell.

"You...you...you... and you, follow me!" An officer in black commanded.

"You...you...you...follow me!" Another officer barked.

The officers in black took groups of us to different areas of the dorm, until all ninety-six of us had been stripped searched; our bodily cavities inspected and our personal belongings rummaged. Booger and I, along with several other guys, were taken to the dayroom.

"Take off every fuckin' piece of clothing you have on! When I come to you, squat and spread your fuckin cheeks! After I examine you, put your clothes back on, and stand by the door in a fuckin single-file line!" A tall officer in black yelled.

I did not like being talked to in the manner that we were, but I had learned early during my incarceration that there was little I, or any other inmate, could do. Any act of defiance would simply land us in the Hole. Being placed in the Hole would be recorded for the parole board or judges to see, jeopardizing our chances of going home early. The COs clearly had the advantage, and they knew it.

After being stripped searched, we were marched back to our cells where we sat waiting for our next orders. We were not allowed to turn on our televisions, so we sat in silence. Eventually, I lay down on my bed. Within a few minutes, I was asleep. I slept soundly for an hour, oblivious to what was going on around me, until I heard a CO's whistle.

"Get your pathetic asses up and out of your rooms! Right now!"

We made our way outside of our cells, where we stood single-file against the wall, again. I looked down the hall to see if I could see Tyler. He looked at me, shaking his head as though he could not believe what we were experiencing. I nodded my head, fully understanding his thoughts.

I wondered how Michael was getting along. His cell was around the corner from mine, so I could not see him from where I stood. I hoped that he was okay. He did not take too well to being spoken to disrespectfully by COs. I did not want him to lose his temper and to find himself in the Hole. I understood that it was difficult to just accept the COs verbal mistreatment, though, if we wanted to see our families anytime soon, we had to endure as much of their abuse as we could handle.

As I looked toward Tyler's direction, I saw the door to the dorm opening, several more black clothed officers entered with huge dogs. The officers led the dogs into each of the cells. An exhausting two hours later, several of the officers and all of the dogs left. We were told to go back to our cells, until yet another hour had passed.

"Line up outside of your cell!" A CO shouted.

"What now?" Logan Anthony, our other cell mate said

aloud.

I looked at him as though he was crazy. The only thing the stupid COs needed was a reason to act like fools. They would take Logan to the Hole and probably beat him to death. Such acts had been committed many times before by COs. They would simply handcuff him and have their way with him. With no witnesses, it would become their word against that of Logan's corpse. Logan had been locked-up long enough to know how the COs were. I could not understand his actions.

"We're going to take you bag of shits to the mess hall to get some slop to eat; walk in a single
file line and, keep your mouths closed! That means no talking for you ignorant bastards that can't understand English!" The CO bellowed.

We walked single-file to the cafeteria, where we were served bologna sandwiches, an apple, and milk. With the institution on lock-down, there were no inmates to cook any food. I gave my sandwich to Logan. I did not have an appetite, especially for a dry bologna sandwich.

After eating, we were told to walk single-file back to the dorm. I saw Michael as I stood up to get in line. I looked in his eyes trying to gage how he felt. He nodded his head, signaling that he was doing fine. I involuntarily sighed in relief.

Eventually the black-clothed officers left the institution, though it was a full two weeks later before they were gone. We learned that the counselor's name was Regina Davis. I did not know her personally, though I saw her in the hallways often. She seemed to be a very pleasant woman: she smiled whenever I passed her and, from what some of the inmates in Sigma Unit expressed, she was always willing to help anyone in need.

It would have been disheartening for any of the employees to be killed, but it was especially saddening when it was one of the few employees who treated us inmates with dignity and respect. Although many of the COs quit their jobs after Ms. Davis' death, those who stayed shared with some of the inmates the horrifying events of how brutally she had been attacked, raped, and murdered by at least fifteen inmates.

"Yeah, they say it happened shortly after four o'clock count," Gonzalez whispered to Booger, Michael, Tyler, and me.

"I guess you guys know that they say the Taylor brothers were involved," Gonzalez said.

"Yeah, those niggas came down with me. I cannot believe they would be involved in some shit like that," Tyler said.

"And, those two older guys came from Lucasville with Rob and Clark," Gonzalez added.

"Those older kats was some fucked up dudes, for real. I used to be on the dorm with them. I ain't surprised at all that they would do something like that. They both some freaky ass dudes! And, they both in here for aggravated murder. That's why some people should be in a maximum security prison, for real!" Michael expressed.

"So what really happened, Gonzalez?" I asked.

"Well, as far as I know, they left their dorm right after count and went to Sigma Unit where Ms. Davis was. No one was working in there with her so they went in there and beat her up pretty badly. A bunch of the guys, about seven or eight of them started to rape her. They say they fucked her in the ass and her pussy, stool was found in her pussy, and part of the lips of her pussy had been bitten off."

I cringed as Gonzalez related the story. I could not believe that someone could do any of what he expressed to another person. Until then, I had only heard of people who did such horrible things, now I knew of people who committed such despicable acts.

"They say that they raped her for hours; many of them leaving and coming back with other people. She put up a hell of a fight, though, from what I hear. They found some of the guys' skin and blood under her nails, and her office was trashed."

"Man, all of that shit don't mean nothing when she lost her life! Them niggas go burn in hell for that shit!" Tyler expressed, angrily.

I was absolutely stunned. *How could they?* I questioned over and over in my mind. Yet, no matter how long I thought about it, I would never know the answer.

In the wake of Ms. Davis' atrocious death, the prison had undergone major changes: cameras and steel bars were placed throughout the corridors; the units' staffs were no longer allowed to work alone in the offices; they all had to carry two-way radios with them; and, as punishment to the inmates, the free-weights and many of the recreational activities were taken.

All of the inmates who were involved in the slaying were transferred to Lucasville; Ohio's maximum security prison. Two of the ring leaders were sentenced to the death penalty. Many of the inmates who were regarded as simply minor threats to the security of Lima were sent to prisons with higher security.

The prison had forever changed on that fateful day during the late summer of 1996.

Chapter Sixteen

The time had finally arrived for me to file for super-shock probation. I had been in school for a year and a half. I was on the Dean's list each semester for having achieved a perfect grade point average of 4.0. I also had successfully completed several institutional programs, including Anger Management, Repeat Offenders, and Victim Awareness. I was hungry for knowledge. Although, it was my prayer that my educational achievements would be looked at favorably and that I would be granted probation, I felt that the knowledge I gained would serve as a catalyst for my self-growth, regardless of whether I went home or not.

Filing for probation was easier than I thought it would be. I had presumed the process would be long and tedious, though it was nothing of the sort. I simply had to fill out a form, stating my intent to file super-shock, enclose any relevant information that may aid the judge in making her decision and that was it. I included my academic and institutional achievements in the motion, along with letters of support from my minister and family members.

Within six weeks of having mailed the packet, I was summoned to the mailroom. After signing a roster, I received an envelope listed as priority mail. I returned to D3 in search of Tyler. I knocked on the door of his cell.

"Yeah?" I heard him yell.

I opened the door. "What's up?" I asked, stepping into the

room.

"Nothing; laying up here watching these Soaps. Victor and Jack bout to go at it!" He said enthusiastically with his eyes glued to the screen, as he watched the Young and the Restless. Tyler, like so many other guys in prison, had been bit by the soap opera-bug. He watched them faithfully every day.

"Is that right?"

"Yeah, these niggas been going at it forever...they finally bout to throw some blows! Jack ass better watch out! Victor ain't to be fucked wit'!"

I could not believe that he was so engrossed in the soap. I used to watch them as a child with my Mama and Mymomme, but, as I grew older, I lost interest in them.

I grabbed a chair. From the look of things, I would be there for awhile.

"What's up, man?" Tyler said during a commercial break. "What you got?" He asked, looking at the envelope in my hand.

"I haven't opened it, yet, but I presume it is Judge O'Connor's response to my motion for super-shock."

"Well, open it, man! What you scared?!" Tyler asked, excitedly.

"Naw, I ain't scared. I was just thinking about what I told you when we first met. You remember?"

"Uhn, Un...What you say?" Tyler asked.

"Uhh," I sighed. Tyler was notoriously forgetful; though, I guess, I was being a bit vague. "Well, I said that I would kill myself if I didn't get shock."

"Oh, yeah! I forgot about you saying that shit!" Tyler exclaimed.

"I was serious. I didn't know how I was going to do it, but I was serious. I couldn't imagine spending another day in here pass the six months that Bradley said I had to wait before I filed. It was too painful. You know, being separated from my family and my friends. I didn't want to deal with this shit, but then God sent you in my life, and it made being here more bearable. Since we've been friends, I hadn't thought about my promise to myself to commit suicide, and I thank you for that," I said, looking up to meet Tyler's eyes.

He was trying his best to contain himself. He was a really good dude. I had not known a guy more compassionate and loving than him. He was the embodiment of what I thought every man should be: manly, yet caring, sensitive, and unafraid of being himself.

"Man, you the best friend I ever had. I thought them other niggas, Jalen and Kevin and 'nem, was my friends, but man you showed me what a real friend is," Tyler said, smiling so broadly that I could barely see the pupil of his eyes.

Without further ado, I took the letter out of the envelope. I quickly read over the contents, looking for the words I had waited nearly three years to read.

"What it say, man?!" Tyler said, excitedly.

"She rejected my motion for an early release. She said that I should be proud of the achievements I made, and that she would write a letter encouraging the parole board to release me when my case was reviewed by them."

Tyler took a long moment before he finally responded, "Man, that's cool! I ain't never heard of no judge saying they would do that. She must really like you!"

"Yeah, but the parole board?! You know they don't care what nobody says, judge or not! Plus, I don't go to the board until two thousand—that's an entire three years away!" I said, forlornly.

"Man, you can handle it," Tyler said, encouragingly.

I thought about the difficult, uncertain rode that lie ahead of me.

"Yeah, I guess you're right. I'll just continue my education. I think I'm going to get a job as a tutor for those dudes trying to get their G.E.D. I need to use what God has given me to help other people," I said, thoughtfully.

"My dude! Man, those cats gone love you. You got so much to offer 'em! I know you helped me a lot!" Tyler said in sincerity.

Tyler really was the best friend anyone could ever want. His support and encouragement of me were invaluable.

~~~

Life is interesting. It seems that as soon as one overcomes one obstacle another stumbling block replaces the previous one.

True to my word, I continued with my college education. I also started working as an Adult Basic Education (A.B.E.) tutor. As an A.B.E. tutor, I instructed student-inmates who performed below the educational level of a sixth grader in reading, writing, and arithmetic.

Although I was given the title of tutor, my duties extended far beyond the perimeter of only being a tutor; I also designed and implemented the curriculum. It was my responsibility to ensure that the students actually learned the material. Each evening, I went back to my living quarters to design daily and weekly lesson plans. I mentally assessed each student's strengths and weakness, seeking ways to best educate them.

In many ways, my responsibilities were like those of a traditional teacher, except my students were far from being traditional students: I instructed student-inmates who were murderers, rapists, robbers, and drug dealers, amongst other offenses; their ages ranged from eighteen to fifty; and, many of them had difficulty reading and writing above that of a third grader. Constructing simple sentences and solving math problems in addition and subtraction proved to be a challenge for many of them.

Several times a week, I would rush to the library in search of books to introduce to my students. It had always been important to me that an individual gain a healthy love and value of himself. In part, the key to accomplishing such a feat resided in familiarizing himself with his ancestry. I had always felt that one of the advantages that Whites had above Blacks was that they could always refer to their lineage and gain a sense of pride from the achievements of their ancestors. Whites could effortlessly go to any American history book and point out a collage of White faces who had succeeded in one way or another; from past presidents to the authors of the Constitution of America to scientists.

Blacks often times had more difficulty in reaching back to their roots to gain such motivation. However, it was my goal to not only encourage my students through the achievements of well-known great African Americans, like Dr. Martin Luther King, Jr., Harriet Tubman, Malcolm X, and Sojourner Truth, but also through the accomplishments of lesser known exemplary African Americans, as George Washington Carver, Mae Jemison, Thurgood Marshall, and Shirley Chisholm.

I thoroughly enjoyed educating my students. It was not only a way for me to help those who sought to further their education, but it also afforded me the opportunity to get to know those with whom I was incarcerated.

While things were progressing well with me in relation to my incarceration, life threw a tragic and unexpected curve ball.

"A, Chris, you seen Tyler?" Chipmunk asked, as I left work.

Chipmunk was a close associate of Tyler's. Chipmunk and my cell-mate, Gonzalez, were alike, in that whenever there was something going on in the institution, they were sure to know about it.

"Naw, I haven't. I just left work," I said, continuing down the hallway to my dorm.

"You need to check on him…they called him down to the unit a little while ago," Chipmunk said.

The thought that something was wrong with Tyler never crossed my mind. I assumed that Chipmunk asked me if I had seen Tyler so that he could borrow something from him, as was his usual.

"Okay," I said, as I quickened my pace.

Seldom was anyone ever called to the Unit, unless there was bad news. The bad news either had to do with the inmate's behavior in prison, or the bad news came from home. Tyler was a model-inmate; he did not do anything against the institution's rule to warrant being in trouble, and so, I assumed something must have occurred with his family.

My immediate thought was that something had happened to Ms. Matthews, Tyler's mother; though, while the news greatly affected Ms. Matthews, she was unharmed.

Walking on the dorm, I went directly to Tyler's cell. He was not there.

"Have you seen Tyler?" I asked his cellmate, Wellman, after knocking on the door.

"No, I think he went to the Unit, Chris," Wellman replied.

"Okay, thanks," I said, as I quickly closed the door.

I rushed from the dorm, en route to the Unit. Once I reached the Unit, I walked straight to Randy Morgan's office, one of the case managers. I looked into Randy's office. To my dismay, Tyler sat with tears streaming down his face. His eyes were blood-shot red. He clenched the telephone receiver in his left hand and a balled-up piece of tissue in his right hand; his left foot tapped the floor nervously. My instinct was to rush into the office to console him, yet I controlled myself. I had no idea what was being conveyed to him on the phone, though whatever it was, I knew that it pained him deeply. I moved away from the doorwell to offer Tyler some privacy.

I waited outside of Randy's office, until Tyler emerged minutes later. Although we met eyes, he walked right passed me without saying anything.

I followed closely behind him, wondering what had happened. After we left the Unit, Tyler shared with me his horrendous news.

"Candice dead," he said flatly, his face filled with pain.

"What?!" I exclaimed.

"M.C. killed her," Tyler said, as we walked in the direction of the gym.

Once there, we sat in silence on a set of vacant bleachers. I did not pressure Tyler into talking. I wanted to give him the space he needed to process what he had just been told. Nearly an hour passed before he finally spoke.

"Him and Candice musta been fighting and he pulled out a gun and pointed it at her. It went off and shot her in the face," Tyler said, as he began to sob.

I quickly, without thinking, grabbed him close, hugging him. His body convulsed heavily. I was unconcerned about the ramifications of my actions: I did not care about going to the hole for hugging him; I did not worry about adding fuel to the rumors that Tyler and I were secretly lovers. My only inclination was to comfort my friend.

Candice was Tyler's younger sister. He and Candice were incredibly close. They were separated by three years in age. Tyler oftentimes told me stories of the mayhem he and Candice committed as children; practical jokes and harmless pranks. They had been an inseparable duo for most of their lives, until Tyler's incarceration.

"I shoulda been there. I coulda stopped it," Tyler expressed.

"How, Tyler?" I asked, releasing him from my embrace.

"I don't know, man. I just feel like if I wouldn't have got myself in this shit and been in here, I coulda did something," he said.

"Tyler, you can't blame yourself for this. You can't assume responsibility for what happened. It wasn't your fault," I consoled.

"She looked up to me, man. Maybe if I had been out and been a better man, she woulda picked a better nigga to be in love wit'. She was out trying to do everything I did; trying to be like me," Tyler shared, as he began to cry again.

I listened to Tyler, allowing him to express his feelings without interruption, until I realized that he would continue to blame himself.

"Tyler, I understand what you're saying, but what happened isn't your fault. You know how Candice was…she was going to do what she wanted to do regardless of what anyone said. Her steadfastness was one of her most endearing qualities."

A whistle blew, indicating that the gym was closing for morning count.

"Thanks, man." Tyler said, looking deeply into my eyes, reaching the depths of my soul.

"Not a problem," I said, grabbing his hand and holding it firmly. After a moment, I released my grip, "Come on, we need to head back to the dorm for count. The gym's closing."

~~~

Death, in its wake, has the power to render the living with feelings of uncertainty and confusion. Past actions are scrutinized more closely; minor failures or shortcomings are sometimes magnified a thousand times; molehills become mountains.

Long before Candice's death, Tyler and I had developed a strong bond with one another's family. It was not uncommon for us to give the phone receiver to each other, encouraging the other to speak to our loved ones. We had come to know and love each other's family as though they were our own. However, with Candice's passing, I became more connected to Tyler's family both emotionally and spiritually.

"Chris, man, say something to momma, man…she blaming herself because of the way Candice lived. I keep trying to tell her how Candice was wasn't her fault, but I can't get the words out to make her understand," Tyler whispered to me as I passed the phone room.

His request caught me off guard. I had literally just entered the dorm. I was unaware that he was on the phone.

I took the phone, unsure of what to say. "Ms. Matthews? Hey, how are you?" I asked.

"Oh, I'm fine, Chris. I didn't know Tyler was giving you the phone," Ms. Matthews said, softly.

"Yeah, I know. I was walking pass the phone room and he told me he was talking to you. How is everybody?"

"We're making it, Chris. You know this is hard on everybody. I mean, I always felt that something like this was going to happen to Candice, because of the life she lived and how she was, but I just didn't really expect it to happen," Ms. Matthews said; her voice breaking.

"I know what you mean," I said, understandingly.

"I just keep thinking that I failed her; that I should have done something different," Ms. Matthews said, crying.

"Ms. Matthews, what happened to Candice is not your fault. You were and are a perfect mother to not just her, but to Tyler and Larry, too. Tyler used to tell me that you would get up every morning to make them breakfast before school; how you bought them the best clothes; how you supported them through all of their issues; how you had the wherewithal to leave your abusive husband to give them and yourself a better life. Ms. Matthews, you are not just a great mother, you are an exceptional woman."

"Thank you, Chris!" Ms. Matthews sobbed. "Thank God for you! You just don't know how much I needed to hear that!"

My skin began to rise with goose bumps. A shiver cascaded through my body. I was being blessed with the presence of the Holy Spirit. I smiled softly, as I whispered thanks to God for His presence.

"It's the truth, Ms. Matthews...I just said the truth," I said, soothingly.

"Oh, God bless you, Chris!" Ms. Matthews expressed, as she continued to cry. "I love you, Chris!"

"You're welcome and I love you, too. I'm going to give Tyler the phone before it hangs up on us. Bye-Bye, Ms. Matthews."

I looked out of the phone room for Tyler. He stood a few feet away.

"Is she okay?" Tyler asked.

"Yeah, here talk to her before the phone hangs up," I said, handing the phone receiver to Tyler.

He took the phone, closing the door as he spoke to his mother. A minute or so later, he walked out of the phone room.

"Man, I don't know what you said, but thanks. She sound a thousand times better. She just kept saying how blessed you is," Tyler said.

"I just told her what was in my heart; about how great of a mother she is to y'all. You know the things I tell you all the time."

"Thanks, man. I knew if anybody could make her feel better it would be you."

After Candice's funeral arrangements had been made, Tyler was allowed to have a private viewing of her. Two armed officers escorted him to the funeral home where he was given an hour to say his last goodbye to his baby sister. Although Tyler was deeply saddened by the experience, seeing Candice gave him a bit of closure.

Over the next few weeks following Tyler's return, I guarded him like a hawk. News of Candice's passing circulated around the prison like wildfire. Guys, who ordinarily did not speak to Tyler, found a reason to say something to him in an effort to gage his mentality. Prison was filled with advantageous people whom sought an opportunity to profit from an individual's weakness. A weakened state-of-mind renders a person vulnerable to an attack.

~~~

Being in a romantic relationship is much like rearing a child: it requires lots of love, lots of patience, and lots of energy to ensure that it grows into a healthy, mature entity. My relationship with Michael was perfect in many ways. Though, like most relationships, ours was not without its share of issues.

Michael was a kind, sensitive, loving, faithful, and a giving man, yet, at times, he was stubborn, moody, and completely unyielding. He also battled with the profundity of his love for me. Michael was not gay in the true sense of the word. He had never been in a relationship with a man before, and, quite possibly, had he not been incarcerated, he would not have entertained thoughts of being involved with a man sexually or romantically. His lack of homosexual experiences came as both a blessing and a curse. On the one hand, I did not have to contend with his previous negative homosexual relations; though, on the other hand, Michael's lack of experiences presented an ignorance with which I was not prepared to deal.

"I don't want you playing basketball with Humpfrey." I said angrily one late afternoon day.

"What? Why not?" Michael asked, exasperatedly.

"Listen, I'm not going to keep going through this with you: the boy likes you!" I nearly shouted.

"Man, that dude don't like me; I ain't gay," he said, by way of dismissal of Humphrey's attraction toward him.

"So what, you think that you have to twist and turn and have a limp wrist for a dude in here to like you?!" I retorted.

"You the pretty one…that nigga like you," Michael replied, matter-of-factly.

"You just don't get it, do you?! You don't have to be effeminate for one of these niggas to like you! You are good looking! And, I'm telling you what I saw! When he guards you, he puts his dick on your ass; when you guard him, he puts his ass up against your dick!"

"Man, that's the game. He just d-ing me up…it's called defense."

"I know the difference between defense and a nigga gettin' his freak on! I'm sitting there on the bleachers watching him! Every time he does something freaky, he looks over at me and smiles! As though to say, 'you see me!'" I was no longer able to control my temper.

"Man, I'm telling you, that dude ain't thinking about me," Michael said, unwilling to accept what I said.

"I don't have to lie about or exaggerate anything, especially some stupid ass shit like this! I'm going to ask him if he likes you, then!"

"Man, do whatever you have to do."

Michael's nonchalance annoyed me. I did not like that I had to go to the lengths I did for him to take what I said seriously. If there was a guy touching me in an inappropriate manner, Michael would be ready to demolish the institution with his bare hands, brick by brick.

It was one thing for two individuals to come together in a romantic relationship; it was a whole other thing to have to combat frivolous things like whether a guy is making sexual advances to his partner.

I really did not want to allow Humpfrey to have a foot-hole in our relationship. Michael and I had agreed that we would not share the status of our relationship with anyone. We believed that one of the quickest ways to ruin a relationship was by allowing other people to be actively involved in the relationship. I needed to deal with Humpfrey's behavior, however. I had always been incredibly possessive in my romantic relationships, and just letting Humpfrey continue with the harmless, though inappropriate, behavior was unthinkable to me.

Things would have been so much easier had Michael simply addressed the situation with Humpfrey. There would be no need for Humpfrey to know about the status of our relationship. Yet, Michael was being obstinate. He refused to believe that Humpfrey saw him in any way other than as opponent on the basketball court.

"Humpfrey, let me talk to you," I said as Michael and I caught up with Humpfrey as he exited the cafeteria.

Humpfrey was about five feet, seven inches tall. He was older than Michael and me by seven years, but like many persons in prison, he had an amazingly well-muscled body.

"What's up, Michael Christopher," Humpfrey joked. He thought that our names were sophisticated and sounded well when spoken together.

"What's up, Humpfrey, man," Michael said, greeting him.

"Do you like Michael?" I said bluntly to Humpfrey. My intentions were not to be rude, but I wanted to get right to the gist of what I wanted to know.

"Whwhwhat?" Humpfrey stammered.

"Do you like him?" I said, pointing at Michael. "Would you have sex with him?" I continued.

Humpfrey was hesitant. He looked from Michael's face to mine, and then back at Michael's. He smiled, shyly, "Yeah."

I looked to Michael, as if to say, I told you so.

"What you mean, you like me?" Michael asked.

Oh, god! "What difference does it make? He said he likes you!" I said, irritatingly.

A lot of people relish in being right, but I did not, especially in an instance like the one we faced. Michael and I had gone back and forth over the issue of whether Humpfrey liked him many times in the past. To have Humpfrey confirm what I knew and had been saying to Michael all along angered me. Again, if Michael had simply taken my word and addressed the issue long ago, we would not have had so many senseless arguments as a result of Humpfrey's behavior.

"Well I'on know what that means?" Michael said, stubbornly.

I looked at Michael through squinted eyes. *Oh, I get it!*

Michael was having a heterosexual moment. He was not so much concerned with Humpfrey's like of him, as he was about the manner in which Humpfrey liked him.

"Humpfrey, Michael wants to know do you want to perform oral sex on him," I asked, impatiently.

"Well, yeah," Humpfrey smiled, mischievously, exposing a missing tooth. Humpfrey was accustomed to my direct manner, but not when it was directed to him or about something so personal.

I looked back at Michael who had a look on his face as though he was not quite satisfied. I turned toward Humphrey.

"Humpfrey, Michael wants to know if you want him to penetrate you."

Humpfrey looked perplexed, "Yeah."

"Okay. Thank you, Humpfrey," I said, as Michael and I turned in the opposite direction, walking away.

The next day I felt horrible about the way I had handled the situation with Humpfrey. I was so spent over how poorly Michael regarded my thoughts and feelings that I just wanted to deal with it and to move pass it. I made a mental note to apologize to Humpfrey when I next saw him.

~~~~

"You gotta understand where I'm coming from, Chris," Michael said to me as we sat in my cell. "I ain't never been with a dude before. All this stuff is new to me!"

"Listen, I didn't ask you to be in this relationship. You chose to be in this relationship! I didn't want to be in a relationship with anyone, especially after the hell I went through with Moe!" I ranted. "I get so tired of you dudes telling me what's new to y'all! Every relationship is new;

every relationship is different! I wasn't given a rule book on how to be in relationship!" I continued, "Mymomme or daddy didn't instruct me on what to do and what not to do in a relationship! Common sense tells me how to behave in a relationship! You treat your partner how you want to be treated. If you know the pain of being cheated on, then don't cheat; if you understand what it feels like to be lied to, then don't lie! It's common sense, Michael! You should have heeded what I said long ago, without our having to come to this. Had the shoe been on the other foot, I would have handled it way before you would have had something to say. And, it has happened! You can't imagine how many people in this place say and do flirtatious crap to me! And, because of my love, care, and dedication to you, I nip the stuff in the bud before it could ever affect you! You are making this relationship a lot harder than it has to be!" I said, angrily.

"Look, Chris, I know you right, but how was I supposed to know the dude liked me?!"

"What?! You supposed to know, because I told you he did!" I said, as I lowered my voice as opened the door to see if anyone was listening. "First of all, ain't no nigga going to be putting his dick on my ass before I know that he likes me. Before he could even think about doing some crap like that I would have known that he liked me! You up here thinking you so rough and tough that these niggas wouldn't find you appealing! They are freaks! They'll fuck anything! Tell me this, how would you have felt if there was a guy putting his dick on my ass, or my ass on his dick?!"

"I wouldn't have liked it…Man, I didn't know," he said, exhausted by the conversation.

"You should have listened to me, then," I said, unwilling to simply accept his call for a truce.

Several months had passed since Candice's death. Although Tyler talked a great deal about Candice and cried occasionally, he appeared to be healing from his loss. He continued to attend his classes, even achieving the Dean's list. He was also scheduled to go before the parole board in a few weeks. Typically, having one's case reviewed by the parole board was a stressful time for most inmates; though, for Tyler, preparing to see the parole board gave him a reprieve from the grief of losing his sister.

In preparation of his hearing, Tyler and I drafted a letter to the Board beseeching them to show favor upon him. We mentioned his academic achievements, the institutional programs he had successfully completed, and that he had never had an altercation of any kind in the five years of his incarceration. By all accounts, Tyler had truly transformed himself while confined.

Ms. Matthews had also worked feverishly to encourage the parole board to grant Tyler an early release. Ms. Matthews' employer wrote a letter on Tyler's behalf, stating that he would provide him with employment upon his release. She also had her pastor and various family members to write letters of support urging the parole board to take into account the positive changes Tyler had made during his incarceration.

I felt that we all had done all we could to ensure that the parole board's decision was a favorable one. It was difficult to gage in which direction the parole board would lean. They were notorious for giving persons hefty sentences of five or more years. For someone who had already served five years, the additional time was disastrous. It took a great deal of mental stamina and spiritual attunement for an inmate to survive while in prison. Being given more time could result in an inmate's ultimate break-down.

Tyler had already endured quite a bit of emotional and mental anguish, from the demise of his romantic relationship with his ex-girlfriend to the separation from his family to the tragic death of his baby sister. His family and I worried about how well he would handle any unfavorable time from the parole board.

As always with time, when one wants it to hurry by, it seems to move at a snail's pace. Though for Tyler, time was his friend; his moment of reckoning had finally come, he was going before the parole board.

"Are you nervous?" I asked Tyler, as he prepared to go the psychiatric unit, where the parole board met.

"Hell, yeah! Look at my hands!" Tyler smiled, as he stretched forth his small hands. Sure enough, they shook like leaves on a tree branch on a windy day.

"You'll be all right...I said a prayer for you. Whatever the outcome, I feel in my spirit that the Creator will sustain you and your family."

"Man, thanks. I need all the prayers I can get!" Tyler said, sincerely.

Tyler was not a religious person, though, over the years, he had become somewhat of a spiritual person. I oftentimes told him that, had it not been for the many Sundays I spent in church and the true love I developed for God long before my incarceration, I would not have been able to deal with any of the events of my incarceration. My faith in God and knowing that He placed certain blessings in my life had helped me to cope with my miserable circumstances.

"Man, I don't know what I'm going to do once you're gone. It seems like you've been here with me every step of the way:

through the crap with Moe; to enrolling in school and tutoring; through my family's issues; and even through my problems with Michael. You've been a rare jewel to me," I said.

"Aww, man. You gone be cool. You got me through a lot of shit, too. I'on know if I woulda ever got over the pain of losing my ex—she was my heart, but through all of yo' hours of counseling!" Tyler laughed. "I got through it. And, we ain't even gone get on how you been here for me and my family after Candice's passing," Tyler began to get emotional. "Man, don't get me started! You know it don't take nothing for me to cry, especially since Candice been gone!" Tyler said, laughing.

"Yeah, I know you a cry baby!" I said, jokingly.

Tyler's ability to cry was one of the things I found most endearing about him. We men had been conditioned to think that crying was an indication of weakness or effeminacy. Tyler, however, knew that his manhood was not contingent upon crying, or, more specifically, a lack thereof.

"Matthews, Jones, Wittenburg!" The CO yelled from his desk.

"Aww, shit! You ready to go? He callin me to go the Board," Tyler said.

"Yeah, I'm ready. Are you?"

Tyler sighed, heavily, "Yeah, let me go get this over with."

Tyler grabbed his pass to get into the Psyc Unit as we passed by the COs desk. We walked to his destination in silence.

"All right. Stay strong. I'll continue to pray for you," I said, once we had reached the Pysc Unit.

"All right. Thanks, man," Tyler responded, nervously.

I went to the gym for several minutes to pass time while Tyler was being seen by the parole board. I watched the guys play a couple games of basketball, until I grew bored. I left the gym to go for a walk. I stepped outside, taking in a big gulp of air. I exhaled slowly, allowing myself to relax.

I wondered for a brief moment what Michael was doing, but I quickly pushed thoughts of him from my mind. We were not on the best of terms. We had gotten into another argument, although I could not quite put my finger about what we argued. It seemed that he had become more irritable and moody. We exchanged a few unpleasant remarks to one another, and I left him to deal with his cantankerous temperament alone.

As I walked around the East Yard, I relished in the beauty of nature. Even the twelve feet high, heavily barbed wire fences could not keep out the sheer magnificence of God's work. I wished that I had gone outside earlier, instead of sitting on the hard bleachers in the gym, watching the guys bounce a ball up and down the court.

I looked at the huge oak trees on the other side of the fence. It was October and the leaves had changed into their usual brilliant autumn colors. I was lost in thought as I walked around the perimeter of the Yard. I loved to think. It was a favorite pastime of mine. I devoted the same intensity to thinking that most people dedicated to a hobby. I would think about everything: past mistakes and joys of mine; present and future endeavors; my family and friends; everything! Nothing escaped my mind.

Suddenly, I realized that quite a bit of time had passed. I did not have a watch to gage exactly how much time had elapsed, so I walked hurriedly into the institution. Once inside, I walked down the corridor and looked at the clock on the wall in 6Dorm. I dared not to step one foot inside the dorm for fear that the CO would think I was exiting the dorm, and place me in the Hole. I squinted as best I could until I was able to focus well enough to see the time. Oh, my God! It was two-thirty!

Two entire hours had passed! Tyler had surely been seen by the Parole Board by then.

I rushed around the circle of the institution. I reached the Psyc Unit.

"Mark, have you seen Tyler?" I asked a friend of mine and Tyler's who stood outside of the Psyc Unit.

"Naw, I ain't seen him. He at the Board, ain't he?"

"Yeah, but he should be out now…okay…thanks…I'm going to check to see if he's in the gym."

"All right. I'll send him around there, if I see him."

"Okay. Thanks."

I walked to the gym, peering over the wall to see if saw Tyler. I did not see him. I walked down to the pool tables. He was not there. I walked down to the weight room; still, no Tyler.

Maybe he was on the dorm.

I left the gym headed for D3. As I rounded the corner, the doors of the Psyc Unit opened. To my surprise, Tyler exited. He did not see me, yet. He stood talking to the CO. I tried to read his face to ascertain what the Parole Board had said to him, but I could not. He was so involved in his conversation with the CO that it masked his feelings. Finally, he looked over his shoulder and saw me.

"All right, Murphy. I'ma holler at you." Tyler said to the CO. Murphy was considered one of the cooler COs. He fraternized with the inmates; playing cards and gambling with them. Although Murphy treated us more humanely than the average CO, I still refused to form a relationship with any of them. I felt that they had a job to do, and it did not involve a friendship with me. Too often, inmates would establish relationships with COs, only to bring undo suffering upon themselves because of the relationship.

It was against the rules for the COs to befriend inmates. When the administrators learned that a CO had established a relationship with an inmate, an investigation began and the CO, more times than not, fabricated his or her way out of the investigation to protect his job. Yet, the inmate was placed in the Hole in violation of whatever rule the CO contrived.

I would not place myself in a predicament to be treated so unfairly, so I steered clear of all COs.

"Okay, Tyler, man. Take care, buddy," Murphy replied.

Tyler and I walked in silence for a moment longer than I could handle. I searched his face trying to ascertain from it the Board's decision. I could not gage anything. He had somehow successfully masked his thoughts and feelings, a feat Tyler had never been able to accomplish. I could not take it any longer. I had to know.

"Well, what did they say?" I asked.

Tyler looked at me, as we continued around the circle of the institution. I looked into eyes looking for a clue as to what he was thinking or feeling. I saw nothing.

"They gave me a projected release date for October of next year." Tyler said solemnly.

The Parole Board had recently begun issuing projected release dates, rather than giving inmates direct paroles. Direct paroles entailed the inmate being released sixty days after his parole hearing. In accordance with projected release dates, an inmate was given a parole for a specified date, typically one year from the date of the inmates' parole hearing, as was the case with Tyler. The inmate's projected release date was contingent upon him refraining from any violations.

Seems easy enough, but prison-life was full of uncertainties. At any given time, an inmate could be placed in the Hole. Prisons were teaming with mean-spirited persons who delighted in a person's misfortune. Inmates who were envious of a paroled-inmate's blessing would initiate fights with him in an effort to make him lose his parole.

In other instances, contraband would be placed amongst the paroled-inmate's possessions. A kite, or prison-institutional letter as they were called, would be sent to the prison administrators, informing them that the inmate was in possession of contraband. The contraband could range from drugs to pornographic magazines. Once informed, the COs would search amongst the inmate's possessions, find the contraband, and reprimand him to the Hole. Any infraction was grounds for the Parole Board to rescind a parole or projected release date, regardless of whether the inmate was entirely engaged in the illicit act.

As was the case in my altercation with Blake; it mattered very little whether an inmate was actively involved in a fight, or if the contraband belonged to the inmate. The fact that he was in a fight, or that the contraband was found among his possessions was all that the COs and RIB used as a basis for their decision. The inmate was at risk of losing his parole for an offense that, in some cases, he had not committed.

COs were not exempt, either. Some of the COs did not want the inmates to be granted paroles. Several of them found joy in mistreating the inmates and keeping them confined. In that regard, COs, too, became a concern for the inmate who had recently been granted a parole or projected release date.

"I know it's not what you wanted, but at least you know that you're going home; before you didn't know if they would make you finish the remainder of your fifteen-year sentence."

Tyler had been convicted of felonious assault for having shot at a guy during a fight. He was given an indefinite sentence of six to fifteen years. He had already served six years of his sentence.

"Yeah, I know, man, but you know how it is in here. Shit, anything can happen. I don't know what I'm gone tell Momma. She just knew I was coming home."

"I know this will be difficult for her, especially after losing Candice last year. Just make sure that you stay connected with her, and let her know that you'll be all right," I offered.

"Man, I'ma try…" Tyler said, dejectedly.

Chapter Seventeen

It seemed that my family had deserted me. With the exception of Raymond, Booger's father, none of my other family members had come to see me in three years. The thought that my grandparents, parents, aunts, uncle, and cousins had abandoned me saddened me deeply. I tried to contact them through letters or phone calls, but my attempts were in vain; most of my letters went unanswered and many of my family members had blocks placed on their phones, restricting all collect calls.

My daddy, Mama, and Aunt Carol were the only persons who did not have restrictions placed on their phones. Yet, I was hesitant to call them for fear that they, too, would place blocks on their phones. I limited my phone calls to those times when I absolutely had to hear their voices. Though, even with limiting the amount of times I called, my phone calls were still met with unveiled irritation.

"Hey, Mama!" I said enthusiastically into the phone receiver, after the automated operator had connected our call.

It had been several weeks since I last called. I missed hearing Mama's all-too-familiar southern drawl.

"Hey," Mama replied, dryly.

My heart quickened. I was expecting to hear her warm comforting, 'Hey, baby.'

"Are you okay? Is something wrong?" I asked in a panic.

"Naw, I'm just tired. You know these bills are sky-high, don't you?" She asked, rhetorically.

"Yeah, I can imagine," I replied, solemnly.

"This phone bill is really getting up there…y'all gone have to stop calling so much," Mama said, pointedly.

Mama had always worried because of her bills. It was not news to me to hear her complain about them. Though, because of my sensitive and vulnerable state of mind, I felt that I was the cause of her grief.

"I haven't called in a while, Mama," I responded, sadly.

"Yeah, but Tookie and Booger calling, too. Y'all don't understand how expensive these phone calls are," she ranted.

The truth was that I did understand how much of a burden the phone calls were, which was why I attempted to limit my calls home.

"Okay, Mama. I'll let you go," I said, dejectedly. My feelings were hurt. I did not know how to deal with being incarcerated. My family had always been my inspiration; my reason for living. Without their love and support, I did not know how I would survive behind bars.

"You don't have to hang up, baby," Mama expressed, realizing that my feelings had been hurt.

"I'm okay, Mama. I'm sorry for calling…I love you," I said, as I placed the phone in its cradle.

I did not know what I was going to do. I did not know what or to whom to turn in my sorrow. I grabbed the phone and began dialing my daddy's number. He always had something positive and motivational to say.

"Hi!" I said, masking the hurt I felt from my conversation with Mama.

"Yeah, what's up, Chris," my daddy said flatly into the phone.

"Hey. How are you?" I stammered.

"What do you want, Chris? Why'd you call?" He asked in an annoyed tone.

A lump rose in my throat; tears threatened to fall from my eyes. "I was just calling to see how you're doing?" I managed to say.

"You just called here last week, Chris," he replied, irritatingly.

"No, I didn't. I haven't called since last month. I'm sorry," I said, hanging up the phone. I did not know what was wrong with him. I did not know why he thought that he had just spoken with me the week before, but I did not care. I felt lost; empty inside. My throat hurt. My head ached from the effort of restraining my tears. I sat on the floor of the phone room for a long moment, as unshed tears flowed from my heart.

~~~

As if things could get no worse, my relationship with Michael had taken a drastic turn for the worse. A gulf had developed between us. We were no longer the loving couple that we once were. We did not laugh as often or as freely with one another. We argued more frequently and seemingly over minute, trivial things.

I did not know what had happened to our relationship. I thought that nothing could come against the love we felt for one another. I looked inward at myself, thinking that perhaps I was to blame. Maybe I was too opinionated; too vocal with my thoughts and feelings; perhaps, I was too spoiled and unyielding. Had I spread myself too thinly? Did I give more attention to my friendship with Tyler than I had with Michael? Did I allow school and work to take precedence over my romantic relationship? I searched my mind trying to figure out where I had gone wrong; where we had gone wrong. Yet, as hard as I tried, I could not say exactly what I or we had done for things to be as bad as they were. All I knew was that Michael had become ill-tempered and irritable. The beautiful man with whom I had fallen deeply in love seemed to abhor my very presence.

"Hey! What's going on?" I said, greeting Michael and his roommate, Donald.

"What's poppin' Chris?" Donald asked.

"Nothing; I just got finished jogging and working-out, and thought I'd come by to see how y'all doing?" I said.

"Everythang, everythang…getting' this scribe out to this female pen-pal," Donald said, smiling. Donald was a cool dude who thought of himself as a lady's man.

"All right, I see you," I replied, laughing with Donald. "What's up, Michael?" I asked, specifically directing my attention to him.

"What's up." He replied flatly, as he watched television.

"What are you up to?" I asked, sitting down on his bed.

"Man, why you sittin' yo ass on my bed?!" Michael barked. "Damn, you see I just washed my blanket!"

I had always been a very sensitive person, yet it seemed that of late I was more sensitive than usual. Possibly being confined was wearing on me. Beds served multiple purposes in prison: they were slept on; breaks were prepared on them; and, they were also used as sofas.

Generally, a towel was placed on the blanket when someone sat down. Though, Michael and I had never observed the unspoken rule with one another. We sat on each other's bed without asking and without placing a towel beneath us, because of the relationship we shared. However, things had obviously changed between us. I sat on the bed a second or so longer, before I got up and walked out of the room.

I went to my cell, pacing the floor of the small room, until I had enough. I left my cell, and, without knocking, I opened the door to Michael's cell. As I opened the door, I overheard Donald saying to Michael, "Man, why you doin' Chris like that?"

I did not give him an opportunity to respond before I interjected, "Listen, I don't know what the fuck is going on with you, but you ain't gone treat me any kind of way yo' ass want to! You ain't gone take yo' shit out on me!"

"Nigga, what you in the hell you talkin' about?!" Michael asked.

"NIGGA!" I said, pointedly. "Just like I said, 'you ain't gone take yo shit out on me!' You can treat your dumb ass girlfriends on the street any way you want to, but that shit ain't flying with me!" I pointed my index finger at my chest. "This shit is over! You hear me?" I said, turning that same index finger and directing it at him. "It's a done mutha-fucka-deal! Don't say shit else to me, and I guarantee you I won't say shit to you!"

I walked from the cell, slamming the thick wooden door behind me as I did. I was incensed. His remark may have appeared minute, but I was tired of dealing with his moodiness and ill-behavior. Over the past few months, our relationship had changed from something people dreamt and prayed about to something depicted in a horror film. We rarely talked anymore; the romantic walks around the East Yard, where we shared our dreams of a life together beyond the concrete walls and barbed wired fences, were extinct; our quick, passionate minutes of love-making had become acts of the past.

I simply could not handle it anymore, not with everything

else that was going on. It was difficult enough maintaining my sanity in an environment as emotionally, mentally, and spiritually draining as prison. I did not have the energy to contend with the issues of an unhealthy relationship.

~~~

The Holy Spirit is always communicating with us; It is always instructing us, comforting us, and directing us. For many of us, we allow life to confound us so that we are unable to hear the Holy Spirit's words, or to feel Its soothing embrace, or to recognize Its guidance. One of the sheer beauties of God is that sometimes He allows us to be placed in a predicament whereby we have no other choice, but to look to Him for our sustenance.

Such predicaments come in the shape of diseases for some, and financial ruin or severed relationships for others. For me, my predicament came in the form of my incarceration. Although I never wanted to be incarcerated, and certainly not for the circumstances in which I found myself confined, I felt blessed to be in prison. Such a statement is not to express that I enjoyed being incarcerated, because I did not. I deplored every day that I was away from my family; separated from the people and things that I loved most. Though, through my confinement, I was able to see the hand of God; the true blessing of His love for me.

I was not new to the power and redemption of God. I studied His word and meditated on His goodness as a very young child and well into my adulthood; long before there was any thought that I would be incarcerated. Yet, being confined allowed me to know Him more intimately and personally for myself. My understanding did not come through the trials and tribulations of the Mothers in church, nor because of the early Sunday morning testimonies of the saints, but from my own experiences with life and His saving grace.

~~~

I had successfully completed all the necessary classes for an Associate's degree in social services. I wanted to complete my Bachelor's degree while I had the time to do so in prison, though, amid protest from Ohio's tax-payers, incarcerated felons were no longer allowed to achieve anything higher than an Associate's degree. As I understood it, tax-payers felt that incarcerated persons should not be allowed to acquire a "free" education, since tax-payers themselves were not able to attend school, without paying the hefty cost of tuition. As a result, thousands of persons who could have bettered themselves through the power of education, and ultimately society upon their release, were unable to do so.

The University of Findlay organized a graduation ceremony for us inmates. Booger, Tyler, and I were all graduating. The graduation was held during the late spring in the visiting room of the prison. The University's president and professors attended the gala. We inmates were allowed to invite two family members. The invitation of two family members was a real treat for Booger and me, since we would be able to invite a total of four of our family members.

I invited my daddy and Mama. I tried to extend one of the invitations to Mymomme, but I could not get in contact with her. She was deeply entrenched in the throes of chemical dependency. I was happy that Mama and my daddy were able to come, though. Mama had a huge fear of prisons, which made her being there to support us that much more special.

Booger invited Raymond and his girlfriend, Niecy; and, Tyler invited Ms. Matthews and his maternal grandmother, Ms. Sheers.

The three of us, along with forty other graduates, walked single-file into the visiting room as our names were called. Donning our black cap and gowns with gold tassels, we individually walked on stage, shook the president's hand and accepted our diploma. I was incredibly excited for my achievement, but also for the opportunity to see my family. It felt like an eternity since I had last seen them.

For the first time in the four years that Tyler and I had been friends, I was finally able to officially meet Ms. Matthews and Ms. Sheers. They were as beautiful and kind as I had imagined from our many phone conversations.

"Hi, Ms. Matthews!" I said, walking to her and hugging her firmly.

"Hi, Chris!" She responded in her beautiful soft voice. "It is a pleasure to finally meet you—face to face!"

"Yeah, it is," I laughed.

"We talked on the phone so much it seems like we already met!" Ms. Matthews smiled, warmly.

"I know. It does, doesn't it?" I asked, as I made my way to Ms. Sheers. "Hi, Ms. Sheers!" I said, as I hugged her.

"I told you don't call me 'Ms. Sheers!' Call me Mother Dear! You like my own grandchild!" Mother Dear said, fervently.

"I'm sorry, Mother Dear!" I said, as we all laughed. "Look at you with all this beautiful hair!" I complimented.

Her long, wavy hair hung neatly down her back.

"You quite a looker yourself, young man!" Mother Dear expressed, exuberantly.

"Isn't he handsome?" Ms. Matthews chimed in from

behind.

"Thank you," I said sincerely as I quickly made my way back to my seat.

We were not allowed to communicate with other inmates' families, but I had to say something to Tyler's family.

For the next hour, we ate cake and punch, as we conversed with our families. As is always the case with visits, the time went by much too fast. Before I knew it, Paul, the University's prison administrator stood on the stage before us.

"Ladies and gentlemen, graduates and special guests, the evening's event has come to an end. I, especially, wanted to thank you for coming and honoring our recent graduates. You should be very proud of the accomplishments that these men have made. They could have easily chosen to stay on their dorms or work in the cafeteria, but instead they chose to further their education. For that, I believe they deserve a round of applause!"

Our families enthusiastically applauded our achievements. It was the first time in the five years of my incarceration that I felt like a normal person; like I was not a criminal. I looked across the table at my daddy, Mama, and Raymond as they clapped their hands. Their faces radiated joy and an immense amount of pride for our achievements. I placed the love and gratitude I felt for them deep within my heart, vowing to allow it to keep me until I returned home to them.

~~~

I could not believe that time had gone by so quickly. Yet, it had. Tyler was leaving. We walked down the long, highly polished concrete floors to the steel gates that would lead him to his freedom. I was immensely happy for the possibilities that lay ahead of him, though I had to admit, my heart ached at the thought of doing my time without him. The mere thought seemed unreal to me.

Every major catastrophe, every true joy, Tyler had been a part of them all. He helped me to get over my relationship with Moe, counseled me through my relationship with Michael, listened to me as a spoke of my family's ills, and supported me as I dealt with the hardships of being incarcerated. Besides my relationship with Booger, Tyler was the most constant figure of my confinement.

"Man, I'ma make sure I send you some pictures and money as soon I get home," Tyler said, as he waited for the CO to unlock the gate that led to his freedom.

"I would love some pictures, but you don't have to worry about sending me some money. I'll be okay. You know Mama still sends me money."

"Yeah, but you can always use more, especially when the mail is running slow as hell or your grandmother ain't got it," Tyler concluded.

I did not know how to respond. Mama was my one secure source of support. We inmates earned a minimum of eighteen dollars and a maximum of twenty-five dollars a month, depending upon our institutional job. The measly funds were barely enough for us to buy our toiletries, so the money Mama sent was a real blessing.

"Thank you," I said, unable to say more.

"Man, you know I'ma look out for you. I know how it is in here." Tyler said, assuredly.

Just then the gate clanked open. A heavy-set CO waddled toward us.

"Matthews!" The CO barked.

"Yeah, that's me!" Tyler said, defiantly. He had never had

much respect for the COs. Although Tyler was a model inmate in many ways, because he did not engage in any misbehavior, I oftentimes had to remind him of his attitude. As I watched him walk down the heavily polished floor, I realized that I no longer had to encourage him to control his temper; I no longer had to worry about being him placed in the Hole for misconduct. He was a free man.

Chapter Eighteen

The New Year was met with a plethora of mixed feelings. It was the new millennium; the year two thousand. Like many people worldwide, we inmates did not know what the future held for us. We wondered if the world was going to come to an end, or if our sentences would be commuted because of the infamous Y2K threat, in which the world's computers would come to a crashing halt.

I did not know what to think or believe. Such information was completely out of my realm of knowledge. I only knew that I wanted to be home with my family, regardless of what was going on in the world. My parole hearing was quickly approaching. Booger and Tookie had already had their cases reviewed. Both of them received projected release dates for the year 2001. It was truly unknown what my outcome would be.

The Parole Board could go any way they wanted in their decision: they could grant me a direct parole, which meant I would be released two months after their decision; I could be given a projected release date; or, I could be denied a parole until my following hearing, which would be three years away.

As was the case when I filed for super-shock probation, I had several things in my favor, including having graduated Magna Cum Laude. The Faulkner family had also somewhat supported my being released, in that they did not challenge it. However, such was not the case with Booger and Tookie. After being notified of Booger and Tookie's impending parole

hearing,
the Faulkners' appeared before the parole panel contesting their release. During the hearing, the Faulkners' expressed that Tookie and Booger showed no remorse for Adam's death. They also positively mentioned the card that I sent to them while I was in the county jail.

I was astounded when I learned of the Faulkners' remarks, and especially stunned that they had spoken favorably of my expression of condolence. As I understood it at the time that I sent the card, they were displeased that I would have the gall to do such a thing. Though, in the end, in following my spirit, they were apparently able to see the true sorrow I felt.

~~~

Tyler had been home for several months. I spoke with him a couple of times during the first week of his release. He had also sent me some pictures, enclosed with a letter and twenty dollars from Ms. Matthews. Though, as time passed, I found it increasingly difficult to reach him. I wrote letters to him, though after a couple of months of not receiving a reply, I stopped writing.

I was devastated, to express the least. It was strange not having Tyler's attentive ear in which to confide, or his laughter to ease away the sorrows of being confined. I could not fathom him deserting me. I had been told that people oftentimes failed to keep in contact with one another once they were released from prison. Though, despite what I had been told, I did not believe it could happen with Tyler and me. We were like brothers. Our every waking day for the past four years had been spent together. I thought that the bond of our friendship was built on foundations so solid that nothing could come between or against it. Yet, something had.

"Hello?" Tyler said into the receiver. After months of not hearing a single word from him, I finally decided to give him another call.

"Tyler?" I queried. His voice sounded strange, unlike the voice I knew. A hollowness or void was present in it that had not existed in all the time that I had known him.

"Yeah, what's up," he responded.

"Hey. Not much. You sound funny. Are you okay?" I asked.

I had always been incredibly perceptive. Tyler used to joke that I was clairvoyant, but I merely read a person's body language or vocal patterns. When doing so, it became easy to know what was going on beneath a person's exterior.

"Yeah…I just got a hang-over," Tyler offered.

"Oh. You drink?"

Tyler used to drink alcohol prior to being incarcerated, though, while confined, he had come to see his drinking as a problem for him, so he vowed not to drink upon his release.

"Yeah, man. I do all sorts of shit that I said I wouldn't do."

I did not know how to respond to his statement.

Should I ask what kind of things did he do? Did I really want to know what sort of things he did?

"What do you mean? What's wrong?" I asked.

"Man, it's fucked up out here. It ain't nothing like we thought it would be. That first week I was home was cool, but after that shit been fucked up."

"What happened? How was your coming-home-party?"

"Man, everything happened," he said with dismay. "Yeah, I had the party. It was cool, man. My mom and 'nem went out they way for me. Caleb and 'nem was there. My son's mama showed up; she still fine as ever. I got a lot of money. Caleb took me shopping at the mall, and told me to get anything I wanted. Man, I ain't seen so much nice shit in so long, I ain't know what to get. I mean, I ain't have shit; no pants, no shoes, not even no draws. Shit, I was gone for seven years, but he kept sayin' 'get what you want'!"

I continued to listen to Tyler without saying a word. He seemed like he needed to get out all that he was expressing. Although we had spoken a couple times when he had first gone home, the conversations were very brief, as he was always in the process of doing something or going somewhere. I did not want to keep him from what he was doing, so I would offer to call him at another time. Yet, when I called him back, I was unable to reach him.

"I moved into the apartment above Randle and Momma's place, but I had to get out of there." Randle was his mother's husbands. "Randle started trippin' soon as I got in there good. You know, you could hear everything from downstairs, so every time a girl came over, we had to be real quiet. But that didn't do shit, 'cause you could still hear us walking up the stairs, and the girls woulda been drinking and you know how girls get when they be drinking. Then he started trippin' on little shit. Tellin' Momma that she baby me too much; that she gotta let me
be a man...but you know how Momma is, she ain't gone let none of her kids go without nothin'! I just got tired of the shit and moved into my own place."

"Mmm hmm," I said into the receiver, acknowledging that I was listening to what he said.

"Man, and, this job shit is fucked up! I tried to get this one job, but I put on the application that I had a felony, so they didn't hire me," Tyler said, dejectedly.

"They said they wouldn't hire you?"

"Yeah, they said they couldn't hire me 'cause I got a felony conviction on my record. Then, I applied to this other job at a factory, but I didn't put nothing in the spot where they ask about felonies on the application. I got the job, but they did a background check, and about a month after I was working, they told me they had to let me go."

"What?! That's unfair. How do they expect us to survive, if we can't work?" I asked, rhetorically.

"Man, they got us hog-tied out here. Shit is fucked up! I'm telling you!" Tyler said, exasperatedly.

"How is Ms. Sheers doing?" I said, hoping to change the subject to something more pleasant.

"Man, that's a whole nother story. We fell out."

"Huh?! Y'all fell out?" I asked, unbelievingly.

How does someone have an altercation with his grandmother, or more to the point, how could Tyler have an altercation with his grandmother? He and Ms. Sheers thought the world of one another.

"Yeah, she told me not to come over to the house no more," Tyler said, with a shimmer of sadness in his voice.

"Why?" I asked, still unable to believe that something could come between them.

"She found out that I was slinging here and there to make ends meet. She said that I was ungrateful and didn't care about what all they had done for me when I was locked up. But, man, she don't understand. She ain't never been locked up. She don't know what it's like to try and get a job and you can't 'cause you been locked-up, or to be fired from a job 'cause you been locked-up."

I did not say anything, although I was thinking that Ms. Sheers may understand his situation from a different perspective. Ms. Sheers was an elderly Black woman. I was sure that she had been denied jobs on the basis of her race. Sadly, felony convictions had replaced race as the tool of discrimination.

"Man, I'ma grown ass man with bills and a son to take care of!" Tyler continued. "I can't be sittin' around hoping one of these hunkies hire me, when I know they ain't! I gotta do what I gotta do to survive out here!" Tyler said, vehemently.

As was always the case, an automated operated interrupted our call, notifying us that we had sixty seconds before the call was terminated.

"I was wondering when that damn operator was going to come on the phone!"

"Yeah, man, remember how we used to hate hearing that shit, 'you have sixty seconds left on your call.' Man, that shit got on my nerves! A, man, call me whenever. I know it's hard getting' in touch with me, but I ain't really stable like I want to be," Tyler said.

"All right, I'll do that. Take care of yourself, Tyler."

"I will, and don't be too disappointed in me, man...I tried to do the right thing."

"I'm not disapp...." The call was disconnected. "Damn, I can't stand these stupid phones!" I said aloud, as I placed the phone in the receiver.

~~~~

I walked briskly down the long corridor of the hallway toward D3. It had been a particularly stressful morning at work. Some of my students were placed in the Hole and several others had been released from the Hole, which usually meant that I had to change my lesson plans to accommodate the recently released students. It was difficult enough trying to encourage my students to do their homework amongst all that went on their dorms, though to expect them to retain any of what they learned after being in the Hole was unrealistic.

"A Chris, you need to go check on your cousin." A guy who lived on D3 said, as I rounded the corner of the hall.

What now? "What's wrong with him?!"

"Something wrong with his eye…"

Ever since Booger was hit in the eye with a rock as a child, his eye had been a source of continuous agony for him. The least little irritant, such as cigarette smoke or sunlight, caused him pain.

I rushed to the dorm. I opened the door to our cell, where I found Booger lying down on his bed, his eye was covered with gauze and tape. I was shocked. I did not expect to find him in such condition. Generally, when his eye bothered him he simply covered it with a towel. Though, with the gauze-covering, he looked injured.

"Booger, what happened?!" I asked in a panic, as I quickly walked to his bed.

"Awww, nothing…I just got a laceration on my eye." He said, nonchalantly, in a slightly humorous tone.

"What?! How did you get a laceration on your eye?!"

"Awww, shit, it ain't nothing…I was just in the gym playing some ball and Phil, one of Pepper's friends, got mad at me 'cause I called a foul on him, and he threw the ball at my eye…it ain't shit."

Pepper was a friend of mine. He used to be a member of the Bloods gang. During the last few years, quite a few of his young, gang-family had come to the prison creating all sorts of mischief.

"What?!" I did not wait for a reply from Booger.

I was seething. I quickly left the cell, nearly slamming the door closed as I did. I walked as fast as I could to the gym, mindful of not attracting the attention of the COs who patrolled the halls. I entered the gym, and leaned over a wall that separated the basketball court from the entrance ramp. I spotted Phil in the distance. I nearly ran down the ramp.

"Did you hit my cousin in the eye?!" I yelled over the clamor of bouncing balls, as I approached him.

"What?"

"Nigga, you heard me! Did you hit Booger in the eye with a basketball?!"

"Whhhaat…" he stammered.

"Don't fuck with my cousin no mo'…if you want to fuck with somebody, fuck with me!" I challenged. "Y'all punk ass niggas always fuckin' with somebody y'all think y'all can get yo' shit off on!" I said loudly, looking in Phil and his friends' faces that were assembled on the basketball court.

I turned from them, exiting the basketball court. I was fuming. As I walked up the ramp leading out of the gym, I heard one of Phil's friends say to him, "Man, I told yo' ass you shouldna done that shit to Boo…his cousin crazy!"

I was not a big and "bad" tough, guy, nor should it been misconstrued that I was, because I was not. Ordinarily, I did not pick fights with anyone, though I refused to allow any of the guys in prison to treat Booger or me any kind of way that they wanted.

Booger had a beautiful, docile personality, yet it irritated me that he would allow the guys to treat him the way he did. Under no circumstances would I permit my cousin or me to be the doormat under such persons' shoes.

It was officially over. My relationship with Michael had come to an end. After our last argument, he had come to my cell and apologized for his behavior. He knocked on my cell door.

"Yeah?" I said, barely concealing my irritation. I had no idea who was at the door, but in my heart I hoped it was Michael. I had already begun to miss him, and only fifteen minutes had passed since I slammed the door of his cell, rushing into my own cell.

"A, baby, I'm sorry for the way I've been acting. I'on know what's going on with me, but I know I love you more than I have loved anybody. I don't want to lose you," Michael said, warmly.

I did not respond to him immediately. In fact, I did not even look up when he entered the cell. I remained rooted in place absorbing his words. In my heart, I believed him; though, more importantly, my mind believed. I knew that he loved me. I also knew that he did not know the reasons for his previous actions. Yet, as I stood resting on the top bunk, with my head lying on my folded arms, a small seed of realization was planted in my spirit; a realization that would soon make known the reasons for his behavior.

At that time, however, my mind and heart were not yet ready to accept what my spirit understood. For the time being, the knowledge remained buried. I turned to Michael, looking deeply into his honey-colored eyes.

"I'm sorry for the things I said," I said, softly. I extended my arm and gently caressed his dark brown skin with my hand. I loved the way his skin felt. His skin was smooth and completely blemish-free. I used to tease him, "What kind of make-up do you wear? I know it ain't Cover Girl! Naw, uhn-uh, that has to be Mac…I think you and Oprah use the same kind of foundation!" He would laugh at my goofiness. He had such a wonderful sense of humor and an extremely good-nature.

This was not the time for jokes, though. An undeniable energy enveloped the air between us. Michael grabbed the palm of my hand, placing my outstretched index finger in his mouth. I closed my eyes. His warm, velvety tongue moved up, down, and around my finger. The sensation caused my knees to buckle. Michael quickly reached out, releasing my finger as he did so, while steadying me by my waist with his huge hands. I held on firmly to his strong shoulders. He pulled me closer to him. The warmth of his body was mesmerizing.

I put my left hand behind his closely shaven head, bringing his lips close to mine. We kissed gently, as we explored the softness of each other's lips.

"I want to make love…" Michael whispered into my ear.

"We can't, baby. We don't have anyone to look out for us," I said, softly.

"We don't need a look-out," Michael said between labored breaths.

Yes, we do. I was going to the parole board in a few months. I could not risk going to the hole for a sex act.

"…I don't know," I said.

"We can put the chair up to the door…" Michael suggested, tickling my neck as he kissed it.

I considered Michael's suggestion for a moment. My stomach felt queasy from the thought of making love with him. The thought sent chills of excitement throughout my body; goose bumps appeared on my arms.

"Okay," I said before I had a chance to reason my way out

of my decision.

That was two months prior. Since then our relationship had returned to its previous state before our moment of ecstasy. However, this time, I was aligned with a different perspective on Michael's ill-temperament. Yet, despite my understanding, I still mourned over the loss of him.

Michael was, all in all, a good dude. He did not have any emotional or mental issues like some of my previous partners. Although, he was protective and possessive of me, he was not so in an unhealthy manner. I loved him. In fact, I loved him like I had loved no other man. It was because of him, the depth of my love for him and the beauty of our relationship, that I began to define my sexual orientation. Before I came to be in-love with Michael, I chose not to label my sexuality.

My choice not to define myself went far beyond the fact that I had loved women romantically. It had more to do with the fact that no man had truly captured my heart. I loved Moe, and even Kevon, but not to the degree, nor with the same freedom that I did Michael. I loved Michael in my soul. After experiencing the veracity of my love for him, I felt no qualms about defining myself as gay.

It took some time for me to realize the reason for Michael's ill-temperament. Though, as I listened and watched him, the truth of my assessment became clear.

"Hey. What's up?" I said to Michael, as I entered his cell.

"What's good?"

"Uhn huh...nothing, I guess. What are you doing?" I asked, watching him intently.

"Reading this letter from Sharon," Michael said, nonchalantly.

"Sharon? Why'd she write you?" I asked, suspiciously.

"I'on know...she wanted to see how I'm doing?" Michael

said, looking up at me.

Michael seemed different; amused; happy, I could not put my finger on exactly what I sensed.

"So what, she just wrote you out of the clear blue after all this time?"

"Yeah…I mean, naw. We been writing each other back and forth for the past couple weeks?"

"The last couple of weeks? And, you didn't say anything to me?" He looked at me stupidly as if he didn't know to respond. "Had you planned on telling me that you all were communicating with one another?" I asked, becoming increasingly upset.

"It's Sharon, man! What's the problem? I can't do shit with her in here?!"

"What?! I don't care if it's Boo-Boo the clown! And, I don't care if she ain't in here…you were romantically linked with her! How would you feel if Moe's ass or Kevon and I were writing each other?"

"I'd be cool with it," he said, flatly.

"You a got damn lie! Yo' ass would be shittin' bricks! You just sayin' that shit, because the shoe is on yo damn foot, instead of the other way around! I'm gettin' tired of yo' double-standards!" I raved.

"Man, it's a damn woman…A woman that I can't see…can't touch, and can't fuck!"

"Nigga, I wouldn't give a damn if it was a got-damn monkey! I'm not gone be sharing my partner with no damn body! You tell my motha-fuckin heart that it's a damn woman! Pain is pain, no matter what gender the damn person is! I'm supposed to feel better 'cause it's a woman you communicating with? Why, cause that's supposed be natural—a man and a woman?! Well, you can take your logic and stick it up your logical ass, 'cause my heart doesn't understand it!" I yelled as I walked briskly from the room.

I could not take being in the relationship with Michael, anymore. The ups and downs of our relationship had become too much for me to endure. Though, more to the point, I suddenly understood the reasons for Michael's mood swings: Michael was not gay, yet he was living the lifestyle of a gay man.

Michael's circumstance, our circumstances, had dictated his actions. Being incarcerated had taken him away from the true desires of his affection—women. While I believe Michael loved me deeply, his love for me was rooted in my spirit; who I was as a person, though not me as a man.

As I thought over his behavior, he had always related some attribute of mine to a woman's: you got soft, smooth skin like a woman; you switch when you walk like a woman; you think like a woman; your ass feel like a woman's pussy'. In a twisted sort of way, he saw me as a woman. He had never been in love with Christopher, the male; but, Christopher, the one he saw as a female. Such were the effects of prison.

I was hurt beyond words, but I really could not be upset with Michael. He simply was not gay. I, nor he, could change his sexuality. Our being incarcerated had brought us together. If I were truly honest with myself, I had to acknowledge that if we were not incarcerated, we would have never had the opportunity to love one another. Loneliness and depravation had driven him to me.

Michael was my one true love. My love for him was the rare, special kind of love that comes along once in a lifetime; the kind of love by which one judges all others. In more ways than not, Michael was perfect: beautifully built; a strong, handsome face; and, a kind, giving, and loving heart. He was attentive to my needs and wants; and, he always sought to make me happy.

Sometimes he would buy Muslim oils and place them under my pillow, surprising me with their sweet fragrances. It was not uncommon for me to walk into my cell to find a bundle of neatly wrapped Snickers (my favorite candy bar) lying on my bed.

Tyler had usually prepared night-time breaks for Booger and me. Though, after Tyler left, Michael assumed the responsibility, creating truly superb masterpieces from the simple meals of noodles and meat.

It seemed futile to remain in a relationship with someone whom I loved with my whole heart, yet whom was only able to love me partly. For days and weeks after I made my decision to leave Michael, the agony of our separation threatened to consume me. I could not seem to escape the memories of our relationship or of my love for him. Yet, despite the pain I felt throughout ever fiber of my being, I resolved to go on with living. I could not allow myself to be lost in what I could not change: Michael would never be mine in the way that I wanted him to be…and so, I moved on.

~~~~

The moment of reckoning had come. I, and hundred or so other inmates, was scheduled to meet with the parole board to determine my fate. I did not know what to expect. The Parole Board was notorious for shocking inmates with paroles or with astronomical time to serve.

I did all that I could do to prepare for that day. I rose early in the morning, and had a substantial breakfast of grits, scrambled eggs, bread, and milk. Once the doors of the dorm were unlocked and the Yards were open, I went for a nice three mile run to clear my mind. I finished running, feeling refreshed and invigorated. I showered, changed into my freshly ironed state pants and shirt, and waited for the CO to call my name for my parole hearing.

Yet, as always is the case when one anxiously awaits the arrival of anything, I seemingly waited forever for them to call me. Hours passed with no word from the Parole Board. I walked to the gym to pass time as I waited. Several guys who had been seen by the Board were in the gym. I walked over to an empty bleacher to sit down.

"A, Chris, you go to the Board today?" One of the guys asked me. I had seen him around the institution over the years, but I had no idea what his name was.

"Yeah, but they haven't called me, yet."

"They runnin' slow...and they got a lot mo' people going up today than they thought. I just saw them," the guy said.

"Oh, yeah? What did they say?"

"They gave me five mo' years," he said, emotionlessly.

"Aww, I'm sorry to hear that," I said, sincerely.

"Aww, shit, it ain't nothin'! I expected them to give me some time, anyway. I was a bad man on them streets."

For the first time since he had spoken, I detected emotion in his voice.

"Oh," I said, not knowing quite what to say.

"Yeah, I deserved to be in here. This place saved my life. I woulda been dead and gone, otherwise."

Over the years, I had heard other inmates express the same sentiment about prison having saved them from a certain death. I thought it was ironic that many of the inmates credited prison for their salvation. Such statements were one more instance as to the reason I felt that prison was the best place for real change to take place in many of the inmates' lives.

For the vast majority of inmates, because we had been stripped of everything that we knew and loved, we were in a unique space in our lives where we were more susceptible to changing our wayward thoughts and behaviors. However, prison administrators did not capitalize on the blessing of their positions. Instead, they simply warehoused us inmates, without offering the true resources to change our behaviors. Rehabilitation was simply a word that was frivolously used by the penal system; the actual act of rehabilitating was never employed.

"Well, I wish you the best. Maybe the Parole Board will call you back in a couple of years and reduce the time they gave you," I said, standing to leave. I wanted to get back to the dorm, just in case I had been called.

"I sho hope so, Chris."

"I'll keep you in my prayers…take care."

I walked back to the dorm. I doubted that the Parole Board had called, but I wanted to make sure. I climbed the stairs to D3. As I walked down the hall, the CO's phone rang. My heart jumped in my chest. The CO took out his pen and began writing on a notebook pad. She put the phone back in its cradle.

"Richardson, Johnson, O'Neil, Price," my stomach did rapid somersaults at the mention of my name. "Phillips, and Tate, head down to the Psyc Department for your parole hearing!" She yelled.

I was nervous; my mind raced. I walked toward Booger's cell. Just as I was about to knock on his door, the door swung open. It was strange not having him as a cellmate, anymore, but a two-man cell had become available. He wisely accepted it, moving out of our four-man cell.

"Yeah, I heard," Booger said, before I was able to say anything.

"Okay," I said, letting out a deep breath. "I'll see you when I get back."

"All right. Good luck, cousin," Booger said, giving me a firm bear hug.

"Thank you, cousin," I said, smiling.

I walked to the Psyc Department, giving the CO who stood outside the department my pass that indicated I was there for a parole hearing. The CO unlocked the gate, granting me passage. I found a seat beside several other guys on a wooden bench. We all waited to be given the news of our lives. Some of the guys waited in silence, as I did; others talked through their apprehension.

"Man, how they acting?" One guy asked.

"Shit, I'on know…" Another guy responded.

"Hey, man. I heard they slammed Everett over there on 3dorm pretty hard!" A White guy said. "They gave him a dime!"

Wow! An entire ten years! I did not know what I would do if I were given that amount of time from the parole board, especially after having already served several years.

"Yeah, but Everett down here on a murder bit. He knew he had it coming," a Black guy said.

I continued to hold my peace. I did not want to even concern myself with the time I could be given, which could have been up to nineteen years. I just sat there praying, until my name was called.

"Price, 307-720!" A CO read from a list.

"Yeah, that's me," I said, calmly.

"You're next to go in. After the next inmate comes out, you go in."

"Okay."

I sat waiting to be seen for an additional hour. We all were growing restless as we waited for the last guy to enter the room. The long wait was not a good sign. We speculated that the board members must be in a poor mood, which was not promising for any of us. Strangely, the wait worked in my favor. It gave me time to think about what lay before me, and my lack of control over the outcome. I resolved that if it was time for me to be released, then it would happen. Fretting over what the Parole Board would say or do did not do me any good.

Just then the door opened. The CO nodded his head at me, signaling me to enter the room. An inmate exited the room. His head was held low. I looked into his eyes as he passed by me. There was a blank, hollow look in his eyes. I closed my eyes for a brief moment, mouthing a silent prayer for him. He looked as though he could use one.

I entered the room. Three board members, two men and a woman, sat behind a long rectangle-shaped table.

"You can sit down, Mr. Price," one of the male members said.

"Thank you," I said as I pulled a chair from the table to sit.

I sat there for several minutes as the members sifted through a folder with my name on it. I wondered what they were thinking. They said nothing to me, and very little to one another. If I had not seen the folder with my name on it, I would have thought they were preparing themselves for the next inmate.

I had heard horrid stories about the Parole Board talking to inmates with little more respect than one would give to a rabid animal. One of my biggest concerns lay in how I would respond to such degradation. I sometimes had a difficult time controlling my tongue.

"Mr. Price, I see that Judge O'Connor has written a letter encouraging your release," the other male member stated.

"Yes, she did."

I made it my business to stay in communication with Judge O'Connor. I began writing her letters when I was in the county jail. I wanted her to know me for who I really was and not who the media or prosecutor said I was. I continued my correspondence with her during my transfer to Lima and several years afterward. I wrote her letters detailing my institutional achievements, including any program I took and that I had graduated from Findlay with a 3.74 G.P.A. I also included that I had worked as a tutor and teacher's aide.

"I also see that your minister, Ryan Donathan, wrote a letter of support as well."

"Yes."

I sat there in my chair for a moment or two longer before the female parole member spoke to me.

"Mr. Price, will you, please, step into the hall for a moment while I speak with my colleagues."

"Yes, ma'am." I said as I stood and exited the room.

I did not know what to make of their virtual silence, nor did I know why they had asked me to leave the room. At first, I was a little concerned about going before the Parole Board for having killed a White guy. It was one thing to go before the Board for having killed a Black person, though it became an entirely different matter when a Black person had committed an act against a White person. The stakes were heightened.

As I entered the hallway, everyone's eyes were on me.

"What happened, man?" A guy whom I did not know asked me.

"Nothing. They asked me to step out here."

"Aww, man," the guy said with a look of dread on his face.

I smiled at him. Ever since I had prayed, I felt at peace about the whole ordeal. I was spiritually prepared for whatever the outcome would be. Just then, a red-bulb light flashed above the door, an indication for me to re-enter the room. I walked into the room and took my seat.

Two of the Parole Board members held their heads down as I walked into the room. They did not acknowledge my presence after I sat down or even after the other parole member began talking to me. Was their failure to recognize my presence an omen?

"Mr. Price, your cousins, Raymond and Raylene Jones, are also incarcerated?"

"Yes."

"Where are they incarcerated?"

"Raylene is incarcerated at the Cleveland Pre-release Center, and Raymond is imprisoned here at Lima," I said, trying to ascertain where he was going with his line of questions. The other two parole members offered no clue, as they continued busying themselves with paperwork.

"Where would you reside upon your release?

My heart skipped a beat. 'Upon your release,' did this mean that I was being granted a parole? Surely he would not be concerned with my place of residence, if I were not being granted a parole!

"With my dad…in Atlanta," I said, trying desperately to contain myself.

"Mr. Price, we, the parole board members, have decided to grant you a projected release date for December 1, 2001. Upon that date, you will be released to the custody of the Adult Parole Authority, granted that you remain free of any infractions."

"Thank you."

"You are free to leave."

I stood up from my seat. The other members had finally raised their heads.

"Thank you," I said, looking at the three of them.

"You're welcome, Mr. Price," the other male member said.

"You're welcome," the female member added.

I walked out of the room. A huge load seemed to have been lifted from my shoulders. The experience was nothing like I thought it would be. The members were not unpleasant in the least. In fact, they were the opposite. I mouthed a silent thank you to the Creator before I stepped into the hallway.

"How'd it go, man," the same guy as before asked me.

"They gave me a projected release date of eighteen months."

"Congratulations, man!"

"Thank you!" I said smiling.

The CO walked me to the gate, unlocking it. I optimistically stepped into the hallway expecting the world to look different, yet it did not. The concrete floors, though they shone brilliantly under the many applications of wax, looked no more radiant than they had any other day. I took note of the walls; the pale, flat paint was still dismal.

I walked to the window desperately searching for an indication that the world around me was somehow different. Though, nothing had changed. The sun still sat high, spreading its magnificent rays across the afternoon sky. The warm air that flowed through the open windows appeared no fresher than it had earlier in the day.

No monumental event had taken place. I was still confined. My life had not altered.

Slowly the magnitude of my release date began to seep into my mind: eighteen months…an eternity in prison. I remembered how optimistic I had been for Tyler when he received a projected release date. I now understood the enormous stress under which he was placed.

Prison life was unpredictable. Anything could happen in a year and a half: a fight; a rape; my death. Each minute of every day I lived with the realization that I could be confined for the rest of my life or killed. During the earlier years of my incarceration, I constantly had to curse out someone to maintain my respect. I had held fast to my refusal to be treated without respect. While I did not have to be on guard as much over the years, I still had to stay mindful of where I was. Every week, younger inmates were being shipped to the institution; inmates whom did not know me; whom did not know my earlier battles; inmates with whom I would have to educate as to who I was and how I demanded to be treated.

I walked back to D3 unnoticed. The halls were empty; a softball game was probably being played. I entered the dorm, no one was in sight. I walked directly to my room, and laid down on my bed to sulk in my misfortune. Just as I was about to doze off, there was a knock on the door. I was tempted not to respond, but I did not want to be rude.

"Yeah?" I called out. The door opened. I looked up to see Booger entering the room. In my sadness, I had not even thought to tell him my news.

"What's up, cousin? What the Board say?"

"Hey. They gave me a projected release date of eighteen months," I said, sadly.

"Eighteen months! That's cool! Why you sound so sad?" Booger asked, confusingly.

"I don't know...I guess I was hoping to get a straight parole."

"Shiiit, I know you was, but, man, that's gravy! Shit, at

least, you know you going home! They coulda gave you more time than that!"

"I know, but you know how it is in here…one of these damn fools can say one wrong thing to me and it can be over! I just don't know how much more of this crap I can take!"

"Man, shiiit, you gone be all right. You just got to stay out of the way," he advised. *Yeah, a lot easier said than done.* "Plus, this way we'll all be going home around the same time. Man, you just never know how Yaweh work. It may not be time for you to go home, no matter how ready you think you are," Booger said, wisely.

He had been practicing the faith of the Israelites, a cross between Christianity and Islam, as I understood it. The teachings were obvious, he was more spiritual and grounded because of them.

"Yeah, I guess you're right. Thank you," I said, standing to hug him. He gave me one of his well-needed bear hugs.

"What you about to do?" He asked, as I began putting on a pair of shorts.

"I'm going outside to do some pull-ups and dips. I need to work off some of this energy. Ain't no need of me lying around crying the blues. What are you about to do?"

I'm about to play bridge with Martin and them. I just came in here to see if you was back, yet. I'll catch up with you later on."

"Okay. I'll see you.

God is truly awesome, I thought, as I walked outside toward the pull-up and dip bars. He always shows His love toward us. We can feel alone and misunderstood at times, but God has a way of making His presence known; of letting us know that we have not been forsaken and that He is always with us; of placing people and things on our paths to help us along our journey.

The year could not have ended more beautifully. I was lying on my bed when I received word that I had a visit. I had no idea who was visiting me, but I welcomed a visit from anyone: man, woman, friend, or foe. I did not care, just as long as I was able to escape the confines of everyday prison life.

I showered and dressed hurriedly. I grabbed my visitor's pass from the CO, and exited the dorm. I nearly ran to the visiting room; I was so excited to receive a visit. I went through the usual routine of being strip searched: took off all of my clothes, opened my mouth, lifted my tongue, turned around, squatted, spread my cheeks, and coughed. As always, no matter how often I performed the act, it always felt demeaning.

I brushed off any irritation I felt, focusing instead on my surprise visitor. I quickly re-dressed, and exited the strip-search room. I walked to the CO's desk to make her aware of my presence. The CO wrote down my name on her pad that she used to keep a count of all inmates who were in the visiting room. The COs had to know where we inmates were located at all times. After checking me in, the CO pointed in the direction of my visitor. I looked in the direction of where she pointed. The table was located clear across the room.

I could barely make out the shape of the person, though I could tell that the person was a woman. Squinting, I tried desperately to see who she was, yet to no avail. I began to walk to the table where my visitor sat. To my surprise and absolute delight, I saw my cousins, Brandy and Casha, sitting at the table. I had not seen them during the entire six years that I was incarcerated. Their smiling faces were not the only surprise I was given, as I looked around the table, I saw not one, but three additional bodies, one of which belonged to Mother.

I quickened my pace. I absolutely could not believe the special gifts I had been given and just one week before Christmas! How appropriate, I thought, as I smiled broadly. Brandy and Casha stood up as they saw me approaching the table. Brandy stood closest to the walkway. We hugged firmly as was our way with one another. I hugged Casha next. I marveled at how small they felt in my embrace. Had I grown that much in the past six years?!

I looked over to where Mother sat. She looked confused, as if she did not know what was going on or what to do. Years later, I would come to understand what the expression on her face meant, though at the time I disregarded the look, focusing instead on the joy I felt at seeing her five feet, eighty-plus year old frame.

After I hugged the three ladies, I turned my attention to the two little people who accompanied them, Sydney and Jared, Casha's daughter and Brandy's son.

"Hey there!" I said, making my way around the table to hug them both. Sydney was born a year before I was imprisoned. Although she did not know me, she was receptive to hugging me. Jared on the other hand, had just been born two years ago. He neither knew me, nor did he have the desire to get to know me!

Brandy, Casha, and I threw ourselves into a lively conversation. They were my closest cousins on the paternal side of my family. They were three years older than me. As children I spent countless nights at Mother's and Aunt Carol's house with them. Years later, as a fourteen year old teenager, they would sneak me into Toledo's young adult clubs.

"Look at you! All buff and everything!" Brandy remarked to me.

"I know, he ain't little Chris no more!" Casha said.

The three of us laughed heartily. Mother sat at the table in a world of her own. I took the opportunity to engage her in our conversation.

"Mother, how have you been?" I asked.

"I been all right. Ready to go," she said.

"You ready to go?!" The three of us asked her incredulously. They had only been there for fifteen minutes.

"Yeah, I'm ready to go!" Mother said, matter-of-factly.

"Well, what's wrong?" I asked her. Mother was infamous for not wanting to be at any place for too long, but fifteen minutes was a little short for even her. Did they search y'all?"

"Ain't nothing wrong. I'm just ready to go," Mother replied, not really offering more feedback.

"Yeah, they searched us, but they searched Mother a little more thoroughly than they did us. The beeper on the metal detector kept going off when she passed through it," Brandy said.

"They made her unhook her bra and a female officer checked under her breast," Casha offered.

"What?!" I exclaimed. "These people get on my nerves! What did they think…that an eighty-year old would hide a machine gun in her bra?!" I said, irritatingly.

I looked over to where the kids sat to see if they were listening to our conversation, but they were happily playing amongst themselves.

Mother did not say a word about what she endured. She looked in another direction, as if she was not listening to what we said. She was an incredibly prideful woman; yet despite her ordeal with the officers, I did not believe that was the reason why she was in such a rush to leave. Something was amiss; there was a distant look in her eyes, as though she was somewhere else in another time and place.

"So, what y'all been up to?" I asked.

"Chile…ain't nothing going on but the rent!" Casha said, laughing. Casha and I had stayed in contact through letters with one another over the years. Her letters were always met with a welcome reprieve. She kept me abreast of all that was going on with our family and in Toledo.

"I heard that. I can't wait to get out of here! I've got one year left!" I enthused.

"I know! Woo! Woo!" Brandy shouted.

"I'm ready to go!" Mother said, again.

"Mother!" Brandy said shocked and irritated by Mother's outburst.

"It's cool, Brandy. If she's ready to go, you all can leave."

I did not want to them to go, but I did not want Mother to be there if she did not want to be.

"Ugh!" Casha said, playfully, "Mother, this is the last time we bring you with us to see your grandson!"

"Fine with me," Mother said in her deep, low voice.

We all laughed at her statement and the serious look on her face. I hugged them all, as they stood to leave.

"It was nice meeting you, Jared." I said, smiling down at him. He looked up at me with a blank stare, as if I had not said anything to him! "Thank y'all for coming!"

"Yeah, next time we'll have to come without you-know-who," Brandy said, winking at me.

"I know who you talkin about," Mother said, rolling her eyes at Brandy. The three of us laughed like old times. Mother was truly something. Even at eighty-five years old, she still had the feistiness of a younger person. It was a blessing to call her my own. Although our visit was short, I was grateful for it. I enjoyed the time we were able to spend with one another. It was the happy ending I needed for yet another year in prison.

Chapter Nineteen

New Year's Eves were like any other holiday in prison: sad, depressing, and monotonous. On those special days in prison, some of us prepared elaborate breaks with our prison friends; others smoked weed, drank hooch, or consumed whatever their drugs of choice were; we all laughed and joked in an attempt to ease the sorrows we felt. As hard as we inmates may have tried, the holidays always fell short of the fervor we felt while home with our families. No amount of laughter or well-prepared meals compensated for the loneliness and void we felt from being separated from the people we loved most in our lives—our families.

The New Year of 2001 was supposed to be different than the previous six New Years that I spent in prison; it was the year of my release from confinement. Gone would be the lonely days and nights; gone would be the feeling of constantly being on guard. I would no longer have to wake each day wondering if it would be my last day alive.

Each day I greeted the rising sun with the realization that I could be raped, assaulted, or disrespected. Subsequently, I realized that, if any of the before-mentioned occurred, I could be killed for defending myself, or, at the very least, incarcerated for the rest of my life for defending myself. As such, I subconsciously lived every hour of each day in fear; not fear of what could be done to me, but fear of what I would do if

I was treated unfairly.

It was my prayer that the year would go by smoothly, though, as was the case with my life, the rough, treacherous road that lay before me was anything but smooth.

For months since Tyler's release, I had fallen on difficult times financially. The measly twenty-two dollars in state pay I received each month did little by way of supplying what I perceived as my necessities: toiletries and food.

Ms. Matthews had faithfully sent Tyler twenty dollars every week. Combined with his state pay, Tyler led a somewhat comfortable existence while confined. While I did not have anyone in my family who sent me money weekly as Ms. Matthews did for Tyler, Mama sent me fifty dollars every four to six weeks. Tyler and I would combine our incomes, and shop for the things we needed from commissary together.

With Tyler gone, I found it increasingly difficult to afford the things Booger and I needed. Booger rarely asked our family for any assistance. Yet, during those times in which he did, they usually told him that they did not have any money, or they would promise to send some money. Though, the money would never arrive.

Mama was no longer working. She had become her Alzheimer's-stricken mother's primary caretaker. As a result, her loss of income made it difficult for her to support me in the manner that she had in previous years. Mymomme and our other family members were so engulfed in their chemical dependency or their own lives that we could not expect any support from them.

I felt as though Booger and I had died. We seldom received visits. We received letters from our family members even less frequently than we received visits. And, now we had no financial support. It was as though we had ceased to exist. I understood full-well that it was our mistake, and our mistake alone, that had placed us in the predicament that we found ourselves, but I assumed that our family would be more supportive of us.

I did not know what to do. I wrestled every day, all day, with what course of action to take. I could not prostitute myself as many of the other gay guys did to survive in prison, nor did I have the street knowledge to do anything illegal to survive while confined.

"A, Chris, what's up?" A guy asked as I walked down the hall after work from the education dorm.

"Hey," I said. I had seen the guy around the institution before, but I had no idea who he was.

"I got a business proposition for you," he said, enthusiastically.

"Yeah, what is it?" I said, disinterested.

I did not know what the business proposition was, but I had no interest in whatever it was at all.

The guy was pleased that I was at least willing to indulge him in conversation. He had apparently heard that I was gay; though, whoever had shared with him the details of my sexual orientation, had failed to tell him more pertinent information about me.

"All you got to do is go on a visit…and get this shit from this nigga…and put it up yo' ass…and bring it out of the visit with you," he whispered, conspiratorially.

I tried as best I could to hold my peace, but I could not. I exploded.

"Nigga, if you don't get yo' stupid ass out my face, you gone wish you woulda. You take yo'
ass out there on a mutha fuckin visit and put some shit up yo' ass! What the fuck I look like?! I wouldn't be a got damn

flunky for none of y'all penny-enny ass niggas!" I fumed.

I was outraged! He had the audacity of a thousand men, assuming, because of my sexual orientation, that I would be willing to place drugs in my rectum for his profit.

For weeks after that incident, the guy had successfully avoided me. When we finally crossed each other's paths, he quickly averted his eyes in the opposite direction. Seeing him, conjured up all of the negative feelings I felt when he offered me his 'proposition.' Many men, whether bound or free, thought of women and gay guys in one way: what can you do for me? I absolutely would not be the coat over the puddle of water for any man to walk.

For a fleeting moment, as I thought of the financial bind in which Booger and I found ourselves, the guy's proposition crossed my mind. Being incarcerated for murder should have taught me to never say what I would not do. Life—poverty/the will to survive—will sometimes lead a person to do that which he ordinarily would not.

I did not know what to do or to whom to turn, but I knew that I could not smuggle drugs into the prison. The fact that the act was illegal was one hurdle I would have had to wrestle with; my nerves would be another. The thought alone sent shivers of apprehension throughout my body.

My pride made my situation worse. I did not like to ask anyone for anything, though it seemed that I had no other alternative. There was one person I could ask, yet the thought of doing so made me quiver.

Again, I thought of our situation. An inmate simply could not survive on the food provided by the institution; the portions were simply too inadequate for an adult male. Oftentimes, in an effort to satisfy his hunger, an inmate would either re-enter the serving line for an additional serving of food, which placed him at risk of being put in the Hole if he was caught, or he begged and borrowed food from his friends to quell his need.

I finally acquiesced: I sat down on my bed and began to write a letter to my daddy. I did not want to ask him for any money, though I felt that I had no other person to whom I could turn. Although my daddy was a very giving man, he had a way of making me feel absolutely awful for asking him for anything. His incessant lectures of how much he had done for his kids and how we unashamedly asked him for money sent bolts of irritation throughout me.

Again, I thought of Booger's and my need. I allowed the thoughts to override my reservations. Our circumstances gave me the focus I needed to put aside my pride. I wrote the letter, sealing it in an envelope to be delivered with the next day's out-going mail.

The letter sat in my locker box for a full two weeks before I had the nerve to send it to my daddy. I just did not want to have to endure a lecture from him. My situation, however, dictated that I mail the letter.

Two weeks after sending the letter to my daddy, I called him to confirm that he had received it.

"Hello?" I said into the receiver after our call was connected.

"Hello," my daddy answered.

"Hey," I greeted. "Did you get my letter?" I asked, getting directly to the reason for my call. I felt uncomfortable with the entire ordeal. It was best to get it over with as quickly as possible, I surmised.

"Yeah, I got…Chris, what makes you think you can write me a letter asking me to send you fifty dollars a month? Did you think about my bills…about my monthly responsibilities?" He asked in a tone of annoyance.

I felt drained. I did not have the energy, or the desire to have a conversation with him about my reason for asking him for the money.

"Yeah, I thought about it," I said, softly as I tried to control my emotions.

"You kids of mine don't have a problem asking me for anything! It's selfish of you to assume that I can afford to send you fifty dollars a month!" He ranted.

I regretted having sent the letter to him; I regretted my phone call to him; and, once again, I thoroughly regretted having gotten myself in the situation in which I found myself incarcerated.

"I do have a problem asking you for money; in fact, I have a problem asking you for anything. I wrote that letter to you weeks ago, and only when I absolutely could not take my situation any longer did I call you…and, I wouldn't have asked you now had Mama not stopped working and could no longer send me any money. I didn't have anyone else I could ask."

There was a thin line between respect and disrespect. I walked closely on that line. Mymomme had raised me to be respectful of my elders, especially my father, but I could not handle his demeaning tone. I felt that he did not really know me. Once before, in times past, he had called me selfish. Anyone who truly knew me knew that I was far from selfish. I had always gone out of my way to make sure someone else's needs were met.

I was incarcerated because of my selflessness: I could have easily run in the opposite direction as Tookie, Booger, and Kim fought the gang of White folk; yet, instead, I stood where I was, yelling for them to run, until all three of them had made it safely behind me. My reason for asking him for money was not only for my needs, but also the needs of my cousin. I had never at any time during my teenaged or adult life operated from a place of selfishness. Mama, the matriarch of my maternal family, had showed me by example how to love and care selflessly.

"I sent the money off to you the other day. You should get it soon," he conceded.

"Thank you. I'm going to go to lie down. I'll talk to you later."

I was extremely grateful for the money he sent, but the conversation had exhausted me.

"Okay…I'm keeping a list of the money you owe me for you to pay me back when you get out!" He joked. His tone had changed; it was lighter, more jovial.

"Okay. I will…bye-bye," I said, prematurely disconnecting the call. Although my daddy's remark was said in jest, he meant every word he said, and I meant every word that I said— I intended to give him every cent that he had given me.

~~~~

Months had gone by since Michael and I separated. Although we both remained on D3, we maintained a safe distance from one another. We were cordial and spoke when we passed each other in the halls; though, beyond that, nothing else seemingly existed between us. It was as though we had become strangers. Then, one mid-afternoon day during the middle of January, the gulf between us was filled…somewhat.

I sat on my bed watching an episode of the Oprah Winfrey Show. As often as I could, I tried to watch the show. No matter what the topic of the day was, I felt that one could always gain something from show. The show could be about something as silly or bizarre as the world's tallest man in the world, yet, by the end of the show, I would have been enlightened somehow.

I heard a soft, familiar tap on the door. My heart leapt within my chest. "Yeah," I shouted loud enough to be heard on the other side of the door.

The door opened, "What's up?" Michael asked, entering the room.

"Hey. What's up?" I responded calmly, trying to contain the excitement I felt from seeing him. He was as sexy as I remembered him in my dreams. During our estrangement, I had tried as best I could to avoid really looking at him.

"Not a lot…I wanted to talk to you about something. How you been?" Michael asked, awkwardly.

He wanted to talk about something. I was suddenly nervous. I wondered about what he wanted to talk.

"I've been cool…maintaining. What's up?" I asked, cautiously. As always, I wanted to get right to the point.

"Damn, you don't waste any time!" Michael laughed.

"Well, you know how I am…I've been through too much these last few years. I can't handle the suspense. I need to know what it is, so that I can begin to tackle it!" I said, laughing.

For a brief moment, I remembered happier times when we were together. A bittersweet thought.

"Yeah, I feel you on that…uhm, I got a letter from a attorney today. I guess, my moms went out and hired one and didn't tell me." He hesitated a moment before continuing, "They lettin' me go…the judge givin' me super-shock."

I sat on my bed, not knowing exactly what to say. I gained my senses, quickly standing up, "Congratulations!" I said, hugging him tightly.

"Thanks, ba…" He caught himself before the word baby

completely escaped his mouth. We still loved each other. The time apart did not change how we felt. In fact, it seemed that our feelings had intensified. The estrangement had given us a better perspective on our feelings and our relationship. The only problem was that we had learned too late.

"So when do you leave for Toledo?" I asked softly, disengaging from our embrace.

Michael looked down, "Tomorrow."

"Tomorrow!" I exclaimed. "And, you just got the letter today?!"

"Yeah; I guess, they rushed through everything and got me the next court date they had available."

"Wow! Are you nervous?"

"A little, but I'm ready for whatever."

"Yeah, I know what you mean. I'm happy for you…I'm going to miss you, but I'm happy for you."

"Man, get outta here. You ain't thinking about me!" Michael laughed. "Yo ass dumped me! You ain't thought two seconds about me in the last four or five months!"

"That's not true," I said quietly. "I thought of you every second of every day…what was I supposed to do? You didn't seem to want me anymore."

"Yeah, I know. I was just fuckin with you about you not thinkin' 'bout me…you did what you had to do, and I don't blame you. That's one of the things I've always loved about you, you ain't gone take nobody's shit, and you ain't gone let nothing stop you from being happy."

I lowered my head in humility; I was both pleased and proud that Michael appreciated me for who I was.

"I'm sorry for taking you through all that shit," Michael said, raising my head and kissing me softly on my lips.

I smiled warmly at him, "It's okay…the ride was worth the journey."

Booger and I had been incarcerated together since our days in the county jail. He was jailed on the seventh of June, and I submitted myself to the authorities on June ninth. There was not a time when we were not accessible to one another.

As I stood at the gate that led to the entrance of the institution, I recalled the times Booger and I had shared over the past seven years: I remembered how we wrote letters of support to one another in the county jail, using the inmate-trustees as our mail carriers; I remembered he and I, and five other guys, eating pizza-breaks on paper bags at C.R.C; I remembered Booger rushing to my side to calm me after Moe and I had tussled—I thought all those things and many more as I watched through the steel bars as my cousin was escorted to a life beyond concrete floors, barbed wire fences, obnoxious COs, and self-serving inmates. The memories seemed like they had occurred weeks ago, rather than years.

While I understood that Booger must leave, it pained me deeply to see him go. He, on the other hand, seemed unmoved by his release. He behaved as if he had only served seven minutes of confinement, instead of seven years.

Though, in actuality, I could not have expected him to act any other way. He had always seemed to deal with our imprisonment far differently than me. When I ranted about our family's virtual desertion of us, he would respond apathetically, "Man, we gone be all right…God gone look out for us."

His attitude always baffled me. I knew in my soul that God would undoubtedly care for us, that He would not forsake us. Yet, even armed with the knowledge of God's ever-abiding presence and undying love for us, I was still hurt by our family's abandonment of us.

At times, I wondered if Booger missed his freedom. Did he not long to eat what he wanted and when he wanted? Did he not miss holidays and birthdays with our family? Did he not dream of long nights with Niecy in his arms?

Years prior, while Tyler and I were engrossed in one of our many passionate conversations of home and the things we missed, Booger walked into the ten-man annex where Tyler slept.

"What's up, y'all?" He asked Tyler and me.

"What's up, Boo?" Tyler greeted.

"What's up, cousin?" I said.

"Nuttin, just seeing what y'all gettin' into," Booger replied.

"Shiiit, nothin'! We just kickin it about home! We ready to get the fuck outta this dungeon!" Tyler said.

"Man, I would do y'all time for both of y'all," Booger said, matter-of-factly, before walking out of the annex. Tyler and I looked at one another, perplexed by Booger's statement. We disregarded Booger's remark, thinking that he was just expressing a bizarre thought of his. Yet, later as I laid on my bed thinking, I believed that Booger was sincere about what he said.

In part, I believed that Booger's statement to Tyler and me was a reflection of the true love he felt in his spirit for us. He saw that our time in prison was agonizing for us, and, because of the magnitude of his love for us, he wanted to ease our burden.

Though, Booger's regard of Tyler and me only explained part of the reason for his expression. The other dynamic, as I believed, was that being incarcerated was not as cumbersome for Booger as it was for us. It appeared to me that he was unaffected by our incarceration; that, though he desired to be home, he was content wherever life found him.

The clank of the gate brought me out of my reverie. I blinked several times to clear my vision. I looked up just in time to see Booger walk through another steel gate, until the only thing that remained was a memory of where he stood.

~~~

I established a new routine after Booger's release. I had to keep myself busy to avoid having to think about how much I missed him. We did not spend our every waking moments with each other, but I felt a comfort in knowing that he was a shout away. Later in life, I would come to associate Tyler, Michael, and Booger's release from prison with the pain of losing a loved one to death.

As with the death of a loved one, I understood that the beloved must go and that where they were going was a far better place than where they were, though, in my innocence, my heart could not quite yet fathom, nor accept, the absence of their presence.

As the days progressed, the sorrow I felt from Tyler, Booger, and Michael's release seemed to overcome me. As hard as I tried, I did not know how to deal with the abyss their absences left. The Creator, however, in His undying love and care for me sent me two special gifts.

I met Hausan when I first moved to D3. He was a close friend of Austin's, my cousin who ensured that Booger and I be placed on the same dorm when we first arrived at Lima. Over the years of being housed on D3, Hausan had become an invaluable friend to Booger and me. He was older than us by seventeen years, so, in some ways he was like an uncle to us. He regarded and protected us as though we were biologically related to him.

My other gift was Kyle. He and I were perhaps two people who were the most unlikely to be friends. Prior to his incarceration, Kyle was a drug dealer. I had little to no respect for drug dealers. I felt that they were self-serving beast who aided in the destruction of the Black family. To make matters worse, Kyle was a womanizer. He, like many men I knew, saw women as simply pawns for their satisfaction. Their behavior teetered on misogyny; they professed to love women beyond measure, yet they treated them with disdain.

I found such mentalities foolish. Not only had women shaped and molded me into the man that I was, but I knew such was the case with many other men as well. Black women were largely the backbone of the African American family. It was because of the sacrifices of Black women that African American doctors, lawyers, educators, entertainers, and athletes existed.

However, in time and through many conversations, Kyle's negative mentality began to wane. He more clearly recognized the sacrifices that his mother made, and he became more conscientious of his choices. I soon learned that he was a funny, intelligent, and warm person who simply needed help in unveiling the treasure within him.

It was December 1, 2001. The day I had awaited seven and a half years for had finally come. I awakened early; lying on my bed thinking. Although that day was supposed to be the happiest moment of my life, it felt very ordinary. I felt none of the excitement I had expected to feel: no butterflies swam in my stomach; no tingling or jittery sensations, just the realization that one door of my life was closing and another door was opening.

For years Tyler and I had planned in our minds how our receptions home would be. We imagined huge, grand parties given in our honor. We would be escorted into a magnificently decorated hall where our family and friends waited anxiously for our arrival.

Stepping into the room, we would be bombarded with love and well-wishes from the attendees. The years of heartache and suffering would dissolve; the feelings of loneliness and desertion would be replaced with love and gratitude. Our eyes would mist as the realization that our tribulations had passed, that we no longer had to endure the hardships of prison.

We envisioned a day of love filled with all the foods we had been denied while incarcerated: golden brown, fried chicken and fish, spaghetti, candied yams, fried okra, macaroni and cheese, dressing, and collard greens. In our minds, there would be mouth-watering desserts: banana pudding, sweet potato pies and peach cobblers, alongside double-chocolate and caramel cakes.

We would look around at the smiling faces as feelings of wholeness enveloped us; we would be complete. The void that had become a natural part of our lives would cease to exist. We would be home.

Yet, as I greeted my special day, a day that was supposed to be saturated with the hope of new beginnings, I did not feel the freedom of liberation. Instead, I felt melancholy and a deep-rooted foreboding.

After hours of thinking, I finally heard the CO blow his whistle, announcing breakfast. It was five o'clock in the morning. I rose from bed, slipped on my robe, and went into the bathroom to brush my teeth and wash my face. I walked into the bathroom, looking down the row of sinks to find an unoccupied one. The second to last sink was free.

Ugh! I thought. I did not like using that particular sink; it drained slowly and water sprayed indiscriminately from the faucet, giving me an unrequested shower.

I walked pass the other sinks to the available sink, speaking to the several of the guys as I passed them. I removed my toothbrush and toothpaste from the pocket of my robe. I turned on the water, rinsing and gargling before I began the task at hand. I looked in the mirror as I brushed my teeth. I quickly lowered my head. Two guys sat on the commodes behind me. Partitions separated the toilets, though there were no doors to offer added cover from onlookers. The last thing I needed to see before I had breakfast was a man wiping himself. The thought would follow me while I ate, ruining any chance of me eating in peace.

After I brushed my teeth and washed my face, I retrieved a comb from the other pocket on my robe. My usual nice, neat taper fade was replaced with a thick, nappy afro. Try as I did, my hair was incorrigible. Every effort I put into combing out the kinks, my hair put forth two times more energy into maintaining the tightly woven coils. It would take a bucket or two of water and an act of congress to get my hair into decent shape. After a few more yanks and pats of my hands, I gave up and walked to my cell to get dressed.

I quickly dressed and exited the dorm. D3 was not far from the cafeteria. It took all of thirty seconds to reach the cafeteria. I entered the cafeteria. Luckily, the serving line was short. I did not have the patience to wait. I looked around to see what was being served. Pancakes! Wow, it may turn out to be a good day, after all. The
pancakes did not taste like they did when Mymomme cooked them, but they were one of the better entrees' served for

breakfast. It definitely beat hard-boiled eggs and cold cereal, which was one of the commonly served meals.

After being served and getting my eating utensils, I entered the dining room in search of a table where I could sit. I saw Kyle sitting by himself at a table along the wall.

"Good morning, Kylie! Do you mind if I sit with you?" I joked.

Whenever a gay guy ate with someone other than his partner or another gay guy, it was assumed that whomever he ate with was a person of interest to the gay guy.

"Man, come on with that bullshit!" Kyle joked. "You know you can sit down!"

"I don't know, but I know how you niggas are…it's all right for you and me to be cool on the dorm, though a whole other story out in population…" I teased.

"Man, I don't give a fuck what these niggas think! Ain't none of them putting no money on my books!" Kyle said, defiantly.

"Uhn-huh, that's what you say now. Let one your homies come around and your tail will be between your legs!" I laughed.

"Man, what's that supposed to mean?! You know I don't know what all them damn parables mean!" He said in mock anger.

"It means, you talking all that ra-ra shit now, but when your friends come around all that courage will disappear!" He looked at me fuming.

We had a special relationship. I loved teasing him, and he loved being teased by me. It kept our moods light. We focused less on being confined and more in the joy of having a friend with whom we connected.

I laughed as I walked to the milk machine to fill my cup.

"Hey, youngster! Today yo big day, ain't it?!" Hausan yelled.

I smiled shyly, "Yeah, but don't tell anyone…it's a secret!" I whispered, jokingly.

"I hear you, young blood. I'll see you on the dorm!" He laughed.

"Okay," I said, laughing with him.

I returned to the table to find Kyle nearly finished with his breakfast.

"Man, you weren't wasting time!" I exclaimed.

"Shit, I was hungry!"

"I guess so…did you leave any syrup on the tray?" I joked.

"Nope, I licked it up!" He grabbed the tray, feigning as though he was licking it.

I frowned my face, "You so nasty!"

He laughed at the expression on my face, "So you excited to be going home?!"

I felt uncomfortable talking about going home with Kyle. He was in prison for murder and given a sentence of life. It was unlikely that he was going home any time soon.

I stammered, "Not really."

"What?! Man, if these mutha fuckas told me I was gettin' the hell out of here, I would be singing all over the place and tellin' every one them ignorant ass COs to kiss my black ass as I walked out of the gate!"

We laughed.

"I don't know what it is. I'm just not excited. It might have something to do with my family's feelings…none of them seem particularly thrilled."

"Man, you crazy! I bet your daddy and 'nem happy as hell!"

"Naw, that's not what I mean. I know that they're happy,

but none of them are ecstatic. You know what I mean?"

"Yeah, but I bet they are and you just don't know it."

"Uhn huh…I don't know. They're not doing any of the stuff that you know people say that their family or friends do for them when they come home. I had to tell Mymomme that I wanted a coming-home party. She hadn't already planned one. Then she told me that my Aunt Trisha was having a birthday party and my party could be with hers. I don't know, maybe I'm being selfish, but I kinda wanted a celebration of my own; to feel special just this one day. I mean, I've been locked up for seven and a half years!"

"Your mom probably just said that. They probably gone surprise you."

"I'on know. I don't think so, but I'll see. You ready?" I asked, picking up my tray.

"Yeah."

We grabbed our trays and cups. We emptied the food from the trays into the garbage container, as we walked out of the cafeteria and headed for our dorm.

"What you about to do now?" Kyle asked me, as I stood outside of my cell door.

"I'm about to lie down for a little while. I've been up since around three or four this morning."

"Man, ain't no way I'd be able to sleep and I knew I was about to go home!"

"I'll be up in about an hour. I just need to rest a little bit. By the time I wake up, it'll almost be time for the halls to open and they should be calling me to go home."

"Okay. I'll see you when you get up."

I closed the door, took off my state clothes, and lay down. Minutes later, I was sleeping soundly when I heard a soft rap at the door. The door creaked open.

"Young blood?" Hausan whispered.

I looked up through bloodshot eyes. I was more exhausted than I thought.

"Huh?" I said in a gravelly voice.

"My apologies. I didn't know you was sleeping."

"It's cool. I'll be up in an hour or so."

"Sleep well, my brother." Hausan said, retracing his steps backwards and softly closing the door behind him.

No sooner than he had closed the door, I immediately fell into a dream-like state.

I walked across a large prairie. The sun was set high in a cloudless, blue sky. A soft, warm breeze enveloped my scantily-clothed body. The lush grass tickled my bare feet. I started to run, enjoying the freedom of the open land. I looked around me; nothing existed, but acres upon acres of beautiful countryside. I took big, deep gulps of the fresh clean air into my lungs. I felt invigorated; alive. I jumped up as high my legs allowed me. I had the sensation that, if I jumped high enough, I could touch the essence of the blueness in the sky.

In this land there was no pain, no fear, no doubt. I could do whatever I wanted; be whomever I wanted without judgment. I danced wildly, with no inhibitions. I was liberated. I laughed loudly; my vibrato melodiously blending in with the symphony of sound around me: the high pitch of birds; the slow flow of a creek; the gentle sway of tree branches in the wind.

I was in awe of all that was around me. I began to run in sheer delight and gratitude of my prosperity. I felt that I could run forever and never tire. I raced full throttle up hills and through unchartered territory. I spotted a tree in the distance. I ran to it. The tree was glorious: a strong sturdy trunk, long out-stretched branches, and broad green leaves adorned it. A small creek flowed beside the huge tree. I knelt down, cupping my hands to drink its water. The water felt cool, smooth, and sweet against my palate.

I rose to my feet to lie down on the blanket of grass beneath the shade of the tree. I closed my eyes, relishing the peacefulness around me.

"Tell your story." A strong voice spoke.

I opened my eyes. "Huh?" I said in bewilderment.

"Tell your story. They need to know your story," the Voice echoed around me, sounding as though it were in a tunnel.

I looked around for the Voice. I did not see Him or Her or It. I moved from under the shade of the tree. I looked across the vast land to the horizon. Nothing...No one...I Stood Alone, under the huge blue sky and life-giving Light. The wind blew. Goosebumps rose on my arms. A breeze flowed around me, piercing my flesh. I felt a tingling sensation that offered a comfort that exceeded my understanding.

"I am with you."

I smiled broadly...I laughed...tears began to replace my laughter. I cried long and hard. I stretched forth my arms to the sky, to the Light, to the wind, to the trees, to the grass around me. I cried vehemently in joy and appreciation of His favor, His protection, His grace, His love. He was with me! I was not alone!

My body heaved as I sobbed at the pure profundity of my blessing. I awakened bathed in tears and sweat. My body shook uncontrollably. I sat up. I wrapped my arms around myself, still feeling the veracity of God's presence. I did not know what roads lay before me, though I knew that, through the blessing of my experience, I could weather whatever the storms that life brought my way. I resolved that I would serve the Creator with every ounce of my being.

~~~

I got out of bed and walked to the door, opening it. I stepped outside of my cell and walked toward the COs desk to look at the clock behind him. Wow! It was eight-thirty! I slept a solid two hours.

"Has anyone called for me?" I asked the CO.

"Not yet, Mr. Price." The CO said. He was an older guy; somewhere in his late fifties. His affable face, smooth and unlined, sat beneath a canopy of silver hair. I still had not changed my mentality in regard to mingling with COs, though he was cool.

"Thank you, Mr. Ferguson," I smiled.

Hmm, I wondered where my daddy was. Usually family or friends of inmate's arrived early to pick up their loved one. I hoped that he was all right. I decided to call him to be certain. Mother had a block on her phone, so I could not call her. I called Mama to see if she had spoken with him.

I worried easily. My incarceration had taught me that in a twinkle of the eye anything can happen.

After a few rings, the automated operator's all-too familiar greeting could be heard, "You have a collect call from 'Chris'... Do you accept the call?

Seconds later Mama was on the phone.

"Hi, Mama."

"Hey, baby. You here already?"

"No, not yet. I'm still waiting for my daddy. I guess you haven't spoken to him, huh?"

"No, baby. I ain't spoke to him since the other day. He stopped by here and said he was going to pick you up."

"Hmm, I hope he's okay."

"C.P., you sound like me with your worrying. I'm sure

he's all right, baby."

"All right. I'm going to take a shower and get dressed. Hopefully, he'll show up soon."

"Okay, baby. If I hear anything, I'll let him know you're waiting."

"Okay, Mama. I love you."

"I love you, too, C.P."

"Okay, bye-bye."

"Bye-bye, baby."

I placed the phone back in its cradle. I still felt a little uneasy. My daddy was notorious for being late, but he was seldom late for important events, like my release.

I walked back to my cell to gather my soap and towel for a shower. As I exited my room, I ran into Hausan.

"I see you woke up, young blood."

"Yeah, I got up a little while ago. I had to call my daddy to see where he is."

"Aww, he probably down there at the gate waiting on you. You know how these guards are."

"Yeah, I hope that's all it is. I better hurry and take my shower just in case he is here."

"Yeah, you sho better."

I got in the stall to shower. I brushed my teeth while in there. I lathered my towel profusely. I liked a lot of suds. I shampooed my hair, and washed and rinsed my body two thorough times before using my wash cloth to dry myself. I was not quite sure why we inmates dried our bodies with our wash cloths, and then with our bath towels. I surmised that it may have been to prevent our bath towels from mildewing, since there was no place to hang them to dry.

I went to my cell, using my bath towel to remove any water residue from my body. After drying off, I lathered on some

lotion. I grabbed my underwear and sweat suit from the bed and began to dress. It seemed hard to believe that this would be the last day I would be in the institution. Although, the place never felt like home to me, I had been there for six and a half years of my life. A lot of my memories were formed within the walls of the prison: I had become a man in there; fallen deeply in love; met some of the best friends
I had ever known; and, yet, I was also forcibly confined in there. I felt a collage of bittersweet moments.

After dressing, I walked from my cell to the CO's desk again to see if there was any word of my dad.

"Hey. They still hadn't called, Mr. Ferguson?"

"No, not yet, Mr. Price. I'll call control to make sure."

"Thank you," I said, feeling honored by his act.

It was completely uncommon for a CO to call the administration desk about something so frivolous. For, while going home was a priority of mine, it was far from being a matter of importance to the administrators of the institution. I felt truly blessed.

"Hi. This is Officer Ferguson up on D3, there is an Inmate Price here who is scheduled to leave for home today. Have you heard anything of his family down there? Uhn-huh…ok…yeah…well, thanks, Jim." Mr. Ferguson hung up the phone. I looked at him expectantly. "No, Mr. Price. Your family isn't down there."

"Okay. Thank you, Mr. Ferguson. I appreciate your effort."

I walked away from Mr. Ferguson's desk. I had no idea where my daddy could have been. I entered the room leading to the phone room and peeped through the window to see if anyone was using the phone. No one was in there. I opened the door, quickly grabbing the phone from the receiver. I

dialed Mama's number, again. I knew that I should not have been calling her for a
second time, but I felt that I had no choice. I was more than ready to go home, but I was also worried that something had happened to my daddy.

Mama answered the phone.

"Mama, you still haven't spoken to my daddy?"

"Yes, I spoke to him, baby. I called him after we hung up the last time."

"Is he okay?" I asked, frantically.

"Yes, he's fine, baby. He just a little behind on time."

Huh? Whose family is 'a little behind on time' to pick them up from prison? In all the years that I was incarcerated, I had never known a person's family or friends to be late getting him. I had waited for this day for seven and a half years! Again, I was struck with the feeling that this day was only significant to me.

"I can call him on this three-way, or whatever it is y'all call it…if I can remember how to work this thing." Mama said.

Her voice sounding distant; she was looking at the phone trying to see how to add my dad to our call.

"Mama, you just have to click over and dial his number. Once he picks up, click back over." I yelled into the receiver so that she could hear me.

"Okay, baby." Click-click. I waited patiently for her to click back over to the line where I waited.

"C.P…C.P?"

"Yes, Mama…Mama…Mama, I'm here. I can hear you."

"Oh, okay, baby. Boy, I didn't think I would ever figure this thing out," she said, referring to the phone. "Your father's on the phone, baby."

"Hello?"

"Chris, why do you keep calling your grandmother?" My daddy asked, irritably.

His attitude caught me off guard. I tried hard to remain composed and respectful. I was tired: tired of being in prison; tired of depending on people; tired of being hurt and disappointed.

"I called because I thought that something had happened to you," I said, thinly concealing my hurt and anger.

"I'm on my way! Your calling your grandmother won't get me there any sooner! I am thirty minutes away!"

"All right. Thank you, Mama," I said, cutting the conversation short.

"You welcome, baby."

"Bye-bye," I said.

"Bye-bye, baby," Mama said before disconnecting the call.

I placed the phone back in the cradle. I did not wait to hear if my daddy had already disconnected the call or if he said good-bye. I felt miserable, as though I was being punished. It seemed to me that my love had only caused me pain: missing and wanting to see my family had only led to my disappointment, for they rarely visited; loving Michael from the depths of my soul had left me alone and with a crumbled heart; something as minute as being concerned about my father's well-being resulted in me being scolded. Perhaps, I was over-reacting…maybe I was just too spoiled, I considered.

I left the phone room and went to Hausan's room. His door was ajar, yet I knocked anyway.

"Youngster!" He said, looking up from a book he was reading, "Come on in!"

"Hey. I just spoke to my daddy and Mama. He's on the way; he said he's thirty minutes from here."

"Well, why do you sound so sad? You should be jumping

off the ceiling!" He laughed.

I thought that I had effectively hidden my feelings, but I guess I had not. I did not like to burden people with my problems.

"I don't know…I guess I expected this day be different. I wanted it to be happier."

"Well, what you mean? Ain't you happy?"

"Yeah, I'm happy that I'm going home; that I'm leaving this place, but I'm not happy with way the day is going," I said taking a moment to gather my thoughts. "Mama called my daddy on her three-way and, as soon as she connected the call, he went off! Talking mess about him being on his way and that my calling Mama won't get him here any faster or something like that."

I continued, exasperatedly, "It's like he misconstrues everything that I do and say. Yeah, I'm ready to get out of here! I don't want to be here a minute longer than I have to, but that's not why I was calling Mama! I wanted to know that he was all right! Anything could have happened to him out on that road! He could have gotten in a car accident or something!"

"Well, youngster, he probably just anxious to see you."

"Huh?" I loved Hausan dearly. He had been a true blessing to Booger and me, though sometimes I did not like talking to him about personal issues. He seemed to miss something in the conversation. I understood that he was an optimistic person and wanted to look at things from a positive perspective, but sometimes I needed him to see a situation for what it was in a real and practical way.

"Okay, Hausan," I gave up trying to express my feelings to him about my daddy, instead I changed the subject. "I know that I've said this to you before, but I wanted to tell you again before I leave…I appreciate the friend you've been to my cousin and me."

"Youngster, you don't have to thank me. I'm a servant that was sent here to serve. See, I'm a real live brotha for the struggle!"

"All right, Hausan," I said, laughing. A lot of people thought Hausan was crazy, but he was far from crazy; peculiar possibly, but not crazy. I hugged him firmly. "Well, I thank you, anyway."

He hugged me back. "You're welcome, young blood."

We disengaged from our embrace. "I'll be back. I'm going to holler at Kyle before I go."

I walked the few short steps from Hausan's room to Kyle's. I knocked on the door. "Come in!" Someone yelled from inside the room.

I walked in, and looked around to see if Kyle was in there. He sat on his bed watching T.V.

"What's up, short-timer?" He said, looking up as I walked pass him to sit on the chair near the end of his bed.

"Short-timer, who? My time ain't short until my daddy out there and I'm walking out of here!" I laughed.

"Shiiiit, you short! Where yo people at?"

"I just spoke to my daddy. He said he's thirty minutes away."

"Damn, this late?! What happened?"

"That's what I'm saying! I don't know what's taking him so long. When I called to check on him, he got all mad, so I got mad and just left it alone."

"Damn, so what he say?"

"Nothing; just that my calling wasn't going to get him any faster and that he was thirty minutes away."

"That don't sound right. Usually cats' peoples be here

waiting on them to get out before they even open the doors of the institution!"

"Yeah, I know. That's what I was trying to explain to you this morning. My family don't seem really excited about me coming home. It's like I'm coming home from school break and they just saw me three months ago! But I ain't coming home from school! I didn't know if this day would ever come! The Board could have made me serve the remainder of my sentence—that's eighteen years!"

"Yeah, that's some shit. Shiiit, if that was me, my moms woulda been here last night sittin' in her car waitin' on them to open the doors to let me go!"

"Hmmm. I don't even have any clothes to wear when I get home. Everybody's saying that they don't have any money. So the only thing I have to wear is this tight sweat suit that I've had ever since I've been here at Lima!" I bowed my head, thinking about the absurdity of my situation.

"I told you that they weren't even going to give me a coming-home party. I mean, when you have to ask someone to celebrate your release, it's like you're alone in the celebration…like it only matters to you. I know times are hard for everybody, and my family ain't in no way rich, but I would have thought that maybe they'd put ten dollars aside here and there, until there was enough to have a party, or so that I would have some money to buy some clothes. I mean, they had a whole year and a half to plan. Booger and Tookie didn't have a party, either. Maybe it's our family…maybe they just don't know any better," I surmised.

"Man, that's how family is. Ain't nobody looked out for me in the ten years I been locked-up in this bitch, but my momma. Shiiit, them niggas left me for dead soon as I left the streets. I don't get shit from none of them niggas I was running with: no letters; no money; not even, a kiss my ass, eat shit and die from them niggas! It's fucked up being in this mutha fucka! And, when I was out all them niggas was in my face! Sucka asses! All them bitches! They all just left me for dead!"

I don't know what I was thinking when I thought to share my blues with Kyle. All it took was a little spark to ignite his fire. He could go on forever talking about how his family and friends had deserted him during his incarceration. Talking to him and Hausan was like being caught between a rock and a hard place; one was an eternal optimist and the other had been so devalued and mistreated that his cup was filled with bitterness and rage. I took both of their sentiments and unique vantages and came to my own conclusions about my family, though, more specifically, about living:

Life was unpredictable. Had someone told me that I would have been incarcerated, I would have laughed in his face; had that same someone told me that I would be incarcerated with a sentence of nine to twenty-five years for murdering someone, I would have insisted that he be taken to the nearest insane asylum to have his head thoroughly examined!

Life was sometimes so beautiful that I did not want to be anywhere but in the midst of its beauty; at other times, it was so painful that I wanted to run into the arms of Jesus and rest my weary soul at the helm of God in a place far from the earthly realm.

One of the many things I learned from my incarceration was that one must always move forward. It was a true blessing to have the love and support of family and friends; though, if ever one should find himself alone in a crowd of thousands, hurt beyond soothing, and maimed beyond recognition, I would encourage him to look within himself to draw upon a love, a power, and a healing that surpasses all carnal understanding, and, from that blessing, find the strength to continue moving forward.

"Price!" I heard the CO yell.

"It must be that time." I got up from the chair and walked to where Kyle stood. I locked my eyes with his. "You keep your head up!" I whispered, passionately. "Don't let life or this place or the people in here make or shape you. Remain the jewel you were born to be." I hugged him tightly.

"Come on, man! You tryin' to get me emotional!" We laughed as I began to walk to the door. I began to think about how fortunate I was to meet the people I had while I was confined.

I stepped into the hallway. Most of my dorm mates were in the hall. I looked around at the smiling faces. I was overwhelmed. I was surrounded by those whom society had written-off: murderers, robbers, drug addicts, and rapist; those whom society said was incorrigible and incapable of compassion; those whom society had said were not worthy to be treated with dignity and respect, yet these same persons had come to wish me well on my journey. Me: a gay, Black man whom society had also deemed a misfit.

I grabbed my bag of personal items from my room, and thanked and hugged my friends as I exited the dorm. I walked to the gate that led out of the institution. I was lost in thought. It was hard to believe that chapter of my life was over and that a new one was beginning.

I waited for the COs to open the gate. *Wow, so this is what it feels like to stand at this gate knowing that you're leaving for home.* Suddenly, the cares of the last seven and a half years began to fall from shoulders. The gate began to clank open. I turned around to face Hausan.

www.ingramcontent.com/pod-product-compliance
Lightning Source LLC
Chambersburg PA
CBHW052010290426
44112CB00014B/2191

"Stay true to yourself," I reminded him.

"I will, young king! I'm looking to see you do great things!"

"I'll try my best!"

I walked through the open gate. I looked back at him as I waited for another gate to open. I nodded my head at him before I walked through the second gate, disappearing down the long corridor.

I stood before a CO behind a Plexiglas window.

"State your name and number!" He barked.

"307-720, Pri..." I stopped before I finished saying my name. "Christopher Price." I said, resolutely. I determined right then and there that I would take back my ownership. I no longer had to identify myself by my last name and number, as though I was cattle on a ranch.

The CO looked at me malevolently. I smiled at him. It was over. I did not have to be subjected to his or any other CO's abuse any longer. The CO slid seventy-five dollars under the window to me; an allowance from the state. I retrieved the money from the counter, smiling like a mule chewing glue as I walked away from the window and through the open doors to my freedom.